# Just A Thought

**Reverend Ernest W "Ernie" Jelliff**

Copyright © 2010 by Ernie Jelliff

*Just A Thought*
by Ernie Jelliff

Printed in the United States of America

ISBN 9781615798346

All rights reserved solely by the author. The author guarantees all contents are original and do not infringe upon the legal rights of any other person or work. No part of this book may be reproduced in any form without the permission of the author. The views expressed in this book are not necessarily those of the publisher.

Unless otherwise indicated, Bible quotations are taken from The New International Version of the Bible, NIV. Copyright © 1973, 1984 by International Bible Society.

www.xulonpress.com

This book is dedicated first to my dear Lord and Savior for His honor and glory. It is my prayer that it will touch your life for Jesus Christ.

Secondly to my precious wife Ruthie and our seven children, their spouses, our fifteen grandchildren, their spouses and our three great-grandchildren, all of whom I love beyond measure.

## Love, love and love some more

**Mark 12:30-31 "Love the Lord your God with all your heart and with all your soul and with all your mind and with all your strength.' The second is this: 'Love your neighbor as yourself.' There is no commandment greater than these."**

**John 13:34-35 "A new command I give you: Love one another. As I have loved you, so you must love one another. By this all men will know that you are my disciples, if you love one another."**

We all know that we're to love others, but let's see how that love works out day-to-day by taking a look at three people Jesus loved on. In John 8:3 we see that, **"The teachers of the law and the Pharisees brought in a woman caught in adultery. They made her stand before the group"** Under the law they were allowed to stone her for what she'd done, but what did Jesus say? **"If any one of you is without sin, let him be the first to throw a stone at her."** (John 8:7) She was repentant and Jesus forgave and loved her. Next look at what we refer to as the woman at the well. After confessing her multiple marriages to Jesus He responded, **"You are right when you say you have no husband. 18 The fact is, you have had five husbands, and the man you now have is not your husband. What you have just said is quite true."** (John 4:18) Then how about Peter who had vehemently denied even knowing His Lord, yet upon His resurrection Jesus told Him, "Simon son of John, do you truly love me more than these?" **"Yes, Lord"**, he said, **"You know that I love you." Jesus said, "Feed my lambs."** (John 21:15) Oh and remember David who said after his confession of adultery and murder, **"Then I will teach transgressors your ways, and sinners will turn back to you."** (Ps 51:13) Repentance brings forgiveness AND restoration that can only come from a loving Savior. No matter the sin He extends the offer AND He expects us to do the same. So the next time you are tempted to look down your nose at another just remember that you, too, have been forgiven.

## As You Go

**Matt 28:18-20 Then Jesus came to them and said, "All authority in heaven and on earth has been given to me. Therefore go and make disciples of all nations, baptizing them in the name of the Father and of the Son and of the Holy Spirit, and teaching them to obey everything I have commanded you. And surely I am with you always, to the very end of the age."**

AS YOU GO (LIVE), MAKE DISCIPLES. Sounds simple enough, but if it is so easy why aren't more Christians doing it? Is it because they are too lazy and selfish to humble themselves before the Lord and be obedient? Is it because they are afraid how they will be seen among peers? Or maybe they think God will just wink at such disobedience when they face Him? Whatever the excuse (however lame) I am sure that when Jesus looks at that excuse and the nail prints in His hands there is no way He will just slough it off. Personally I am always acutely aware of His suffering for me and the responsibilities that come with all God has promised to those who believe in Him. Some would say that they believe and that settles it, but what does it mean to believe? Consider these two verses, **"Simon Peter answered, "You are the Christ, the Son of the living God."** (Matt 16:16) **"Repent of this wickedness and pray to the Lord. Perhaps he will forgive you for having such a thought in your heart."** (Acts 8:22) In religions without Christ those who believe are willing to destroy their own lives for their god, and yet many a Christian hides their faith lest they be laughed at or worse. I read daily of those in China and other nations who are persecuted and killed just because they believe in Jesus. Now that is true belief. How about you? Do you really believe and are you spreading the good news of Jesus Christ and His love every step of your way?

## You Will Obey!

**John 14:15 "If you love me, you will obey what I command."**

**1 John 5:2-5 This is how we know that we love the children of God: by loving God and carrying out his commands. This is love for God: to obey his commands. And his commands are not burdensome, for everyone born of God overcomes the world. This is the victory that has overcome the world, even our faith. Who is it that overcomes the world? Only he who believes that Jesus is the Son of God.**

**"If you love me, you will obey what I command."** YOU WILL OBEY IF YOU LOVE ME. Try reading these verses over several times and see what the Lord says to you. Draw a picture in your mind of Jesus hanging on the cross, nails through His hands and feet, a crown of thorns on His head, fresh blood from all His wounds and dried blood from the awful beatings He had endured, and THIS IS THE SON OF GOD. Only one thing held Him there and it wasn't the nails; it was His love for you and me. The assignment given Him by the Father was to pay the price for our sin (death) that we might not die. And even in the garden as He wrestled with what the night would hold He said, **"Father, if you are willing, take this cup from me; yet not my will, but yours be done."** (Luke 22:42) Love for His Father was so great that disobedience was never in the picture. How then can you or I do any less? How can we claim to love Him and appreciate His gift and still let selfishness rule our lives? The honest answer is WE CANNOT. I ask myself, if I don't obey God am I really saved and I challenge you to do the same. If your spouse claimed to love you yet stayed three or four nights a week with someone else would you believe their profession of love? Yet many of us treat God with the same disregard. Please do not allow this to be the case in your life.

*Just A Thought*

## One secret to being able

**Phil 4:8 Finally, brothers, whatever is true, whatever is noble, whatever is right, whatever is pure, whatever is lovely, whatever is admirable-if anything is excellent or praiseworthy-think about such things.**

**1 Thess 5:21-22 Test everything. Hold on to the good. Avoid every kind of evil.**

Oh how often we say, "I can't tell when something is right or wrong", or "I really don't think such and such is sin". Well think on this, ANYTHING that puts a blotch on the absolute purity of God is sin. Through the years a lot of us have been given incomplete lists of do's and don'ts of what is sin and what is not. Again, sin is ANYTHING short of God's perfection. That means for instance that if I say something disparaging about another person I have sinned. And quite a different example; Corkie Hahn, founder of the Presidential Prayer Team, says that many Christians (???) have withdrawn from the team since January of 2009 because they refuse to pray for Mr. Obama. Friends, that is sin. **"I urge, then, first of all, that requests, prayers, intercession and thanksgiving be made for everyone for kings and all those in authority,"** (1 Tim 2:1-2) We tend to pick and choose what we see as sin, but we had better look at The Bible and weigh everything in light of what GOD says. When we begin to trust the Lord and His Word instead of our personal thoughts and preferences we will live free from the bondage of legalism and trying to measure up. **"He has made us competent as ministers of a new covenant-not of the letter but of the Spirit; for the letter kills, but the Spirit gives life"**.(2 Cor 3:6) No list and no self effort will ever bring contentment or fulfillment. We need to realize that Satan and the demonic world love it when we all follow some list instead of the Word of God for then we are weak and ineffective. If we measure everything against God's standard and allow Him to direct our every step, then we will know the abundant life He intends for us.

*Just A Thought*

# Watch your tongue!

**2 Cor 12:20-21 For I am afraid that when I come I may not find you as I want you to be, and you may not find me as you want me to be. I fear that there may be quarreling, jealousy, outbursts of anger, factions, slander, gossip, arrogance and disorder. I am afraid that when I come again my God will humble me before you, and I will be grieved over many who have sinned earlier and have not repented of the impurity, sexual sin and debauchery in which they have indulged.**

**Rom 1:29-30 They have become filled with every kind of wickedness, evil, greed and depravity. They are full of envy, murder, strife, deceit and malice. They are gossips,**

I once heard a radio skit that was about the passing on of a prayer request. By the time it got to the last person the poor husband who had been downsized was being gossiped about as if he were a lazy bum. It doesn't matter if it's a prayer request or an "innocent" conversation; we need to watch what we say. Any time our talk puts down another person in any way we are gossips, plain and simple. The other matter is that sometimes we tell things that have been shared with us in confidence. We live in an age where endless information is all over the place. Just take a look at Twitter or Facebook and you will see things from "I'm brushing my teeth" all the way to "I wrecked my car today". Info told by the person is one thing, but usually it is not OK for us to share it. Jesus had the perfect answer to all this when He said, **"in everything, do to others what you would have them do to you, for this sums up the Law and the Prophets."** (Matt 7:12) Before you and I talk about some tid-bit, we should consider if this were about me would I want everyone to know it? Remember the pain you felt when some hurtful event became the topic of conversation around the area for months? So we should watch our tongues lest others have that same "WONDERFUL" experience. Proverbs 12:23 (The Message) says, "Prudent people don't flaunt their knowledge; talkative fools broadcast their silliness". Let us be prudent.

## A sounding gong

**1 Cor 13:1 If I speak in the tongues of men and of angels, but have not love, I am only a resounding gong or a clanging cymbal.**

**Mark 12:33 To love him with all your heart, with all your understanding and with all your strength, and to love your neighbor as yourself is more important than all burnt offerings and sacrifices."**

As I get "more mature" I find it harder and harder to distinguish words from background noise. The music often makes it hard to hear the words. Yes, I'm aware that some current music is designed that way, but I am not referring to that. The background noise in a movie or even from our TV sometimes blurs the words someone is speaking. At times this can be embarrassing or confusing if I think a person said one thing and it turns out they said something entirely different. Oh my, how confusing is the message we send to the world if we say one thing with our mouths and our life is saying something else so loudly that our words are being hidden. A Sunday Christian verbally says that one must show kindness but lives the rest of the week being anything but kind, or only "performs" for show (You know who you are). Genuine kindness makes a difference in our world. Phillips Brooks said – "No man or woman of the humblest sort can really be strong, gentle and good, without the world being better for it, without somebody being helped and comforted by the very existence of that goodness." Paul said – **"Love is patient, love is kind. It does not envy, it does not boast, it is not proud. It is not rude, it is not self-seeking, it is not easily angered, it keeps no record of wrongs. Love does not delight in evil but rejoices with the truth. It always protects, always trusts, always hopes, always perseveres. Love never fails."** (1 Cor 13:4-8) Are you making a difference or just making noise?

# Don't you know?

**1 Cor 6:19-20 Do you not know that your body is a temple of the Holy Spirit, who is in you, whom you have received from God? You are not your own; you were bought at a price. Therefore honor God with your body.**

**2 Cor 6:16 What agreement is there between the temple of God and idols? For we are the temple of the living God. As God has said: "I will live with them and walk among them, and I will be their God, and they will be my people."**

**Rom 6:3 Or don't you know that all of us who were baptized into Christ Jesus were baptized into his death?**

    I can see it now; you just received a letter announcing that a famous person whom you greatly admire wants to stop by for a visit. Oh my, windows to wash, painting that needs to be done, oh and we have to have a new welcome mat; the to-do list goes on and on because we want to impress this special visitor. Paul asked the Corinthians, "don't you know that your body is the temple of the Holy Spirit?" In light of that question, here is another. Why do we think we can continue with bad habits, little "harmless" sins, attitudes of harshness, purely selfish goals and no more than a Sunday religion and still expect God to find us totally acceptable? A third question: why is it that we will work harder at fitting in and being admired by the world than we will at living pleasing to the very One who indwells us? If we claim to be a Christian, we are claiming His precious spilt blood. Having made that claim, we are **"not our own"**. If we truly BELONG to Him, we OWE it to Him to be all that He expects of us. No longer can we be in first place. He is the Supreme One and either we live for Him or we do not.
    "Lord Jesus, help us put You above all else and live like we are Your dwelling place." Amen

## LIVE by Faith

**Heb 10:38 But my righteous one will live by faith. And if he shrinks back, I will not be pleased with him."**

**Hab 2:4 "See, he is puffed up; his desires are not upright- but the righteous will live by his faith**

**Phil 3:16 Only let us live up to what we have already attained.**

**Heb 3:12 See to it, brothers, that none of you has a sinful, unbelieving heart that turns away from the living God.**

It's amazing to me the number of email chains floating around that promise some miracle from God if you will just forward them to seven or maybe ten of your friends. Oh, and if you don't, your cat will die or some other crazy harmful thing will happen to you. We are told over and over in the Bible that we are to live by faith and that faith is to be based on and in Jesus Christ. He's the One who left heaven to come to earth and in the most vulnerable form possible, a baby. It was of Jesus that John wrote, **"He the creator of all "In the beginning was the Word, and the Word was with God, and the Word was God."** (John 1:1) God the Son gave His all for us and when we place our faith in anything other than Him we are sinning and rejecting Him. Doing so in the Old Testament was referred to as divination. Samuel wrote, **"For rebellion is like the sin of divination, and arrogance like the evil of idolatry. Because you have rejected the word of the LORD, He has rejected you as king."** (1 Sam 15:23) Saul lost his throne for just that reason. Oh precious ones, don't let sin creep into your lives, but rather live by faith in the One who loves you so. Do what I do and hit delete as fast as possible instead of relying on what some email says. If we trust God to get us to heaven, we can trust that He CAN and WILL take us through this life.

## Give God His Due

**Matt 12:31-32 "And so I tell you, every sin and blasphemy will be forgiven men, but the blasphemy against the Spirit will not be forgiven. Anyone who speaks a word against the Son of Man will be forgiven, but anyone who speaks against the Holy Spirit will not be forgiven, either in this age or in the age to come."**

**Matt 11:19 "The Son of Man came eating and drinking, and they say, 'Here is a glutton and a drunkard, a friend of tax collectors and "sinners." ' But wisdom is proved right by her actions."**

Today there is great interest in the supernatural. As Christians we know that THE Supernatural deserving of attention is GOD. It is He who spoke this world into being, implanting into to it both newness and antiquity. But because man is under the curse he has a hard time giving God credit for it all. People have their preconceived ideas of how things are and should be so they refuse to give God His due. This can happen in the Christian realm as well, for instance denial of the Holy Spirit and His working among us. The word "blaspheme" seems to carry two main connotations. ONE is the misuse of the name of God in any form and the SECOND is to give credit for the works of the Spirit to the demonic world. Both occur often. Those who refuse to accept that the Holy Spirit does many wondrous things today deny it by calling the person through which the work was done evil. "God doesn't do that stuff anymore", they say. These people may be well intended but so were the Pharisees, and they both are wrong. God DOES heal, He DOES deliver from demonic oppression and possession and He DOES give all the gifts AS HE SO CHOOSES. He always has and always will and even more so as we approach the return of our Lord Jesus. What men do not understand they mock and ridicule, but denying God and TRUE WORKS of the Holy Spirit is blasphemy and probable eternal death. Give God credit for His actions and exercise faith in who He is and what He does and you will be free from this trap of Satan.

## You can be a winner

**John 15:5-8 "I am the vine; you are the branches. If a man remains in me and I in him, he will bear much fruit; apart from me you can do nothing. If anyone does not remain in me, he is like a branch that is thrown away and withers; such branches are picked up, thrown into the fire and burned. If you remain in me and my words remain in you, ask whatever you wish, and it will be given you. This is to my Father's glory, that you bear much fruit, showing yourselves to be my disciples."**

**Phil 4:13 I can do everything through him who gives me strength.**

"I just can't do this Christian life thing!" We've all heard it, said it, or at least thought it. But believe it or not that's good news to the Lord. It is the one who thinks he or she has it nailed that has a problem. Truth is, we can't do it on our own. No more can we walk on water than we can live the way we should apart from the Holy Spirit. We need Him and His wisdom and help. Solomon wrote, **"The proverbs of Solomon son of David, king of Israel: for attaining wisdom and discipline; for understanding words of insight; for acquiring a disciplined and prudent life, doing what is right and just and fair; for giving prudence to the simple, knowledge and discretion to the young let the wise listen and add to their learning, and let the discerning get guidance for understanding proverbs and parables, the sayings and riddles of the wise."** (Prov 1:1-6) Only God has the wisdom that enables us to be what we should be and the only way we can gain that kind of wisdom is to SEEK it. We have to spend (invest) time in the Word and in prayer AND at times accept counsel from godly people. There are two ways to pass a test in school, study hard or cheat, but there is only one way to live the Christian life and that is to gain wisdom.

# Through HIM!!!

**Phil 4:13 I can do everything through him who gives me strength.**

**John 15:4 "Remain in me, and I will remain in you. No branch can bear fruit by itself; it must remain in the vine. Neither can you bear fruit unless you remain in me."**

**2 Cor 3:4-6 Such confidence as this is ours through Christ before God. Not that we are competent in ourselves to claim anything for ourselves, but our competence comes from God. He has made us competent as ministers of a new covenant-not of the letter but of the Spirit; for the letter kills, but the Spirit gives life.**

"Pastor, you just don't understand; there are things that are just too much for me". Well I couldn't agree more. After all, we're human beings and broken vessels even though we're created in the image of God. From the time Adam and Eve chose that fruit and doomed all of us to be born sinners, we have existed under sin's curse. As sinners we cannot fight the forces of evil in our own strength, our innate desire for sin is so strong. BUT, the good news is that we can win, for we have the resources at hand that can enable us to defeat our overwhelming urges for sinful ways. All we must do is CHOOSE to allow Jesus Christ through the power of His Holy Spirit to guide every step of our lives. If when our old habits, addictions, lusts etc. come calling we send HIM to answer the door instead of wrongly thinking that **we** have to do this ourselves, He will give us victory. You may say, "I have my own plan" and maybe so, but you've heard about the "best laid plans of mice and men". If you really want to lose those pounds, to end that addiction, to be all you can be, etc., then let HIM work HIS plan. He has the very best track record, He never misses the mark and He always scores. So why not let HIM fight your battle?

## TRADITIONS

**Acts 2:41 Those who accepted his message were baptized, and about three thousand were added to their number that day.... 47 praising God and enjoying the favor of all the people. And the Lord added to their number daily those who were being saved.**

**Acts 4:4 But many who heard the message believed, and the number of men grew to about five thousand.**

Every day souls die and enter into a Christless eternity in hell. That very thought should cause us deep sorrow and pain. The only reason we are here on earth is to give the good news of the gospel to the lost and dying. What is the church in large part doing about it? We are more concerned with our traditions of church décor, dress style, worship style etc. and in general that our judgmental attitudes and opinions are kept intact. We should hang our heads in shame. Peter preached his first sermon in the outdoors and 3000 were saved. Listen to his opening lines**, "Therefore let all Israel be assured of this: God has made this Jesus, whom you crucified, both Lord and Christ."** (Acts 2:36) The first communion was held in an upper room and somehow I doubt that anyone wore three-piece suits and sat on padded pews. They said of John the Baptist that he had a demon because he ate wild locusts and honey. The problem is like that of the Pharisees, TRADITION. **"Why do your disciples break the tradition of the elders? They don't wash their hands before they eat!"** (Matt 15:2) I think we would be hard pressed to find a sanctuary design or a dress code in the Bible. What does it matter if we sit in pews in a "proper sanctuary" or chairs in a multi- purpose area? It is OUR tradition and while we are fighting with each other to preserve it, souls are dying. Tradition that hinders our mission is wrong and we are wrong. Shame on us! We need to confess and repent of our sin, for if we do not willingly change, God may bring about changes for us and/or withhold His blessing from our land as well as us.

## The love of Christ constrains

**2 Cor 5:14 For Christ's love compels us, because we are convinced that one died for all, and therefore all died.**

**Matt 10:37 "Anyone who loves his father or mother more than me is not worthy of me; anyone who loves his son or daughter more than me is not worthy of me;**

**Job 32:18 For I am full of words, and the spirit within me compels me;**

**Acts 4:19 But Peter and John replied, "Judge for yourselves whether it is right in God's sight to obey you rather than God. 20 For we cannot help speaking about what we have seen and heard."**

In the original, the word constrain is *"'sunechoo' which means, to hold together, to press together, to shut up; then to press on, urge, impel, or excite. In the verse above the meaning is that the impelling or exciting motive in the labors and self-denials of Paul was the love of Christ for mankind. Christ so loved the world as to give Himself for it. His love was a demonstration that people were dead in sin. We, being urged by that same love, are prompted to like acts of zeal and self-denial to save the world from ruin."* (Barnes Notes) What we are to see here is that we also must be driven with an undeniable zeal for the lost. Our every thought and action in life is to be centered on what Jesus has done for us, then out of sincere appreciation we must dedicate every moment to Him and what is dearest to His heart. Rick Warren states in The Purpose Driven Life *"The church that does not want to grow is saying to the world, 'you can go to hell'"*. The church is made up of individuals, therefore it follows that those who do not make their lives an example of Christ's sacrifice are saying the same. What or who is the focal point of your life? Is it love for Christ and the lost that moves, motivates and drives you day after day, or is it something else?

## Where your treasure is

**2 Cor 4:18 So we fix our eyes not on what is seen, but on what is unseen. For what is seen is temporary, but what is unseen is eternal.**

**Matt 6:21 "For where your treasure is, there your heart will be also."**

**Phil 3:14 I press on toward the goal to win the prize for which God has called me heavenward in Christ Jesus.**

No one likes to talk about the brevity of life. We praise the medical industry when they find a cure for some disease or a better surgical procedure. We take special vitamin concoctions and supplements, all in an effort to live longer. The truth of the matter is that life is short and death will come. In fact the Bible makes this clear, **"The length of our days is seventy years or eighty, if we have the strength; yet their span is but trouble and sorrow, for they quickly pass, and we fly away."** (Ps 90:10) Today the average life expectancy is a little over eighty but though that figure be extended in years to come, death is imminent. Even if we live to be more than one hundred, it is still just a speck in time. For the Christian this is not bad news at all for we will immediately be united with our precious Jesus. The only question we need to consider is this; did I use my time here effectively for HIM? Matthew recorded Jesus' words **"For where your treasure is, there your heart will be also."** The truth of that statement is self-defining. I can be all consumed with things of this life that will take up my thoughts, time, money and strength, OR, if I am focused on Jesus and His kingdom, I can live a life that above all else seeks to honor HIM. We need to ask ourselves, am I living with the things of eternity in view. Are my eyes fixed on Him and is He my daily treasure? Am I living in view of the fact that all that I am and all that I do affects both now and eternity?

## Your body is holy ground!

**Matt 22:21 "Give to Caesar what is Caesar's, and to God what is God's."**

**Matt 4:10 "Away from me, Satan! For it is written: 'Worship the Lord your God, and serve him only."**

**Matt 22:37 "Love the Lord your God with all your heart and with all your soul and with all your mind."**

**1 Cor 6:19 Do you not know that your body is a temple of the Holy Spirit, who is in you, whom you have received from God? You are not your own;**

"It's my body and my life and no one is going to tell me how to live." Sound familiar? We all as humans are prone to thinking we should be able to control everything that happens in our lives, the events, the people and even God. When we take the seat of authority away from our rightful King, the Lord Jesus, we set ourselves up for trouble. The really weird thing is that when things go from bad to worse we strive even harder against Him, instead of yielding our wills and letting Him control the situation and us. He said, **"give to God what is God's"** and then the Apostle Paul told us, **"Do you not know that your body is a temple of the Holy Spirit."** As believers our bodies are the Temple of the Holy Spirit. If we are to give to God what is His, it only stands to reason that we surrender ourselves totally to the Lordship of Jesus Christ. Our bodies are Holy Ground and as such when we refuse Him full control we are literally slapping God in the face and denying ourselves joy, peace and freedom from stress and grief. If things in our lives are going from bad to worse, we first have to take a look and see who is in charge, Him or us. Isn't it a no brainer for us to quit our struggling, confess our sin, stay close to the Lord in every way possible and allow our wise, all powerful and loving God to handle EVERYTHNG?

## If we don't love, we don't know God

**1 John 4:7-12 Dear friends, let us love one another, for love comes from God. Everyone who loves has been born of God and knows God. Whoever does not love does not know God, because God is love. This is how God showed his love among us: He sent his one and only Son into the world that we might live through him. This is love: not that we loved God, but that he loved us and sent his Son as an atoning sacrifice for our sins. Dear friends, since God so loved us, we also ought to love one another. No one has ever seen God; but if we love one another, God lives in us and his love is made complete in us.**

Today as in the past many people have some weird ideas of what Christianity is all about. A pastor once told me how it offends him when he hears someone say to a lost person "God loves you". I hope he didn't mean by that that God does not love people who do not know Him. I for one am sure glad that Jesus loved me when I was lost in my sin, for long before my birth He paid the penalty for that sin. The truth is that GOD IS LOVE, loving even the vilest of sinners and here is the kicker, He expects us to love as He did. Our verses for today go so far as to say that if we don't love others, ALL others, we cannot claim to love Him. The list of those who are loved by God includes killers, prostitutes, druggies, and gossipers, overeaters etc. If we can see people as souls that are lost and bound for hell, God's love for them will fill us in a flash. The Apostle Paul says of himself, **"I was shown mercy so that in me, the worst of sinners....".** (1 Tim 1:16) He who penned a major portion of the New Testament saw and never forgot his sinfulness, as should we. As the old saying goes, "there but for the grace of God go I". God expects us to pass along the love He has shown us to those still living in their sin, so that they may also accept His gift of love and redemption.

## Lust is what?

**1 John 2:16 For everything in the world the cravings of sinful man, the lust of his eyes and the boasting of what he has and does-comes not from the Father but from the world. 17 The world and its desires pass away, but the man who does the will of God lives forever.**

**Num 11:5 We remember the fish we ate in Egypt at no cost, also the cucumbers, melons, leeks, onions and garlic. 6 But now we have lost our appetite; we never see anything but....this manna!**

The Psalmist cried out to his God for protection from lust, **"Turn my heart toward your statutes and not toward selfish gain. Turn my eyes away from worthless things; preserve my life according to your word."** (Ps 119:36-37)" Turn my heart, turn my eyes". This writer knew the source of the evil in his life. Understand that lust is never only sexual in nature. Lust covers a whole realm of sin. The Israelites lusted after melons and cucumbers and complained because all they had to eat was manna. Whenever we stray from the Lord it is because "each one is tempted when, by his own evil desire, he is dragged away and enticed." (James 1:14) My own evil desire! Yes, we all have deep desires within us that must be controlled or we will easily lapse into sin and that from within. Jesus also told us that we can lust in our minds. "But I tell you that anyone who looks at a woman lustfully has already committed adultery with her in his heart." (Matt 5:28) Breaking free from the sin that plagues us takes work and devotion to Jesus. Paul said that true Christians have crucified this sinful nature and the evidence of such crucifixion is how I react when my old desires rear their ugly heads. When this happens, do I immediately feel sorrow, repent and get rid of the very thought, or do I consider it for a while, increasing the possibility of acting upon it? Jesus asked Peter three times "do you love me". Is an evidence of your love for God horror and disgust at the temptations that rise up from your old self?

## Humble, but the GREATEST!!

**Phil 2:5-11 Your attitude should be the same as that of Christ Jesus: Who, being in very nature God, did not consider equality with God something to be grasped, but made Himself nothing, taking the very nature of a servant, being made in human likeness. And being found in appearance as a man, He humbled himself and became obedient to death even death on a cross! Therefore God exalted him to the highest place and gave him the name that is above every name, that at the name of Jesus every knee should bow, in heaven and on earth and under the earth, and every tongue confess that Jesus Christ is Lord, to the glory of God the Father.**

It's really amazing what people will do to draw attention to themselves. Human nature seems to desire that five minutes in the sun; just watch some of the reality (?) shows on television these days. BUT, the greatest man who ever lived and walked the paths of this earth never wanted or needed such acclaim. He knew the mission he had been given and what He sought beyond all else was to do the will of His Father. He made Himself of no reputation and obeyed the order to die on the cross when He had every right to demand all glory and honor, not death. He knew that true greatness is found in being totally humble. Now what about us? The one who would be a true servant of Christ is ministering and just as much at home cleaning toilets as fulfilling the role as worship leader or standing behind a pulpit preaching God's Word. True glory and honor only comes from our GOD. We can do no better than to bury all ego and self-promotion and seek the glory that only HE can give to whomever He pleases. Will you follow the example of the "King of kings" and "Lord of lords" and in humble obedience serve wherever He places you?

*Just A Thought*

## What Would Jesus Do?

**John 8:3-4 The teachers of the law and the Pharisees brought in a woman caught in adultery. They made her stand before the group and said to Jesus, "Teacher, this woman was caught in the act of adultery.**

**John 4:17-18 "I have no husband," she replied. Jesus said to her, "You are right when you say you have no husband. The fact is, you have had five husbands, and the man you now have is not your husband. What you have just said is quite true."**

**John 21:15 When they had finished eating, Jesus said to Simon Peter, "Simon son of John, do you truly love me more than these?" "Yes, Lord," he said, "You know that I love you." Jesus said, "Feed my lambs."**

We live in a day when many find it hard to take a stand for Jesus Christ. Whole denominations refuse to call sin sin and the "politically correct" way has long since taken over. Looking, though, at the other end of the spectrum it is also common to totally bash and belittle those who are trapped in certain sins. But, WHAT WOULD JESUS DO? Today's verses answer that question and they give us a good idea of how we are to handle the presence of sin. One day the Pharisees thought they could trap Him by setting up a woman taken in adultery, but He showed her love, not condemnation. His response to her and her sin led this broken woman to repentance, after which He said, **"Go now and leave your life of sin."** (John 8:11) Everyone knew her sordid past and after seeing this dramatic change because of Jesus' love and kindness, many others came to know Him as well. **"Then, leaving her water jar, the woman went back to the town and said to the people, "Come, see a man who told me everything I ever did. Could this be the Christ?" They came out of the town and made their way toward him"**. (John 4:28-30) Peter denied ever knowing his precious Lord, yet He told Peter, **"Feed my lambs."** Never does Jesus abuse or cajole anyone into following Him and consider this; Jesus loved you and me so

*Just A Thought*

much that before we even existed **He paid** the penalty for our sin. Now as you go and live life, LOVE as **He** did.

## Awesome "Charges"

**Eph 6:1-4 Children, obey your parents in the Lord, for this is right. "Honor your father and mother" which is the first commandment with a promise "that it may go well with you and that you may enjoy long life on the earth." Fathers, do not exasperate your children; instead, bring them up in the training and instruction of the Lord.**

**Col 3:21 Fathers, do not embitter your children, or they will become discouraged**

**Prov 22:6 Train a child in the way he should go, and when he is old he will not turn from it.**

**Prov 19:18 Discipline your son, for in that there is hope; do not be a willing party to his death.**

Ask the mother of one or the mother of a dozen (maybe that's a stretch) and both will tell you that children are truly a blessing from the Lord, even though some seem to work hard to be otherwise. With the joy of having children comes the awesome responsibility of teaching and guiding them to one day live on their own. Solomon wrote that we are to "train a child in the way he should go" and the Apostle Paul reminded us to not "exasperate" them, meaning frustrate or infuriate them. At times these two requirements seem like oxymorons. Many parents think that any discipline at all will make their kid mad, but it is possible to do our job in such a way that will ease much of the tension. Parents are usually trying to conform their children to their own preconceived idea of how that child should turn out. But the actual wording of Solomon's command indicates that we are to "train" them in keeping with their natural gifts and the particular bent for which they were created. A parent may believe their child should be a doctor, but that may not have one iota to do with their real calling. The valedictorian of his class may really want to be a plumber and not a rocket scientist. Parents, we need to identify and encourage our kids' particular and special talents and gifts.

Doing so will make our job a whole lot easier. Don't try to live out your dreams through your kids; they have their own. Do everything you can to encourage them in the way that God has made them and you will not only find life with them a whole lot easier, but you may even find them more eager to learn from you about Jesus.

## FORGIVE?

**Matt 6:9-15 "'Our Father in heaven, hallowed be Your name, Your kingdom come, Your will be done on earth as it is in heaven. Give us today our daily bread. Forgive us our debts, as we also have forgiven our debtors. And lead us not into temptation, but deliver us from the evil one.' For if you forgive men when they sin against you, your heavenly Father will also forgive you. But if you do not forgive men their sins, your Father will not forgive your sins."**

**Matt 18:32-35 "Then the master called the servant in. 'You wicked servant,' he said, 'I canceled all that debt of yours because you begged me to. Shouldn't you have had mercy on your fellow servant just as I had on you?' In anger his master turned him over to the jailers to be tortured, until he should pay back all he owed. "This is how My heavenly Father will treat each of you unless you forgive your brother from your heart."**

"Forgive or you will not be forgiven." Yesterday a pastor shared the story of how the Lord convicted his heart regarding this subject of forgiveness. My friend had a very real dislike and lack of forgiveness for another. Some will ask if an unforgiving person will lose their salvation. I am very glad I don't have to answer that one, but in Matthew 18 Jesus brings to our attention a person who was forgiven, but because he withheld forgiveness from someone else his forgiveness was canceled and he ended up being tortured until he paid back what he had owed. We choose to not forgive for many reasons and more than likely some of the problems in our lives are the result of the attitude, "I deserve to be angry and upset over this." Maybe so, but that "right" may well be causing us pain and grief, another visit to the situation may be in order. There is no way we can take a lax attitude toward this issue. Jesus said, "Christian, forgive or you will suffer", physically, emotionally, spiritually etc. etc. If you are nursing any grudges, you need to forgive and let go; and if you know someone who is harboring the sin of unforgiveness (it is a sin), do them a favor and with Jesus' love share this with them.

# ROB God, "ME"?

**Mal 3:8 "Will a man rob God? Yet you rob me.**

**Ps 29:2 Ascribe to the LORD the glory due his name; worship the LORD in the splendor of his holiness.**

**Matt 22:21 Then he said to them, "Give to Caesar what is Caesar's, and to God what is God's."**

**Luke 11:42 "Woe to you Pharisees, because you give God a tenth of your mint, rue and all other kinds of garden herbs, but you neglect justice and the love of God. You should have practiced the latter without leaving the former undone."**

"ME? I would never even think of robbing God. I'm a good Christian and stealing is sin, so no way." In theory that sounds great and honorable, but is it true? The Malachi statement refers to tithing so the question is "do you tithe?" But wait, there's a lot more here than tithing. Jesus accused the Pharisees of giving their tithe yet ignoring justice, compassion and love. Paul said, **"Give everyone what you owe him: If you owe taxes, pay taxes; if revenue, then revenue; if respect, then respect; if honor, then honor"**. (Rom 13:7) So it seems that when we fail to give God the honor due Him, when we fail to worship Him, when we are not compassionate, when we could care less about justice and when we neglect to honor and show respect to our fellow human beings, we are in fact robbing God. Sorry to say, even Christians look down on other people. We see a street person, a drug addict, someone out of work and needy, those who dress differently from us or anyone else we view as a lost cause ("after all they could help themselves"), BUT JESUS CHRIST loves that one the same way He loves you and me. He knows the real reason they are as they are and still loves them. Aren't you glad that YOU never made any poor choices and can smugly take pride in where you're at today?

## ME Serve? – YES YOU!!

**Mark 10:45 For even the Son of Man did not come to be served, but to serve, and to give his life as a ransom for many."**

**Luke 22:26-27 "But you are not to be like that. Instead, the greatest among you should be like the youngest, and the one who rules like the one who serves. For who is greater, the one who is at the table or the one who serves? Is it not the one who is at the table? But I am among you as one who serves."**

**John 13:14 "Now that I, your Lord and Teacher, have washed your feet, you also should wash one another's feet."**

Somehow humans prefer to be served rather than serve. Hosts of us prefer to have the honorable seat at the table than be the one serving the food. The more the perceived glory, the more we want the position. But Jesus, though He was King of kings, taught and set the example of servanthood by washing the feet of his disciples, even those of Judas' only hours before he would kiss Him with the kiss of death. There is no greater display of humility and service than to get down and wash the feet of another. Somehow we have developed an attitude of BEING SERVED rather than that of SERVING. All sorts of relationships suffer because this important virtue is so lacking, including marriages that fall apart because one or the other expects total service from their mate. Paul admonishes us men to love our wives, **"However, each one of you also must love his wife as he loves himself,"** (Eph 5:33) A great way to show that love is to bow before her and wash her feet. Does she deserve it? Maybe or maybe not in your mind, but guys we need to forget the deserving part and demonstrate our appreciation of her. After all, they put up with us, don't they? If Jesus served, and He did, why not do as He did? Oh, and I will never forget the initial look of shock then love and respect on Ruthie's face the Sunday I washed her feet in front of our church family.

## For GOD so loved <u>your name</u> !

**John 3:16 "For God so loved the world that he gave his one and only Son, that whoever believes in him shall not perish but have eternal life."**

**Rom 5:10 For if, when we were God's enemies, we were reconciled to him through the death of his Son, how much more, having been reconciled, shall we be saved through his life!**

**Rom 8:32 He who did not spare his own Son, but gave him up for us all-how will he not also, along with him, graciously give us all things?**

Some people today, as in ages past, go around saying that God hates sinners, at least certain types. I'm not sure where they get their theology, but the truth straight from the WORD is that GOD LOVES all people, though not their sin. Jesus Christ came to earth for one express purpose. **"For God did not send his Son into the world to condemn the world, but to save the world through him."** (John 3:17) Nowhere in the Bible does it say that there is anyone that God does not love, either individually or as a group; in fact that love is so deep that He gave His SON. Having said that, there **are** things that God does hate, **"There are six things the LORD hates, seven that are detestable to him: haughty eyes, a lying tongue, hands that shed innocent blood, a heart that devises wicked schemes, feet that are quick to rush into evil, a false witness who pours out lies and a man who stirs up dissension among brothers."** (Prov 6:16-19) It is sin He hates, not the sinner, and He extends His salvation to any and all who will come to Him. So whether you and I are prone to overeating, misstatements (lying) or whether we're part of a hated segment of society, it matters not. He hates ALL sin, but we can be assured that He loves us and has no desire to see us die without the certainty of eternal life with Him. His offer is for everyone and the decision is ours, not His. Have you accepted His love and free gift of salvation? If not, why not?

## Be Content WHATEVER Circumstance

**Phil 4:11-13 I am not saying this because I am in need, for I have learned to be content whatever the circumstances. I know what it is to be in need, and I know what it is to have plenty. I have learned the secret of being content in any and every situation, whether well fed or hungry, whether living in plenty or in want. I can do everything through him who gives me strength.**

**2 Cor 8:9 For you know the grace of our Lord Jesus Christ, that though he was rich, yet for your sakes he became poor, so that you through his poverty might become rich.**

**Phil 3:13-14 Brothers, I do not consider myself yet to have taken hold of it. But one thing I do: Forgetting what is behind and straining toward what is ahead, I press on toward the goal to win the prize for which God has called me heavenward in Christ Jesus.**

We sure do like to complain. The weather, our checkbook, our neighbor or a thousand other things we're not happy with at the moment. The Apostle Paul learned that whatever his circumstance he was content. We in America, at least until lately, have enjoyed mostly unlimited freedom. On the other hand our Christian brothers and sisters in China, Sudan, Iran, Iraq and countless other places are regularly imprisoned, beaten, tortured and murdered just because they love the Lord. Oh and by the way, they stay true to Him. We get hung up in traffic, see our vacations dreams go up in smoke, lose some material possession or just aren't able to do what we want when we want and we become irate. Eleven of the Apostles were murdered for their faith, John was exiled to Patmos and Paul was beheaded, but they knew the secret of contentment. They knew that God was the center of everything and that no matter what, He is to be trusted. Life carries with it changes and problems and we must walk the path before us. The early saints relied on the Holy Spirit for strength and wisdom for each and every day. We have the same God, the same Savior, Jesus Christ, and the same Holy Spirit so why can't we trust like they did?

## Pseudo Christians

**2 Tim 3:1-5 But mark this: There will be terrible times in the last days. People will be lovers of themselves, lovers of money, boastful, proud, abusive, disobedient to their parents, ungrateful, unholy, without love, unforgiving, slanderous, without self-control, brutal, not lovers of the good, treacherous, rash, conceited, lovers of pleasure rather than lovers of God having a form of godliness but denying its power. Have nothing to do with them.**

**Isa 29:13 The Lord says: "These people come near to me with their mouth and honor me with their lips, but their hearts are far from me. Their worship of me is made up only of rules taught by men.**

A few years ago our church began praying specifically for God to reveal to us the reason or reasons for the oppression in our area. He showed us three things. Two of them had to do with drugs and witchcraft. These things can be expected as we do live in a fallen world, but the third was quite alarming. He showed us that even within churches many do not truly know Him. Our scriptures today tie in with that fact. The Apostle Paul warned Timothy of this and told him to "have nothing to do with them." While we cannot treat such ones as brothers and sisters in Christ, we can and must pray for them and show them His love. True followers of Christ are the opposite of 2 Tim. 3:1-5 and are humble and kind and loving, unconditionally loving others and God. Real Christians honor God with their heart rather than with actions to be seen and approved of by men. Real Christians bear "fruit" and are different from the world around them. They may seldom speak a word, but their daily walk shows that they have something, SOMEONE, very special. There is no room for hypocrisy in our lives or in the church. Jesus' response for some when they face Him one day will be, **"Then I will tell them plainly, 'I never knew you. Away from me, you evildoers!'** (Matt 7:23) Are you what you say you are before men and God?

## Glorify Your God!

**2 Thess 1:11-12 With this in mind, we constantly pray for you, that our God may count you worthy of his calling, and that by his power he may fulfill every good purpose of yours and every act prompted by your faith. We pray this so that the name of our Lord Jesus may be glorified in you, and you in him, according to the grace of our God and the Lord Jesus Christ.**

**2 Thess 1:10 on the day he comes to be glorified in his holy people and to be marveled at among all those who have believed. This includes you, because you believed our testimony to you.**

**1 Peter 4:14 If you are insulted because of the name of Christ, you are blessed, for the Spirit of glory and of God rests on you.**

Very few of us would come right out and say that we do not want God to be glorified in our lives, but sometimes that is exactly what we show by our actions. The real source of glory to God is His people. If we have accepted His gift of salvation we are forever indebted to Him and just like we must pay those pesky mortgage payments we owe God our allegiance and devotion. Some will say, "I don't know how". Okay then, what do you do at work when you don't know how to do something? You learn. RIGHT? In the same way, **"Do your best to present yourself to God as one approved, a workman who does not need to be ashamed and who correctly handles the word of truth".** (2 Tim 2:15) It's hard work, but isn't God's love, His presence and eternal life here and the blessed assurance of a home with Him in the future worth some effort? It is entirely possible that someone you love dearly will be in heaven just because you worked at living your life for the Lord. If you have trouble understanding the Bible ask a pastor for help. A few tips, don't try to read the whole Bible in one sitting, rather read one passage until you get it. Get involved in your church and a small group. Contact your pastor or me for help. Do these things NOW. He died for you and the least we can do is get to KNOW HIM.

## LET your light shine!

**Matt 5:16 "In the same way, let your light shine before men, that they may see your good deeds and praise your Father in heaven."**

**Eph 5:8-14 For you were once darkness, but now you are light in the Lord. Live as children of light (for the fruit of the light consists in all goodness, righteousness and truth) and find out what pleases the Lord. Have nothing to do with the fruitless deeds of darkness, but rather expose them. For it is shameful even to mention what the disobedient do in secret. But everything exposed by the light becomes visible, for it is light that makes everything visible.**

When was the last time the electric was off at your home? I can see it all now as you stumble through the darkness trying to remember where that flashlight is supposed to be. Ah, there it is, but the batteries are dead. You actually jump for joy because you are still in the dark? NOT, because of course when you finally get your hands on the light you expect this whole problem to go away. Far more serious, there are lost family members, co-workers and friends that stay as they are because we are not shedding light on their lostness. We may be making an attempt to reach them by preaching at them when what they need is to see that this Jesus is real and that He can be everything to them. Our lives must display, **"the fruit of the Spirit is love, joy, peace, patience, kindness, goodness, faithfulness, gentleness and self-control. Against such things there is no law. Those who belong to Christ Jesus have crucified the sinful nature with its passions and desires. Since we live by the Spirit, let us keep in step with the Spirit. Let us not become conceited, provoking and envying each other."** (Gal 5:22-26) The Holy Spirit will give us the ability to SHINE if we will allow Him too. People can ignore preaching and often will, but it is impossible for them to argue with the fact that you and I are different from what we once were. Is your light a soft glow or is it burning brightly, breaking up the darkness around you?

# I will trust Him!

**Job 13:15 Though he slay me, yet will I hope in him;**

**Job 16:17-21 yet my hands have been free of violence and my prayer is pure. "O earth, do not cover my blood; may my cry never be laid to rest! Even now my witness is in heaven; my advocate is on high. My intercessor is my friend as my eyes pour out tears to God; on behalf of a man he pleads with God as a man pleads for his friend.**

**1 John 3:20 whenever our hearts condemn us. God is greater than our hearts, and he knows everything.**

There is quite a widespread belief that accepting Christ as Savior will take away all of one's problems. While this is true on a spiritual level, that will not be the case in practical day-to-day life. People and situations still cause us problems, we get sick and the list could go on, but when Jesus is our Best Friend we are free to lean on Him and know that He will handle everything. A lady once told us that she came home late one evening to find a message on her answering machine alerting her to a serious contention that was going on in her family. Having to be at work early the next day, she told the Lord, "I have to get some rest so I'm giving this to You to handle". While in the shower the next morning another message came in telling her that this huge problem had been resolved while she trusted and slept. Our woes can go away but not always in the way we expect. God wants to take care of us, but as our pets totally trust us for their care we must throw ourselves on Him to do the same. Is Jesus Christ your Best Friend and your Everything in EVERY circumstance or is He only your Savior? One life leads to dilemmas and the other to complete peace. Why then not choose peace?

## Bridle That Tongue?

**James 3:3-6 When we put bits into the mouths of horses to make them obey us, we can turn the whole animal. Or take ships as an example. Although they are so large and are driven by strong winds, they are steered by a very small rudder wherever the pilot wants to go. Likewise the tongue is a small part of the body, but it makes great boasts. Consider what a great forest is set on fire by a small spark. The tongue also is a fire, a world of evil among the parts of the body. It corrupts the whole person, sets the whole course of his life on fire, and is itself set on fire by hell.**

**Ps 64:3 They sharpen their tongues like swords and aim their words like deadly arrows.**

**Prov 15:1 A gentle answer turns away wrath, but a harsh word stirs up anger.**

Oh my, how much trouble we get ourselves into with words that so easily fly off our tongues. Many times things are said in jest, but the "victim" doesn't always see the humor. I have been guilty of that with my precious wife. I am quite prone to humor and don't always think ahead, so I know how challenging it is to "bridle that tongue". By the way, I here apologize to her in public and ask everyone to hold me accountable. The good news is that the Holy Spirit is more than willing to help every one of us if we will let Him, but our allowing that is our choice. James says that the tongue is a small part of the body and likens it to a spark of fire that can cause major problems. Solomon gave words of wisdom when he said, "a gentle answer turns away wrath (anger)". Relationships will heal and trouble will be avoided if only we will be careful of what we say in the first place. Jesus said, **"This is my command: Love each other."** (John 15:17) Real love puts me in the position of weighing how I would feel if I were the brunt of that joke or that harsh word. Oh and by the way, if you ever notice me being unkind to my Ruthie, please let me know. OK?

## Not my will!

**Luke 22:42 "Father, if you are willing, take this cup from me; yet not my will, but yours be done."**

**Ps 40:8 I desire to do your will, O my God; your law is within my heart."**

**John 6:38-40 "For I have come down from heaven not to do my will but to do the will of him who sent me. And this is the will of him who sent me, that I shall lose none of all that he has given me, but raise them up at the last day. For my Father's will is that everyone who looks to the Son and believes in him shall have eternal life, and I will raise him up at the last day."**

The question today is this; is there anything keeping us from living totally for God? Many things in this life can stand in the way such as our social standings, careers, ambitions, trusting ourselves instead of Him. I don't know exactly what Jesus was struggling with in the garden that night, but I do know that if I had been facing the pain of being beaten half to death and nails driven through my body I would be asking, "Isn't there another way?". Whatever was going on He chose the right answer, **"Yet not my will, but yours be done."** How about you and me? If the Lord were to ask us to change or alter anything in our lives would our willing response be, "Not my will, but Yours". If Jesus had failed His Father, you and I would not have the gift of salvation. If we refuse to do what He asks of us, there will be serious consequences, not the least, lost souls who may never come to know Him. One more question is this; do we want Jesus for our own selfishness or do we want Him for HIS purposes? Aren't you glad that Jesus chose the will of the Father?

*Just A Thought*

## Does your heart pound for HIM?

**Rev 3:20 "Here I am! I stand at the door and knock. If anyone hears my voice and opens the door, I will come in and eat with him, and he with me."**

**Song of Solomon 5:2-4 I slept but my heart was awake. Listen! My lover is knocking: "Open to me, my sister, my darling, my dove, my flawless one. My head is drenched with dew, my hair with the dampness of the night." I have taken off my robe- must I put it on again? I have washed my feet- must I soil them again? My lover thrust his hand through the latch opening; my heart began to pound for him.**

Oh how we look forward to the arrival of a loved one who's long been absent. We've all waited at the door and ran out to meet them, holding them in an embrace as our hearts pound with joy. The separation at last has ended. What a picture of Jesus as He patiently waits for lost sinners to repent and come home, home to the One who created them and for whom He gave his life. An old TV ad portrayed a substitute family providing a hug as a guy decides to take a certain cell contract offer. As the hug ends the teenage son coldly says to the salesman, "I'm going to lunch now." This is just about all that an empty relationship provides, a hug totally devoid of meaning. The enemy would have us think that his embraces are real but he knows what some people have yet to learn. Remember, he tried to get rid of our Lord that day on the cross because he knows that the love and devotion of Jesus is the only real source of a meaningful relationship. Solomon's description of a lover anxiously awaiting the appearance of his beloved one is a clear picture of how God feels about us. The sad thing is that many, including some who claim to know Him, are living as if He were still in the tomb. He died yes, but the joyous news is that He rose again to give us victory over sin and death and intimacy with Him. Do you know the overflowing greatness of His love?

## Where is your faith?

**Matt 6:33 "But seek first his kingdom and his righteousness, and all these things will be given to you as well."**

**Prov 3:9 Honor the LORD with your wealth, with the first fruits of all your crops; 10 then your barns will be filled to overflowing, and your vats will brim over with new wine.**

**Ps 37:3 Trust in the LORD and do good; dwell in the land and enjoy safe pasture.**

**Ps 37:25 I was young and now I am old, yet I have never seen the righteous forsaken or their children begging bread.**

Seek first!!! The story is told of "Pistol" Pete Maravich who as a young lad would lean out the window of his dad's car and dribble his basketball all the way to town. As a result he became one of the all-time best players. He wanted to be good at his craft and was willing to do whatever it took. Likewise he strived to be a good Christian and gave it that the same kind of devotion. It is when we really want and go after a sincere deep relationship with the Lord Jesus that it becomes possible. Saying a "sinners prayer" may get one into heaven, only God knows its sincerity, but becoming a true intimate friend of Jesus calls for a lot more effort. What kind of relationship do we want with Him? It's only when a seed falls into the ground and dies that it can know the joy of growth and new life The same holds true for us when we die to our own desires. Jesus himself said, **"And everyone who has left houses or brothers or sisters or father or mother or children or fields for my sake will receive a hundred times as much and will inherit eternal life."** (Matt 19:29) Simply put, He must be above all else and most important to us to the extent that we would willingly give up any person or any thing that He'd ask of us. Let's "get with it" and also motivate someone else to "lean out the window and dribble the ball" for the One who died and rose again for all of us.

## Love not, know not!

**1 John 4:8 Whoever does not love does not know God, because God is love.**

**1 John 2:4 The man who says, "I know him," but does not do what he commands is a liar, and the truth is not in him.**

"I just can't stand _____. If you knew what they've done you wouldn't like them either." Usually the target of such venom is someone who has offended us in one way or another. But John makes it clear that an attitude of contempt indicates one thing and one thing only, we don't know God. We may attend church every week, tithe and do all the "right things", BUT we do not know God. I am not the one saying this, the WORD does. No use in mincing words because the WORD is explicit. **"Anyone who claims to be in the light but hates his brother is still in the darkness"** (1 John 2:9) and John adds, **"No one who lives in Him keeps on sinning. No one who continues to sin has either seen Him or known Him."** (1 John 3:6) We don't have to be in such bondage as this because Jesus has provided a way of escape. **"He was delivered over to death for our sins and was raised to life for our justification."** (Rom 4:25) If we claim to love Him we must accept His justification and love our brothers through His power. Yes, there are those who are hard to love and they may try hard to be unlovable, but love them we must. Jesus set the example when He washed Judas' feet and when He loved those who had just nailed Him to the cross by asking the Father to forgive them. If you are reading today's Thought it is clear that no one has driven nails into your body or killed you. You may choose to not expose yourself to more harm from someone who has hurt you, but you must love them and pray for them.

## God meant it!

**Gen 45:4-7 Then Joseph said to his brothers, "Come close to me." When they had done so, he said, "I am your brother Joseph, the one you sold into Egypt! And now, do not be distressed and do not be angry with yourselves for selling me here, because it was to save lives that God sent me ahead of you. For two years now there has been famine in the land, and for the next five years there will not be plowing and reaping. But God sent me ahead of you to preserve for you a remnant on earth and to save your lives by a great deliverance.**

Friends betray us, families at times turn their backs on us, spouses inflict pain beyond belief, and so on. In this life there will be those who will cause us sorrow and grief, but what they do is not the important thing. Let's review Joseph's life. He was daddy's favorite, even had a special coat. In his naivety he shared a dream with his brothers who reacted in harsh anger and sold him into slavery. Winding up in Egypt, he was imprisoned on false charges and forgotten by one he had befriended, yet eventually he became literally the ruler of the land. With all the betrayal and lies told of him if anyone had a "right" to be angry and vindictive it was Joseph, BUT because his attitude was so far from that. What a challenge he is to us. He had the wisdom to know that what others meant against him for evil, God intended to use for good. In this case it resulted in the saving of an entire nation. Had not Joseph been so influential in Egypt the Jews would have starved to death. From the cross Jesus said, "Father, forgive them, for they do not know what they are doing." (Luke 23:34) Not unlike Joseph's brothers, those who hurt us do not really know all the consequence of what they are doing, but oh our God knows and will use it for our good. The only question is "will we be as wise as Joseph?"

*Just A Thought*

## Even if He slays me?????

**Job 13:15 Though he slay me, yet will I hope in him; I will surely defend my ways to His face.**

**Job 19:25-26 I know that my Redeemer lives, and that in the end He will stand upon the earth. And after my skin has been destroyed, yet in my flesh I will see God;**

**Ps 23:4 Even though I walk through the valley of the shadow of death, I will fear no evil, for You are with me; your rod and your staff, they comfort me.**

**Rom 8:38-39 For I am convinced that neither death nor life, neither angels nor demons, neither the present nor the future, nor any powers, neither height nor depth, nor anything else in all creation, will be able to separate us from the love of God that is in Christ Jesus our Lord.**

"God knew this was coming long ago. We will trust Him and go on", said an Amish man as he spoke of the school shooting tragedy in Nickel Mines, PA. Job said, "Though He slay me" and David said, "Through the valley of death I will not fear". The Biblical patriarchs and many others down through the years knew something we need to know and remember. God will not desert us; He will never leave us to our own devises. We may not always understand the events of our lives, but truly God already knows long beforehand what will come our way. Our responsibility is to rely on Him even when it seems He is not meeting our needs, the pain does not go away, the cancer is not cured, or whatever. He has a much higher purpose, **"For my thoughts are not your thoughts, neither are your ways my ways," declares the LORD. "As the heavens are higher than the earth, so are my ways higher than your ways and my thoughts than your thoughts."** (Is 55:8-9) "God is too wise to be mistaken, God is too good to be unkind; For when you don't understand, When you don't see His plan, When you can't trace His hand, Trust His heart. (from the song "Trust His Heart" by Babby Mason)

## Glorify God

**Col 3:17 And whatever you do, whether in word or deed, do it all in the name of the Lord Jesus, giving thanks to God the Father through him.**

**Prov 3:6 in all your ways acknowledge him, and he will make your paths straight.**

**1 Cor 10:31 So whether you eat or drink or whatever you do, do it all for the glory of God.**

**Col 3:23 Whatever you do, work at it with all your heart, as working for the Lord, not for men.**

I once heard a preacher tell that he had done extensive research on the root meaning of the word ALL, wanting to know exactly what it meant. Not surprisingly, what he found was that ALL means exactly that, ALL. So it would appear that when the Bible says, whatever we do we must do it all as unto the Lord, that applies to everything. Literally, whether we are eating, drinking, sleeping, walking, talking, working, hiking etc., in all of living we must not just do it FOR Him, but WITH Him and IN HIS POWER. Our lives have to be bringing honor to our Lord in everything, even our choices of entertainment, movies, TV shows, internet, sporting events and so on. Anything we do that contains sin will not be honoring to Him. If anything, ANYTHING), we do is not glorifying to God, it is our responsibility to change what we are doing. If we claim Jesus as Savior, He must also be LORD. Yes, we must be prepared to make correct choices, even though they appear to be small ones, if God is truly our God. If we are His children how can we justify bringing ANY shame on His good name? The Psalmist said, **"Better is one day in your courts than a thousand elsewhere;"** (Ps 84:10) The world can look threatening and appealing as well, but He is the final victor and I would rather stand for the ultimate winner than enjoy temporary pleasure. How about you?

## Praise Him

**Hab 3:17 Though the fig tree does not bud and there are no grapes on the vines, though the olive crop fails and the fields produce no food, though there are no sheep in the pen and no cattle in the stalls, 18 yet I will rejoice in the LORD, I will be joyful in God my Savior.**

**Job 13:15 Though he slay me, yet will I hope in him; I will surely defend my ways to his face.**

**Phil 4:4 Rejoice in the Lord always. I will say it again: Rejoice!**

The trooper only gave a warning ticket "praise the Lord". The mailman brought an unexpected check "praise the Lord". The doctor announced there is no more cancer "praise the Lord". BUT, what about the ticket for speeding, the lack of money or when doc says "the picture looks dire". Do we still "praise the Lord"? Is God still good? YES, He is. Our God is always good. This is the lesson I have been learning for years. Nearly thirty long years ago I herniated a disc when I fell. Since that time my back has continually degraded until the latest MRI shows more arthritis that causes increased constant pain. Yet, I am so grateful to my God for He knows the total picture and I have learned to trust Him regardless. I can honestly say I would rather have this situation and Him than to be out there in perfect health without Him. It is not convenient and it is not really something wildly enjoyable that's for sure, but after being anointed several times and tons of prayer it is my lot, at least for now. I praise my Lord every day that He is at my side and makes life very good anyway. There are days when I have to remind myself of all this, but He is Lord and He is good. Do YOU know this truth?

## Not against flesh and blood!

**Eph 6:11 Put on the full armor of God so that you can take your stand against the devil's schemes.**

**2 Cor 10:4 The weapons we fight with are not the weapons of the world. On the contrary, they have divine power to demolish strongholds.**

**1 Cor 10:13 No temptation has seized you except what is common to man. And God is faithful; he will not let you be tempted beyond what you can bear. But when you are tempted, he will also provide a way out so that you can stand up under it.**

Wrestling against flesh and blood is completely different than wrestling with sin and temptations. Many a contact sport person has gone undefeated in their battles simply because they are physically strong and have an ability to withstand any encounter. To do this they invest many hours maintaining their bodies in championship form. But when it comes to spiritual battles we face another kind of enemy and normal weapons will not do the job. He knows our weak spots, he knows the Scriptures and he is not above distorting the truth just enough to trip us up resulting in defeat. Just as the athlete must train, train and train some more to keep the winning form, so WE MUST train - train - train. We do this by INVESTING in our Lord with prayer, Bible study and intimate time with Him as well as fellowship with His people. This enables us to put on the armor against Satan that He offers us and this is how we become winners. God demands obedience and our allegiance and He provides not only the weapons but also the power we need. How good is this, to be on a team that will never lose?

## "I will remove this "king" – Herod

**Luke 1:39-44** At that time Mary got ready and hurried to a town in the hill country of Judea, where she entered Zechariah's home and greeted Elizabeth. When Elizabeth heard Mary's greeting, the baby leaped in her womb, and Elizabeth was filled with the Holy Spirit. In a loud voice she exclaimed: "Blessed are you among women, and blessed is the child you will bear! But why am I so favored, that the mother of my Lord should come to me? As soon as the sound of your greeting reached my ears, the baby in my womb leaped for joy.

**Matt 2:16** When Herod realized that he had been outwitted by the Magi, he was furious, and he gave orders to kill all the boys in Bethlehem and its vicinity who were two years old and under, in accordance with the time he had learned from the Magi.

What a striking contrast between the attitude of Mary and Elizabeth and that of Herod. When the angel appeared to Mary with the news of her baby she was no doubt confused by such a message but answered, "be it unto me." Upon hearing Mary's greeting Elizabeth felt her child leap for joy in her womb. Despite the circumstances, both of these women rejoiced at the events unfolding in their lives and felt privileged to be honored by God as their part of history unfolded. One other player in all this was Herod. In his ignorance and worldly attitude he felt a threat to his power upon hearing the news of a king. He was an evil man and we know now that his jealously caused a lot of suffering in Bethlehem as his soldiers mercilessly slew all the baby boys two years old and younger. Added to that, Herod rejected the only One who could pay the price for his sin, as do many in our day. But instead of casting stones at those who are like him we would do better to cry over the Herods in our world and pray that they find love, mercy and forgiveness in God's Son, Jesus.

## What's in your heart?

**Matt 15:18-20 "But the things that come out of the mouth come from the heart, and these make a man 'unclean.' For out of the heart come evil thoughts, murder, adultery, sexual immorality, theft, false testimony, slander. These are what make a man 'unclean'; but eating with unwashed hands does not make him 'unclean.'"**

**Gal 5:19-23 The acts of the sinful nature are obvious: sexual immorality, impurity and debauchery; idolatry and witchcraft; hatred, discord, jealousy, fits of rage, selfish ambition, dissensions, factions and envy; drunkenness, orgies, and the like. I warn you, as I did before, that those who live like this will not inherit the kingdom of God. But the fruit of the Spirit is love, joy, peace, patience, kindness, goodness, faithfulness, gentleness and self-control. Against such things there is no law.**

A young person commits a hateful crime and the media and some of the public immediately blame it all on "that horrible music". The sad part is, they may be correct. Repeatedly the Scripture tells us that sin and evil comes from the heart. The heart according to Mr. Webster is "the whole personality, the emotional or moral as distinguished from the intellectual nature, one's innermost being". Just as people filled with hate, street gangs and others, act out of the content of their hearts so do Christians. Problem is that many of us do not fill our hearts with "the right stuff". What are the buttons on your radio set to? What do you watch on TV? How often to you read your Bible? When was the last time you read the words of a hymn? Are you struggling with a particular sin? Are you feeling down, defeated, dejected and generally discouraged? The old saying is "garbage in, garbage out". Not that secular music, TV etc. is all garbage, but if that is all we take in how can we expect to bring joy, peace, and security out? If you feed on a constant diet of foul language, illicit sex, negativism and other stuff that is palmed off as entertainment, your actions will be adversely affected. BUT, if your "favorite foods" are the Lord Jesus and good things, His Word, church and fellowship, the benefits will be great. Sooooo, what is in your heart?

## Love = respect = joint heirs

**1 Peter 3:7 Husbands, in the same way be considerate as you live with your wives, and treat them with respect as the weaker partner and as heirs with you of the gracious gift of life, so that nothing will hinder your prayers.**

**Matt 5:23-24 "Therefore, if you are offering your gift at the altar and there remember that your brother has something against you, leave your gift there in front of the altar. First go and be reconciled to your brother; then come and offer your gift."**

"If you only really knew my wife." That is the way many a husband begins a self-justification statement. I am sure there are wives that are less than pleasant to live with, but at times that is the fault of the husband. Paul told us, **"However, each one of you also must love his wife as he loves himself, and the wife must respect her husband."** (Eph 5:33) I found a wheel-shaped illustration that said, "He reacts without love, She reacts without respect, He reacts without love, She reacts without respect" etc. over and over until the wheel is spinning about one-hundred fifty miles per hour. There are no winners when that happens and we are setting ourselves up for big trouble as well as rejection by the Lord. A husband, wife, friend, fellow Christian or anyone who fails to understand and practice this truth is sinning in many ways. Two of these sins are disrespect of a fellow heir and exaltation of self. Any person who accepts Jesus Christ as LORD and SAVIOR is an heir of His and when we act in a cruel way toward another believer, or even a non believer, it is no wonder our prayers are blocked. The opposite of the wheel illustration is one where love results in respect that results in love that results in respect etc. When this second wheel starts spinning, blessings flow in ways we cannot begin to imagine and such a home or friendship will yield unbelievable joy and peace. And the added blessing, He WILL hear our prayers.

## HIS Ways!!!

**Is 55:8 "For my thoughts are not your thoughts, neither are your ways my ways," declares the LORD. 9 "As the heavens are higher than the earth, so are my ways higher than your ways and my thoughts than your thoughts.**

**Hos 14:9 Who is wise? He will realize these things. Who is discerning? He will understand them. The ways of the LORD are right; the righteous walk in them, but the rebellious stumble in them.**

"This just doesn't make sense", "I can't see any way this could be right" or "Where is God? Doesn't He know I am in trouble here?" We have to admit that we've all been there, which brings to my mind a few thoughts. There was no human sense to Job's trials either. It didn't fit that it took forty years for the Israelites to walk what should have taken them less than a couple weeks. Oh, and it makes no sense that the Son of God would die for my sin. The thing we lose sight of is that God's ways and thoughts are so superior to ours, there is really no comparison. He sees the end from the beginning while we only see what's gone before and what is happening today, no, make that this moment. All too often we get our minds made up to what God should do and how He should answer our prayers, when in His wisdom He answers with the best overall reply. Remember that Jesus actually allowed Lazarus to die and that sounds crazy to us. **"Jesus loved Martha and her sister and Lazarus. Yet when he heard that Lazarus was sick, he stayed where he was two more days. After he had said this, he went on to tell them, "Our friend Lazarus has fallen asleep; but I am going there to wake him up."** (John 11:5-6 & 11) He knew how to bring the most honor to the Father. So the question is this; are we willing for God to do WHATEVER IT TAKES to be honored in our lives? Job said, 'Though he slay me, yet will I hope in him." (Job 13:15a)

## Walk in the LIGHT!

**John 12:35-36 Then Jesus told them, "You are going to have the light just a little while longer. Walk while you have the light, before darkness overtakes you. The man who walks in the dark does not know where he is going. Put your trust in the light while you have it, so that you may become sons of light."**

**Eph 5:14 for it is light that makes everything visible. This is why it is said: "Wake up, O sleeper, rise from the dead, and Christ will shine on you."**

**1 John 1:6-7 If we claim to have fellowship with him yet walk in the darkness, we lie and do not live by the truth. But if we walk in the light, as he is in the light, we have fellowship with one another, and the blood of Jesus, his Son, purifies us from all sin.**

Walking in the light is not and never has been purely an intellectual decision but rather a heart decision. The Christian life is not the journey of an intellect, which can leave one empty, but the journey of ones HEART for God. It is significant that Jesus did not pick the academically elite for His right hand team. In that day those who couldn't make it to the position of upper or even middle class became fishermen. They were the dregs of society but they TRUSTED THE LIGHT so implicitly. I recently heard about a guy who attended a worship service in Argentina, at which time the Lord distinctly told him that he needed to get out of his head and into his heart if he really wanted to know and serve Him. Enough of our judgmental, elitist attitudes. We must forget the thoughts of "they're not perfectly on key, the speaker doesn't use proper English", and the like. It is time to get beyond our preconceived notions of the proper way things ought to be and focus on what is important to God. This man did just that and found a deeper understanding of what God wanted for him. Only when we get into the Lord with our hearts more than our heads will we know the greatest joy, peace and love and only then will we be able to go from having a knowledge of God to really knowing the Lord. It is easy to talk ABOUT God, but quite another to have complete trust in Him as LORD. So which is He to you?

## HE will lift you up!

**Luke 14:10-11 "But when you are invited, take the lowest place, so that when your host comes, he will say to you, 'Friend, move up to a better place.' Then you will be honored in the presence of all your fellow guests. For everyone who exalts himself will be humbled, and he who humbles himself will be exalted."**

At wedding receptions there is usually a table assigned to the wedding party and another one or two reserved for family and other special people. While attending a wedding a few years ago we were invited to sit at such a table with our friends. As the celebration progressed I got the impression that, even though it was not marked and no one said anything, we were sitting where we should not have been. I had noticed some family members squeezing chairs in at other tables and it was embarrassing to think that we had taken seats reserved for others. That happened by accident, but many times folks intentionally take a seat of honor thinking they deserve it. Jesus said that we should not be conceited enough to think we merit a place of honor. Not that a certain seat is a bad thing, but rather pushing ourselves into it when it is not our place is where the problem lies. Solomon puts it this way, "The fear of the LORD teaches a man wisdom, and humility comes before honor." (Prov 15:33) We may well deserve a special place, but oh how much better to take a lower position and be asked to move up than to take another's seat and have to be asked to move down. Be sure of this, if we have earned honor it will be given to us and the real way to do that is this, "So whether you eat or drink or whatever you do, do it all for the glory of God." (1 Cor 10:31)

# Be Holy

**Lev 20:7 "'Consecrate yourselves and be holy, because I am the LORD your God"**

**Eph 1:4 For he chose us in him before the creation of the world to be holy and blameless in his sight. In love**

**Col 3:12 Therefore, as God's chosen people, holy and dearly loved, clothe yourselves with compassion, kindness, humility, gentleness and patience.**

Some days it seems that this Christian life is so complicated and hard. How does God expect me a sinner, even as a redeemed sinner, to "be holy"? How could He even think that I can meet all His requirements? I mean, loving those who are unlovable, having a personal time with Him daily, watching my every thought to be sure each one is pure, forgiving those who do not merit forgiveness and on and on. Good news, God knows that I am unable to be and do all these things, that is why He says, **"Come to me, all you who are weary and burdened, and I will give you rest. Take my yoke upon you and learn from me, for I am gentle and humble in heart, and you will find rest for your souls. For my yoke is easy and my burden is light."** (Matt 11:28-30) Did you hear that? He says that His yoke is easy. Truth is, we make it harder than it needs be. We try to live this life in our own power and Jesus is saying, "Let Me Live My Life Through You". When things get overwhelming the first thing we should realize is that we have been focusing on ourselves, not Him. When we empty ourselves of all our own agendas, desires, lusts and other self- fulfilling ideas, we are free and have cast all our cares on Him. It is only then that we can have the life He wants us to have, a life that is easier and joyful, for He is carrying our load. Even better than a cane helps one walk, He helps us LIVE.

## Don't you know?

**1 Cor 6:19-20 Do you not know that your body is a temple of the Holy Spirit, who is in you, whom you have received from God? You are not your own; you were bought at a price. Therefore honor God with your body.**

**2 Cor 6:16 What agreement is there between the temple of God and idols? For we are the temple of the living God. As God has said: "I will live with them and walk among them, and I will be their God, and they will be my people."**

Interesting how when some people are invited to church they respond with "I don't have good enough clothing to go there." Somehow the very mention of church conjures up this feeling of needing to respect the institution in a special way by dressing "properly" and kids are told, "don't run in church". You know what I'm talking about. But the Word says, "YOUR BODY is temple of the Holy Spirit". Our bodies are His actual abiding place yet we do not respect them nearly as much as we do "the church". We overeat, smoke, drink to excess, don't get enough rest and in many other ways expose our temple to danger and destruction. If we fully realized that WE ARE that temple wouldn't you think we would take better care of ourselves? For the one who says, "I've tried to stop abusing my body and I just can't", here is the good news. You have just taken the first step to healing by acknowledging that YOU CAN'T DO IT and the necessity of giving it to God because HE CAN. All you have to do is yield it to Him. Will you, will you right now? I pray that each and every one of us will respond to the Holy Spirit's conviction and love, let go and let God.

## "It's MY life"

**John 15:8 "This is to my Father's glory, that you bear much fruit, showing yourselves to be my disciples."**

**Matt 5:16 "In the same way, let your light shine before men, that they may see your good deeds and praise your Father in heaven."**

**1 Cor 6:20 you were bought at a price. Therefore honor God with your body.**

**1 Cor 10:31 So whether you eat or drink or whatever you do, do it all for the glory of God.**

"Nobody tells me what to do, it's my decision!" "I don't have to if I don't want to!" Sort of sounds like the typical kid doesn't it? Sad, but true, it also sounds like some who say they are Christians. Oh, they will no doubt use different words. One of the favorite phrases is, "I'll have to pray about this!" It's for sure good to pray about everything, but that may just be a cop out that loosely translates, "NO WAY". Paul said that we are bought with a price, so whatever we do must be done for God's glory. Jesus said that we are to glorify God by bearing fruit. If our lives are not totally different from the world around us we may want to take another look at whether we have ever accepted Jesus as Savior and Lord in the first place. Jesus also said, **"But whoever disowns me before men, I will disown him before my Father in heaven."** (Matt 10:33) By refusing to glorify God by living out our witness for Him before the world, we are denying Him. Read that verse again. It can't get much plainer than that.

## If you know HIM, you are without excuse!

**Luke 6:47-48 "I will show you what he is like who comes to me and hears my words and puts them into practice. He is like a man building a house, who dug down deep and laid the foundation on rock. When a flood came, the torrent struck that house but could not shake it, because it was well built."**

How many times God's messenger is roasted for lunch and I fear that may be your reaction today, but please hear me out. Jesus is the One who said, **"if a servant knows and does not he will be punished."** (Luke 12:47) One who claims to know Jesus as Savior yet continues to sin is headed for trouble. It is that simple. I hear comments like, "well I don't kill, commit adultery, or any of those "bad" sins so I am OK, right?" Let me ask, do you harbor any unforgiving spirit? **"For if you forgive men when they sin against you, your heavenly Father will also forgive you."** (Matt 6:14) Have you ever gossiped? Oh I forgot, you were only passing on prayer requests. **"Besides, they get into the habit of being idle and going about from house to house. And not only do they become idlers, but also gossips and busybodies, saying things they ought not to."** (I Tim 5:13) Do you ever look lustfully on one who is not your spouse? **"But I tell you that anyone who looks at a woman lustfully has already committed adultery with her in his heart."** (Matt 5:28) Are you taking care of the temple of the Holy Spirit? **"Do you not know that your body is a temple of the Holy Spirit, who is in you?"** (1 Cor 6:19) Anything and everything that is less than pure is sin, period, and Jesus Himself said, **"But the one who hears my words and does not put them into practice is like a man who built a house on the ground without a foundation. The moment the torrent struck that house, it collapsed and its destruction was complete."** (Luke 6:49) Are you hearing or HEARING the words of Jesus?

## But not THEM

**Jonah 4:1-2 But Jonah was greatly displeased and became angry. He prayed to the LORD, "O LORD, is this not what I said when I was still at home? That is why I was so quick to flee to Tarshish. I knew that you are a gracious and compassionate God, slow to anger and abounding in love, a God who relents from sending calamity.**

**Ps 86:5 You are forgiving and good, O Lord, abounding in love to all who call to you.**

Sad as it is many of us know people that we consider as "them" or "that kind". Maybe it is a homeless person, a drug user or someone we just don't like. For Jonah it was "those Ninevites". He had an intense dislike for them and he did not want them to be forgiven by God of their sin. What's more, he strongly disliked the idea of being the agent of that forgiveness. So much so that his next words were **"Now, O LORD, take away my life, for it is better for me to die than to live."** (Jonah 4:3) He would have rather died than witness the events that were to come. Jonah was a Hebrew and as such had known God's mercy many times, but still his self-righteousness wanted to deny that same grace to "them". John says that there is a command associated with love, **"We love because he first loved us. If anyone says, "I love God," yet hates his brother, he is a liar. For anyone who does not love his brother, whom he has seen, cannot love God, whom he has not seen. And he has given us this command: Whoever loves God must also love his brother."** (1 John 4:19-21) There cannot be an attitude of "them" in our lives. They are God's creation and Jesus died for them as well as us. If you know you have a "them" in your life I plead with you to confess it to God and seek His mercy and grace, then go out and love ALL people.

## You failed to consult The One

**Is 22:10-11 You counted the buildings in Jerusalem and tore down houses to strengthen the wall. You built a reservoir between the two walls for the water of the Old Pool, but you did not look to the One who made it, or have regard for the One who planned it long ago.**

**James 4:17 Anyone, then, who knows the good he ought to do and doesn't do it, sins.**

It is amazing how many times we think we know exactly what aught to be and just how to do it. Usually what we have in mind are very good things. The Israelites fortified the wall of Jerusalem, which would seem like a good thing, but God told them, **"Beware, the LORD is about to take firm hold of you and hurl you away, O you mighty man.** (Is 22:17) Recently I heard a young man testify that God spoke to him to think with his heart and not with his head. God gave us minds and we are to use them, but what this fellow meant was that he needed to listen to God and follow the HIS leading in his heart, putting complete trust in the Lord. God will never fail the one who consults Him, the one who implicitly trusts Him. Why do we find that so hard? I think it may be because His plans don't coincide with ours. God's people in Jerusalem needed to trust Him for deliverance, but chose to trust their own puny efforts more. We may think we know best, but ultimately it is God who is faithful, able and willing to be our all in all. So where is your trust? Is it in God, the One who created all things and perfectly maintains the whole universe, or are you trusting your own wants and desires? Remember, **"Anyone, then, who knows the good he ought to do and doesn't do it, sins."** Are you and I sinning?

## Does HE know me?

**Matt 7:21-23 "Not everyone who says to me, 'Lord, Lord,' will enter the kingdom of heaven, but only he who does the will of my Father who is in heaven. Many will say to me on that day, 'Lord, Lord, did we not prophesy in your name, and in your name drive out demons and perform many miracles?' Then I will tell them plainly, 'I never knew you. Away from me, you evildoers!'"**

**Matt 25:11-12 "Later the others also came. 'Sir! Sir!' they said. 'Open the door for us!' "But he replied, 'I tell you the truth, I don't know you."**

**John 10:14 "I am the good shepherd; I know my sheep and my sheep know me"**

**2 Tim 2:19 Nevertheless, God's solid foundation stands firm, sealed with this inscription: "The Lord knows those who are his," and, "Everyone who confesses the name of the Lord must turn away from wickedness."**

A few years ago the Lord revealed to us at Daybreak that there are many people in churches and even whole assemblies who are playing games with Him. They faithfully attend services, say all the right things and play the part oh so well, claiming to know Him, but Jesus does not know them. Simply put, they have never truly repented of their sin and turned their back on their past. Amazing isn't it that we say we want to live in heaven with Jesus and share His glory, but we seem to want to be with Him only in the future. Right now we have our lifestyle, desires, friends, and other preferences that we are unwilling to give up. They are more important to us than Him. Thing is, often these personal agendas tear us apart and we are totally unaware of our real problem. We can't understand why God doesn't get us out of this or that or do such and such for us, but fail to understand that He cannot work if we continue to play our games. The Christian life is a one hundred percent calling. **"Everyone who confesses the name of the Lord must turn away**

**from wickedness."** We cannot keep our "little white sins". Either He is Savior AND LORD, or He is nothing at all.

## The least of these!!!!!

**Matt 25:40 The King will reply, 'I tell you the truth, whatever you did for one of the least of these brothers of mine, you did for me.'**

Whatever the time of year, we would do well to read and ponder these words of Jesus. There are millions upon millions of kids around the world, including right here in the USA, who have never had a "good" Christmas or birthday or anything else. Some of them have never been given a gift of any kind. Many do not know love from ANYONE and it's safe to say that the majority have never heard of JESUS and HIS love for them. When Christmas season rolls around again I urge you to pack one shoebox, at the very least, for Operation Christmas Child (Franklin Graham's Samaritan's Purse), this tremendous ministry that annually blesses millions of kids all around the world. My next suggestion is to look around your own community for a family in need and do something to love and bless them in Jesus' name. Parents are struggling with all the effects of economic crises and an enormous number of kids are suffering from loss of parents. In short, whole families need something, somebody to encourage them and it takes so very little time, effort or money to share the love of Jesus. His words to those who withhold compassion were in His day and will be in the future, **"Depart from me, you who are cursed, into the eternal fire prepared for the devil and his angels. For I was hungry and you gave me nothing to eat, I was thirsty and you gave me nothing to drink, I was a stranger and you did not invite me in, I needed clothes and you did not clothe me, I was sick and in prison and you did not look after me.' "They also will answer, 'Lord, when did we see you hungry or thirsty or a stranger or needing clothes or sick or in prison, and did not help you?' "He will reply, 'I tell you the truth, whatever you did not do for one of the least of these, you did not do for me."** (Matt 25:41-45)

## "Neither do I condemn"

**John 8:11 "No one, sir," she said. "Then neither do I condemn you," Jesus declared. "Go now and leave your life of sin."**

**John 3:17 "For God did not send his Son into the world to condemn the world, but to save the world through him."**

**John 8:15-16 "You judge by human standards; I pass judgment on no one. But if I do judge, my decisions are right, because I am not alone. I stand with the Father, who sent me."**

**Luke 15:7 "I tell you that in the same way there will be more rejoicing in heaven over one sinner who repents than over ninety-nine righteous persons who do not need to repent."**

Jesus was always full of compassion for everyone He came in contact with. John records the story of the woman taken in adultery in chapter eight. Jesus knew her whole story and refused to be taken in by those trying to trap her AND Him. I have often wondered where the guy was; after all it takes two to be in an adulterous situation. The Pharisees were so much like many today in that they desired to use one letter of the law to justify their position. I know someone who was told, "You committed adultery twelve years ago so you need to realize that God expects you to sit in the corner, useless to Him." I'm so glad that God is not like that at all. When we repent our past sins, He erases them from the record. He says to us as He did to that woman **"Go now and leave your life of sin."** He judges by the Father's standard and not man's. Two lessons should be learned from this. One, do not suppose to judge another, leave that to God, and two, do not let anyone hold repented sin over your head. If God has erased it, nothing is left. NOTHING.

# Run do not walk!!!!!!!

**2 Tim 2:22 Flee the evil desires of youth, and pursue righteousness, faith, love and peace, along with those who call on the Lord out of a pure heart.**

**1 Tim 6:11 But you, man of God, flee from all this, and pursue righteousness, godliness, faith, love, endurance and gentleness.**

**1 Peter 2:11 Dear friends, I urge you, as aliens and strangers in the world, to abstain from sinful desires, which war against your soul.**

We all struggle with various sins in our lives. For some it is overeating, lack of exercise, gossip, a judgmental attitude, anger, lust, an addiction, etc. Is it possible that we do not really FLEE from those things that drag us down? James tells us that, **"When tempted, no one should say, 'God is tempting me.' For God cannot be tempted by evil, nor does he tempt anyone; but <u>each one is tempted when, by his own evil desire</u>, he is dragged away and enticed."** (James 1:13-14) So when we sin, it is our own fault. Yes, the enemy will try to entice us, but to be victorious two things must happen. 1— We have to flee the initial sinful thought. 2 — We have to take the double barrel approach of submitting (giving ourselves) to God AND resisting the devil. And I might add, in the Holy Spirit's power, not ours. Look again, **"<u>Submit</u> yourselves, then, <u>to God</u>. <u>Resist the devil</u>, and he will flee from you. Come near to God and he will come near to you."** (James 4:7-8) God has given us very specific instructions for defeating sin in our lives, BUT we have to apply what He has commanded. Only when we consistently take ownership of our failures, confess them and flee from them, will we experience joy and victory.

## Oh how we trust ourselves

**Prov 3:5-7 Trust in the LORD with all your heart and lean not on your own understanding; in all your ways acknowledge him, and he will make your paths straight. Do not be wise in your own eyes; fear the LORD and shun evil.**

**Prov 28:26 He who trusts in himself is a fool, but he who walks in wisdom is kept safe.**

**Jer 10:23-24 I know, O LORD, that a man's life is not his own; it is not for man to direct his steps. Correct me, LORD, but only with justice not in your anger, lest you reduce me to nothing.**

I've been pondering the subject of thinking with our hearts rather than our heads. Many times we do think with our hearts all right, but I fear it is not with a heart that is attuned to God. Problems arise that are really internal and we fail to get God's input regarding a situation. We start thinking we would be happier in another job, another marriage or whatever, but if we have shut the door on the Lord's guidance nothing will change. It may appear to, in the short haul, but not over the long one. At that point whatever exterior change we make in our lives won't bring about any difference for us if we don't address the negative things inside, primarily because we will carry the same old baggage from our former life into the new. I read yesterday about a lady who was very upset because her husband showed no interest in a project she was into. She soon learned that God would supply the answer to her prayers if all she did was wait for Him to work. How about those times when we know we are doing what will bring pain to the One who died for us? We know we are failing Him, but proceed anyway. It could be likened to buying your child a very expensive gift only to watch them stomp it to bits. Jeremiah cries out for God to show justice rather than anger. Is there a good chance we need just that? Yes, for if we are sinning and are well aware of it, we so much need His mercy. How about it, do you need to repent of something right now? He will gladly forgive and restore us if we just call on Him, own and confess our sin and turn a complete 180 from it.

## Expect Trouble

**Matt 5:11-12 "Blessed are you when people insult you, persecute you and falsely say all kinds of evil against you because of me. Rejoice and be glad, because great is your reward in heaven, for in the same way they persecuted the prophets who were before you."**

**Matt 19:29-30 "And everyone who has left houses or brothers or sisters or father or mother or children or fields for my sake will receive a hundred times as much and will inherit eternal life. But many who are first will be last, and many who are last will be first."**

"Just accept Jesus and your trials will be over". This is what many today are being duped into believing. But Jesus told us that when the world abuses us we would be blessed. When we take a stand for Him and are not afraid to let it be known that we love our blessed Son of God, we will be attacked. Satan hates Jesus and anyone who loves Him, so he is not happy when we live our lives for our Savior and not him. Jesus made some statements that apply here, **"Whoever finds his life will lose it, and whoever loses his life for my sake will find it."** (Matt 10:39) **"Then you will be handed over to be persecuted and put to death, and you will be hated by all nations because of me.** (Matt 24:9) **"If the world hates you, keep in mind that it hated me first.** (John 15:18) Only in Jesus do we find life and because the world hated Him we should not be surprised when it hates us. Every day in places like Sudan, India and China folks are imprisoned, starved and even killed for their faith in Christ. What a challenge to us. Do we love Him that much? He died so that He would not have to live without us; is that love reciprocated? Would we rather die than deny the One who loved us so? Being a citizen of a country comes with responsibilities and being a citizen of heaven requires that we surrender our all.

## What Sin?

**Mark 14:72 Immediately the rooster crowed the second time. Then Peter remembered the word Jesus had spoken to him: "Before the rooster crows twice you will disown me three times." And he broke down and wept.**

Chuck Swindoll once said that the church seems to want to keep all of our past offences in a "brown paper bag" which is checked before we're allowed to again serve the Lord. If we have committed certain sins we are then relegated to sitting in a corner and prohibited from ever serving God again. Oh, the monies we give will be gladly accepted but that's about it because back in 19__ we _____. Praise the Lord that Jesus never said anything like that. He even made a point of making sure that Peter knew he was still loved and useful after he had "majorly" sinned and assigned him to be a great worker in the Kingdom. When God forgives sin it is gone, never to be mentioned again. 1 John 1:9 says that, **"If we confess our sins, He is faithful and just and will forgive us our sins and purify us from all unrighteousness."** When a person is cleansed and purified they are just that, clean and pure. Jesus forgave the woman taken in adultery and told her, **"Go now and leave your life of sin."** (John 8:11) And after being confronted by Nathan, the prophet, David said, **"Create in me a pure heart, O God, and renew a steadfast spirit within me. Do not cast me from your presence or take your Holy Spirit from me. Restore to me the joy of your salvation and grant me a willing spirit, to sustain me. Then I will teach transgressors your ways, and sinners will turn back to you."** (Ps 51:10-13) He had full assurance of total forgiveness and knew that God would use him to teach and warn others of the dire outcome of blatant sin. How about you; have you been shelved? If so, do not be afraid to seek and pursue God's will for your life, whatever it is. If God calls a person clean how can any man do differently?

## Fear the Lord

**Prov 1:7 The fear of the LORD is the beginning of knowledge, but fools despise wisdom and discipline.**

**Job 28:28 And he said to man, 'The fear of the Lord-that is wisdom, and to shun evil is understanding.'"**

**Ps 111:10 The fear of the LORD is the beginning of wisdom; all who follow his precepts have good understanding. To him belongs eternal praise.**

**Prov 9:10 "The fear of the LORD is the beginning of wisdom, and knowledge of the Holy One is understanding.**

Every day fear eats away at many many people and "phobias" abound, phobia being defined by Webster as an irrational persistent fear or dread. The key word here is irrational. Most phobias are just that and keep us from enjoying life. **"There is no fear in love. But perfect love drives out fear, because fear has to do with punishment. The one who fears is not made perfect in love."** (1 John 4:18) This powerful emotion of fear is a very effective tool of the enemy of our souls and again we look to Mr. Webster for its meaning. As a verb, one definition of fear is *to have a reverent awe of* and as a noun it is a *profound reverence especially toward God*. Understandably some people do live in a phobia-type fear of God, but actually the "fear" of Him is to be more like an awesome reverence. There was once a man who could not find the words to tell the Lord how much he loved Him and words do very often fail us. But once we truly get a view of our Holy, Holy, Holy God our intense thankfulness will go far beyond any words to action, showing Him how we feel by giving every bit of our lives to Him. When others see such a sense of love and reverence for Him in us they will be attracted to this awesome Lord and Savior. What are they seeing of Him in us?

## Your first love

**Rev 3:15 "I know your deeds, that you are neither cold nor hot. I wish you were either one or the other! 16 So, because you are lukewarm-neither hot nor cold-I am about to spit you out of my mouth. 17 You say, 'I am rich; I have acquired wealth and do not need a thing.' But you do not realize that you are wretched, pitiful, poor, blind and naked."**

**Phil 1:9 And this is my prayer: that your love may abound more and more in knowledge and depth of insight,**

**2 Thess 1:3 We ought always to thank God for you, brothers, and rightly so, because your faith is growing more and more, and the love every one of you has for each other is increasing.**

**Rev 2:4 "Yet I hold this against you: You have forsaken your first love."**

If you are like me you know the ugh feeling of picking up a cup of coffee or hot chocolate and taking a sip, only to find it has cooled off to a point where the taste is actually disgusting. If it were ice cold or still hot, okay, but this Luke-warm stuff is awful. Jesus told John to write to the Laodicean church that they were neither hot nor cold so He was about to spit them out. Unfortunately many people in the church today would cause Him to make that same statement. He told the Ephesians that they had left their first love. They had drifted away and allowed the cares of daily life to eclipse their once sincere love for the Savior. When we say we are just too busy to spend time with our Lord, what we are really saying is that other things have become more important to us and we have lost interest in knowing Him more. It was He who said, **"Remember the height from which you have fallen! Repent and do the things you did at first. If you do not repent, I will come to you and remove your lampstand from its place."** (Rev 2:5) Return, oh weary one, return and enjoy the intimacy with Jesus you first knew.

## "Be it unto me"

**Luke 1:38** "I am the Lord's servant," Mary answered. "May it be to me as you have said." Then the angel left her.

**Gen 24:58** So they called Rebekah and asked her, "Will you go with this man?" "I will go," she said.

**Ps 116:16** O LORD, truly I am your servant; I am your servant, the son of your maidservant; you have freed me from my chains.

**Rom 4:20-21** Yet he did not waver through unbelief regarding the promise of God, but was strengthened in his faith and gave glory to God, being fully persuaded that God had power to do what he had promised.

    Most of us will do whatever we are asked if certain criteria are met and as long as it doesn't take me out of my comfort zone, like having to learn a new skill or be put in an embarrassing situation. But could we review for a moment some of the greatest figures in the Bible. Job lost everything but his integrity (Job 1 & 2), Joseph was in jail under false charges, Rebekah married a man she didn't know, David was the Lord's anointed yet was hiding for his life, and Isaiah went around stripped and barefoot for three years. (Is. 20:3) Then along comes Mary, somewhere in the thirteen to fifteen age range, who mysteriously goes away to visit a cousin only to return home visibly pregnant, then tries to tell everyone that she is yet a virgin. Joseph, a just man, so loved Mary that he sought to protect her through it all by getting a quiet divorce. BUT GOD intervened. All of these knew that God was faithful even though it was hard for them. HE was the source of their salvation so HE was to be obeyed. The Apostle Paul reminds us in Romans that Abraham was so sure of God that he did not waver nor entertain disbelief; rather he was strengthened in his faith. Closely following Christ may well cost us, but it is the only way that has a "lived happily ever after" ending. God is all-powerful and He will see us through all of life's hard spots, if not deliver us from them.

## DESPERATE!!!!!

**Ps 42:1-2 As the deer pants for streams of water, so my soul pants for you, O God. My soul thirsts for God, for the living God. When can I go and meet with God?**

**Matt 5:6 Blessed are those who hunger and thirst for righteousness, for they will be filled.**

One evening in Bible Study while studying intimacy with God we talked about being desperate for Him. The first stage of desperation is to realize we have wandered away from Him and NEED to go home, but it goes much farther than that. Michael W. Smith well described this state in the song, "Breathe", *"This is the air I breathe. This is the air I breathe, Your holy presence living in me. This is my daily bread. This is my daily bread, Your very word spoken to me. And I, I'm desperate for you. And I, I'm lost without you. This is the air I breathe. This is the air I breathe, Your holy presence living in me. This is my daily bread. This is my daily bread, Your very word spoken to me. And I'm, I'm desperate for You. And I'm, I'm lost without You. And I'm desperate for You And I'm, I'm lost without You."* If that describes you or me then we are truly living in that state of desperation, knowing we cannot exist apart from Him. While step one brings us INTO Him, there has to be a step two of TOTALLY LIVING Him. We consciously decide that no one or no thing is going to be more important or come between Him and us. If you've worked out with weights you know you have to start with smaller pounds and work up gradually or you may become discouraged and even give up. In the same way, I suggest that you begin by spending consistent short times with the LORD. You will find that in time the more you do the more you'll want. The more you KNOW Him the more you'll WANT to know Him. So if you have never invested yourself in the Lord, why not start today?

## "Do not be afraid"

**Matt 1:18-21** This is how the birth of Jesus Christ came about: His mother Mary was pledged to be married to Joseph, but before they came together, she was found to be with child through the Holy Spirit. Because Joseph her husband was a righteous man and did not want to expose her to public disgrace, he had in mind to divorce her quietly. But after he had considered this, an angel of the Lord appeared to him in a dream and said, "Joseph son of David, do not be afraid to take Mary home as your wife, because what is conceived in her is from the Holy Spirit. She will give birth to a son, and you are to give him the name Jesus, because he will save his people from their sins."

**Is 51:7** "Hear me, you who know what is right, you people who have my law in your hearts: Do not fear the reproach of men or be terrified by their insults.

Mary endured quite an ordeal to become the mother of our Lord Jesus, but Joseph did not get a free ride either. He had some hard decisions to make. Joseph is described as a righteous man. He had carefully chosen Mary to be his wife and then to find her with child, before their marriage had been consummated, left him in a quandary. This decent pure girl he thought he had married appeared to be anything but decent and pure. Then the angel told him not to fear to take Mary home with him as his wife. I'm sure the gossip mill ran wild that day far more than it does today. More than likely he was accused of being with her anyway. BUT Joseph made a choice to believe God no matter the consequence and raise this child as his own. What an example of obedience both of them are to us. They both chose to follow the Lord no matter what the outcome. We have little Biblical information on either of them, but tradition and normal human behavior give us some good ideas of the price they paid. Are we willing to follow such an example?

## LOOK alive or BE alive?

**Rev 3:1-3 "I know your deeds; you have a reputation of being alive, but you are dead. Wake up! Strengthen what remains and is about to die, for I have not found your deeds complete in the sight of my God. Remember, therefore, what you have received and heard; obey it, and repent. But if you do not wake up, I will come like a thief, and you will not know at what time I will come to you."**

**2 Cor 3:3 You show that you are a letter from Christ, the result of our ministry, written not with ink but with the Spirit of the living God, not on tablets of stone but on tablets of human hearts.**

How is it that a person can look like they are alive, but be anything but? Yet, this is the charge that Jesus, **"Him who holds the seven spirits of God and the seven stars"**. (Rev 3:1) had against the church at Sardis in Rev. 3. He is speaking directly to a church that could well exist today, a body of people who say and do all the right things, that would give the appearance of being Christian yet they have no relationship with the King. It is as if they think all their good deeds and words will win them points with the One who controls their destiny. But He is not easily taken in as men often are. The world may look on and say "oh what a wonderful church", but He sees perfectly and says, "I don't know who they are". Because the church is made up of individuals it then follows that if the body is spiritually dead so also are the people. Two things then come to mind, the need for individuals to get into right relationship with the Lord Jesus and the church coming to life as a result. Merely looking alive may impress men, but it will not lead to genuine life in Christ and a home in heaven.

## New day – clean slate

**Eccl 1:9 What has been will be again, what has been done will be done again; there is nothing new under the sun.**

**Is 43:19 See, I am doing a new thing! Now it springs up; do you not perceive it? I am making a way in the desert and streams in the wasteland.**

**Rev 21:1 Then I saw a new heaven and a new earth, for the first heaven and the first earth had passed away, and there was no longer any sea.**

Solomon was so right when he said "there is nothing new under the sun". In a world of sin and pain it's true that what goes around comes around. If we continue to walk in the path of the world we will continue to experience the same old pain and sorrow. BUT, we do not have to hang onto our past way of living. God provided a new way when He offered His own Son, Jesus, as an atoning substitute for our sin. In so doing He made a way of joy, peace, rest, safety and assurance, freeing us from the bondage of doing the same ol' stuff. But it's our choice. Today you can launch a brand new life, a new start with the One who so loves you. May I suggest that in place of trying to keep some list of do's and don'ts, you just hand God the reins of your life and let him handle everything from here on out. Things won't always be easy but He will make all things new and never leave you; all you have to do is get with Him and follow His leading every moment of every day. It may cost you some temporal earthly things, but giving Him His proper place of authority will fill the void and deep longings of your heart with His abiding presence. For sure nothing in all this world can buy that.

## Though He slay me????

**Job 13:15 Though he slay me, yet will I hope in him; I will surely defend my ways to his face.**

**Job 23:10 But he knows the way that I take; when he has tested me, I will come forth as gold.**

**Ps 23:4 Even though I walk through the valley of the shadow of death, I will fear no evil, for you are with me; your rod and your staff, they comfort me.**

Just what's this life all about? The way we act at times one would think it has everything to do with our own individual comfort. Oh sure, we may boast like the disciple Peter that we would even die for Christ; but what about those times when the IRA doesn't grow as fast as we think it should, when our property values are affected by external events, when the car, the computer, and the fridge all break in the same week or when the promotion goes to someone else? Are we willing to surrender everything to Him including our comfort, our fears, our will? In the closing line of the movie "The Second Chance" the older pastor says, "I long to fear nothing but God Himself" and Jesus said, **"Do not be afraid of those who kill the body but cannot kill the soul. Rather, be afraid of the One who can destroy both soul and body in hell."** (Matt 10:28) So what is in control of your life, the problems you now face or total trust in the One who gave His very life for you? Paul wrote, **"For I am convinced that neither death nor life, neither angels nor demons, neither the present nor the future, nor any powers, neither height nor depth, nor anything else in all creation, will be able to separate us from the love of God that is in Christ Jesus our Lord."** (Rom 8:38-39) If NOTHING can separate us from HIM, what else matters? Why do we get concerned with the possible loss of creature comforts when in short they are temporary and it is the soul and spirit that are eternal?

## A sacrifice of praise

**Ps 145:1-7 I will exalt you, my God the King; I will praise your name forever and ever.
Every day I will praise you and extol your name for ever and ever. Great is the LORD and most worthy of praise; his greatness no one can fathom. One generation will commend your works to another; they will tell of your mighty acts. They will speak of the glorious splendor of your majesty, and I will meditate on your wonderful works. They will tell of the power of your awesome works, and I will proclaim your great deeds. They will celebrate your abundant goodness and joyfully sing of your righteousness.**

"Praise the Lord, oh my soul; let all that is in me praise His Holy Name." David prayed this song over and over. Perhaps he knew something we would do well to learn. There are times when praising the Lord has to be a deliberate choice, times when we get bad news, when all seems to be caving in around us. It is at those times that it is hardest to praise Him, but it is then that we MOST NEED to give Him praise. Our God is God of all gods and He is worthy of all honor and glory. He created us knowing full well that we would reject Him and He willingly gave His one and only Son to pay the price we could never pay. Through the precious shed blood of Jesus we've been given life, new life, eternal life in Him. If He never did one more thing for us we would still owe Him a sacrifice of praise. So choose today and all the days that lie ahead to give Him your FULL heart's devotion and praise in EVERY circumstance.

*Just A Thought*

## ALL things are possible

**Matt 19:26 Jesus looked at them and said, "With man this is impossible, but with God all things are possible."**

**Job 42:2 "I know that you can do all things; no plan of yours can be thwarted.**

**Luke 18:27 Jesus replied, "What is impossible with men is possible with God."**

"This is a hopeless situation and I just don't see any way this can work out." How easily we cave in and yield to the urge to doubt, fear and give up. When we think logically with our HEADS and fail to allow God to show us His power by hearing what He is saying to our HEARTS, things may well look impossible. It's at those times that we have forgotten that our God is the God who allowed Sarah to bear Isaac in her 90's? **Abraham fell facedown; he laughed and said to himself, "Will a son be born to a man a hundred years old? Will Sarah bear a child at the age of ninety?"** (Gen 17:17) Have we forgotten that our God caused the ravens to bring Elijah bread and meat? **The ravens brought him bread and meat in the morning and bread and meat in the evening, and he drank from the brook.** (1 Kings 17:6) Paul reminds us in Romans how Abraham could trust God and that there is no such thing as impossible, **"being fully persuaded that God had power to do what he had promised."** (Rom 4:21) Do we fail to see God's miracles in our lives because of our unbelief that "God has power to do what he had promised"? No, not necessarily. Maybe it's a case of not WANTING to see ourselves as so needy that the ravens would have to feed us, which might well be called PRIDE on our part. What it all comes down to is this, "With man this is impossible, but with God all things are possible." and believe it or not, that's the truth.

# A house of prayer!

**Mark 11:17 "Is it not written: "'My house will be called a house of prayer for all nations'?"**

**Is 56:7 these I will bring to my holy mountain and give them joy in my house of prayer. Their burnt offerings and sacrifices will be accepted on my altar; for my house will be called a house of prayer for all nations."**

Are our churches "houses of prayer"? Steve Kendrick who with his brother, Alex, and the people of Sherwood Baptist Church in Albany, Georgia made the movies, "Flywheel", "Facing the Giants" and "Fireproof". has stated numerous times that these projects are always completely bathed in prayer. The outcome has been that the Lord greatly honored their prayers and their availability to produce great movies that are impacting the world for Him. We seem to have a lot of stuff going on in our churches, but there is way too little prayer. Jim Cymbala, author of books including "Fresh Wind, Fresh Fire", wrote "If we call upon the Lord, He has promised in His Word to answer, to bring the unsaved to Himself, to pour out His Spirit among us. If we don't call upon the Lord, He has promised nothing— nothing at all. It is as simple as that. No matter what I preach or what we claim to believe in our heads, the future will depend upon our times of prayer. That is the engine that will drive the church." I firmly agree and the truth is that when we pray and pray and pray some more THINGS WILL HAPPEN. Programs, plans, plots, and anything we can come up with on our own will fall short. Only as we pray and follow the leading we receive from the Lord will we have the right impact in our world. Is prayer first and foremost in your church, in your life? Paul said "PRAY CONTINUALLY". (1 Thess 5:17), SO DO IT!

## Do you really know Jesus Christ?

**Matt 10:32 "Whoever acknowledges me before men, I will also acknowledge him before my Father in heaven."**

**Rom 10:9-10 That if you confess with your mouth, "Jesus is Lord," and believe in your heart that God raised him from the dead, you will be saved. 10 For it is with your heart that you believe and are justified, and it is with your mouth that you confess and are saved.**

**2 Tim 1:8 So do not be ashamed to testify about our Lord, or ashamed of me his prisoner. But join with me in suffering for the gospel, by the power of God,**

There are a lot of people out there who claim to be Christians and on their way to heaven, but who never say a word or show in any way that they know Jesus. I am reminded of the story of a young lad who went off to basic training. His family and friends were afraid for him because of his Christian witness. Upon arriving home the question was asked if he had had to endure some abuse due to his faith. His reply was "no, they haven't found out about me yet". There is no such thing as an under-cover Christian. If our co-workers and associates do not know where we are in the Lord we may need to look at whether we really do know Him. Peter and another apostle, having been instructed by the Sanhedrin not to teach about Jesus, responded - **"We must obey God rather than men!"** (Acts 5:29) They knew a truth some have yet to learn. In Matthew Jesus said, **"But whoever disowns me before men, I will disown him before my Father in heaven."** (Matt 10:33) If we are not acknowledging God, we are disowning Him; the choice is up to us. If we're only going about our own agenda and trying to please men rather than God, we may not actually know Him. How about you?

## Kids learn oh so well!

**Phil 3:18-20 For, as I have often told you before and now say again even with tears, many live as enemies of the cross of Christ. Their destiny is destruction, their god is their stomach, and their glory is in their shame. Their mind is on earthly things. But our citizenship is in heaven.**

**Matt 5:19 Anyone who breaks one of the least of these commandments and teaches others to do the same will be called least in the kingdom of heaven,**

"Well, I don't understand. I tried to raise my kids the way they should go, but they've gone off to live in sin and it hurts." This is the experience of far too many parents these days, but here is the rub. Our children learn far more from example than from what they are told. Parents tell their kids so many things but do the very opposite, like Daddy tells his son that lying is wrong yet his boy hears dad call off sick from work so he can play a round of golf. Consequences are, they're seeing everything from lying to the boss to changing lovers for whatever reason whenever the urge strikes. So why should kids do any different than what they see? If we really want the next generation to know the truth of God's Word and to live a pure life, WE have to set the example. Those of us who have messed up need to repent our sin, allow the Lord to be our "lodestar" (focus point) from here on, and live as we would have those we love live. If you are lying, are involved in an affair, cheating on your taxes or doing any other sinful activity, I challenge you to get on your knees before God Almighty, confess to Him and repent and do whatever it takes to get back on track for the sake of your children, nieces, nephews and any one else who is precious to you. If you need help to sort things out contact your pastor, me or someone who can give you wisdom and direction and with God' strength GET BACK TO WHERE YOU WANT THE YOUNGER SET TO BE.

## One Flesh

**Mark 10:7-9 'For this reason a man will leave his father and mother and be united to his wife, and the two will become one flesh.' So they are no longer two, but one. 9 Therefore what God has joined together, let man not separate."**

**1 Cor 7:1-5 for the matters you wrote about: It is good for a man not to marry. But since there is so much immorality, each man should have his own wife, and each woman her own husband. The husband should fulfill his marital duty to his wife, and likewise the wife to her husband. The wife's body does not belong to her alone but also to her husband. In the same way, the husband's body does not belong to him alone but also to his wife. Do not deprive each other except by mutual consent and for a time, so that you may devote yourselves to prayer. Then come together again so that Satan will not tempt you because of your lack of self-control.**

So often when a man and a woman come to the wedding ceremony they have paid excess attention to making the day "something to remember", but have put very little if any effort into understanding the covenant they are about to enter. We take it all so lightly, but God looks upon marriage as two literally becoming one flesh. God created the most wonderful gift of sex and expects a married couple to fully enjoy their union, only with each other. In Hebrews we are told, **"Marriage should be honored by all, and the marriage bed kept pure, for God will judge the adulterer and all the sexually immoral."** (Heb 13:4) There were reports a few years ago of a runaway bride. News of the wedding plans showed that the whole event was to be an enormous affair, way over the top, and many wondered if it all hadn't gotten to be too much for her. Question is, had she concentrated so much on the planning that there was nothing left in her to give to her intended? Maybe, maybe not. But Creator God laid out the plan for marriage and if we will put even half as much into our marriage as we do the wedding AND all of the activities of our busy lives thereafter, far fewer of us would end in divorce. May I even be so bold to suggest that we, especially as Christians, set standards that match God's, get in tune with His plan and live out the wonderful life of love and joy He has for all of us.

## Lukewarm – neither hot nor cold

**Rev 3:15-18 I know your deeds, that you are neither cold nor hot. I wish you were either one or the other! So, because you are lukewarm-neither hot nor cold-I am about to spit you out of my mouth. You say, 'I am rich; I have acquired wealth and do not need a thing.' But you do not realize that you are wretched, pitiful, poor, blind and naked. I counsel you to buy from me gold refined in the fire, so you can become rich; and white clothes to wear, so you can cover your shameful nakedness; and salve to put on your eyes, so you can see.**

**Matt 24:12 "Because of the increase of wickedness, the love of most will grow cold,"**

Speaking to John, the Lord Jesus who is **"the Amen, the faithful and true witness, the ruler of God's creation."** (Rev 3:14) warned the church at Laodicea of their lack of zeal for Him. The fact that they were not cold seems to indicate that they were saved and going to heaven, BUT on the other hand, and that is a big but, they did not burn with desire for the One who was the Source of their salvation. While Jesus was here on earth He warned that the love of most would grow cold from increased wickedness. Is not the reverse also true that one reason we are seeing ever increasing evil in our world including the United States is because the Church, the Body of Christ, has lapsed into a state of tepidity? For sure we all want to go to heaven, but do we thirst for Him here and now? Far too many of us are satisfied to go to church on Sunday, and maybe Wednesday, but the rest of the week is our own time. Little do we realize how we are robbing ourselves of intimacy with the One who so loved us that He chose to die rather than live without us. Is He so important to us that we would we rather die than live without Him? **"Come near to God and he will come near to you. Wash your hands, you sinners, and purify your hearts, you double-minded."** (James 4:8)

# Walk Worthy

**1 Thess 2:12 encouraging, comforting and urging you to live lives worthy of God, who calls you into his kingdom and glory.**

**Eph 4:1 As a prisoner for the Lord, then, I urge you to live a life worthy of the calling you have received**

**Col 1:10 And we pray this in order that you may live a life worthy of the Lord and may please him in every way: bearing fruit in every good work, growing in the knowledge of God,**

**Gal 5:16 So I say, live by the Spirit, and you will not gratify the desires of the sinful nature.**

I'm sure that most of us would not keep it a secret if we met some noted political figure, maybe even show all our friends a picture of ourselves with that person. The politician may be a nonentity tomorrow, yet no doubt we'd always be proud of having been given this opportunity. For some reason we are not always nearly as enthusiastic about sharing and serving the God of all eternity. Peter tells church leaders to **"Be shepherds of God's flock that is under your care, serving as overseers-not because you must, but because you are willing, as God wants you to be; not greedy for money, but eager to serve;"** (1 Peter 5:2) ALL of us should be more than willing to serve God, not from compulsion but out of gratitude, love, and appreciation for who He is, first of all, and then for what He has done for us. Service begins with our realizing just what we were and where we were headed before He came into our lives. Fact is, we were vile wretched people heading straight for hell when in love He rescued us and set us on the path to life with Him for all eternity. That alone is more than enough reason for us to completely give ourselves and stay close to God every minute of every day and **"live by the Spirit"** through HIS strength and power, not our own. That is the way, the only way, to joy, peace and fulfillment beyond belief.

## Life MUST to be different

**John 8:11 "No one, sir," she said. "Then neither do I condemn you," Jesus declared. "Go now and leave your life of sin."**

**John 4:28-30 Then, leaving her water jar, the woman went back to the town and said to the people, "Come, see a man who told me everything I ever did. Could this be the Christ?" They came out of the town and made their way toward him.**

Many Christians live in a state of naivety; they've accepted Jesus as Savior, that settles it and they're now free to live any ol' way. Jesus told the woman caught in the very act of adultery that He forgave her, BUT He also told her **"to leave her life of sin"**. Today's other scripture is about a woman who had been married five times and was at the moment living with a man to whom she was not married. She was "one of those women", the kind everybody knows and talks about. Jesus extended forgiveness to her and she immediately went to tell the very ones she knew were whispering about her to "Come, see the man who told me everything I ever did". When was the last time you were glad someone told you about your sin? Many a pastor has been roasted for Sunday dinner because he stepped on the toes of "the roaster". Jesus said, **"If anyone loves me, he will obey my teaching. My Father will love him, and we will come to him and make our home with him. 24 He who does not love me will not obey my teaching. These words you hear are not my own; they belong to the Father who sent me."** (John 14:23-24) When He becomes our LORD and Savior we must leave our sinful ways, share the news and keep His commands. There are no options. So where does that leave you and me? Have we separated ourselves from the sin that would destroy us to live entirely for the one who died and rose again to pay the penalty we could never pay? Our perfection will never happen until we get "home", but we can and had better strive to be different now.

## Be ye Holy

**1 Peter 1:14-16 As obedient children, do not conform to the evil desires you had when you lived in ignorance. But just as he who called you is holy, so be holy in all you do; for it is written: "Be holy, because I am holy."**

**Matt 5:48 "Be perfect, therefore, as your heavenly Father is perfect."**

"BUT, I really enjoy a little ___(sin)___ every now and then." Too many of us believe that it's OK to live like the world, just a little. We will never know sinless perfection in this life but we MUST strive to live pleasing to God and the WORD tells us over and over to "be holy". Stated plainly, live as if Jesus were right by your side, He is anyway. It is told of Henry Clay that as he was about to introduce a particular bill in Congress, some of his friends warned that it would damage his ambitions. *"If you do this, Clay," said one colleague, "it will kill your chance for the presidency."* Clay asked, *"But is the measure right?"* When his friend agreed that it was the right thing to do, he replied, *"I would rather be right than be president."* I don't know why we're afraid to take a solid stand for Jesus, but if we don't we may suffer shame when we see Him face to face. Paul Harvey is reported to have prayed on air a prayer that closed with, *"We know Your Word says, "Woe to those who call evil good," but that is exactly what we have done. Search us, Oh God, and know our hearts today; cleanse us from every sin and set us free. Amen!"* Oh church, we cannot continue to live on both sides of the fence. Let us be like Isaiah, "Woe to me!" I cried. "I am ruined! For I am a man of unclean lips, and I live among a people of unclean lips, and my eyes have seen the King, the LORD Almighty." Then one of the seraphs flew to me with a live coal in his hand, which he had taken with tongs from the altar. With it he touched my mouth and said, "See, this has touched your lips; your guilt is taken away and your sin atoned for." Then I heard the voice of the Lord saying, "Whom shall I send? And who will go for us?" And I said, "Here am I. Send me!" (Is 6:5-8)

## BUT they're not loveable

**1 John 2:9 Anyone who claims to be in the light but hates his brother is still in the darkness**

**1 John 3:15 Anyone who hates his brother is a murderer, and you know that no murderer has eternal life in him.**

**Matt 5:22 "But I tell you that anyone who is angry with his brother will be subject to judgment. Again, anyone who says to his brother, 'Raca,' is answerable to the Sanhedrin. But anyone who says, 'You fool!' will be in danger of the fire of hell."**

I picked up the paper this morning to see a dozen or so pictures of what looked like good kids who had been nabbed in a drug operation. My heart melted in my chest. These kids made some bad choices and now will have to deal with the fallout for the rest of their lives. I prayed for them and thought of words that I've heard in the past, like, "well, it serves them right". Words like these come from folks who go to church no less, but Jesus made it clear that all men are our brothers (See Luke 10:31-36) and what John learned at the feet of Jesus He repeatedly tells us. If we do not love our brothers, we do not love Him. **"Whoever loves his brother lives in the light, and there is nothing in him to make him stumble. But whoever hates his brother is in the darkness and walks around in the darkness; he does not know where he is going, because the darkness has blinded him."** (1 John 2:10-11) If we do not love others and we do not love Jesus, then it follows that it is entirely possible we ourselves are not saved. It matters not whether people are loving in return. I think it is safe to say that perhaps the guy who was helped by the Samaritan was out of it and not acting very loving, but the Samaritan loved him anyway. Jesus loved those who crucified Him and sought His Father's forgiveness of them from the cross. (Luke 23:34) Oh brothers and sisters, we must love.

## You have to love!

**1 John 4:8 Whoever does not love does not know God, because God is love.**

**1 John 2:4 The man who says, "I know him," but does not do what he commands is a liar, and the truth is not in him.**

**1 John 2:9 Anyone who claims to be in the light but hates his brother is still in the darkness.**

**1 John 3:6 No one who lives in him keeps on sinning. No one who continues to sin has either seen him or known him.**

"I praise God for my salvation and I believe I'm on my way to heaven, but I just can't love _____." That statement appears to be an oxymoron because John makes it clear over and over again that we cannot have it both ways. If we want to claim that we love God we must (that is MUST) love everyone else. This does not mean that we have to gush sweet ooey gooey over them, but is does mean that we will not be negative toward them either. Even the most hardened serial killer is created in the image of God and Jesus died for that one just as much as He died for me. A friend of mine once fell badly into sin and it was not a huge pre-planned crime that got him. It was a heat of the moment opportunity to sin that took him down. My heart is broken for him and his family, and at the same time my heart is reminded to love him and appreciate his honesty when facing what he had done. He has confessed to God and others publicly, but my how stones are being hurled at him. Oh my friends, there but for the grace of God go you and I. Hatred and abuse never won one soul to the love of Jesus, but love in spite of sin has won many. Jesus loved Jerusalem so much that He cried over her sin. As for me, I choose to weep over sinners rather than cast stones at them. How about you?

## "Were not ten cleansed?"

**Luke 17:12-19 As he was going into a village, ten men who had leprosy met him. They stood at a distance and called out in a loud voice, "Jesus, Master, have pity on us!"**

**When he saw them, he said, "Go, show yourselves to the priests." And as they went, they were cleansed. One of them, when he saw he was healed, came back, praising God in a loud voice. He threw himself at Jesus' feet and thanked him-and he was a Samaritan. Jesus asked, "Were not all ten cleansed? Where are the other nine? Was no one found to return and give praise to God except this foreigner?" Then he said to him, "Rise and go; your faith has made you well."**

Does this happen yet today? Are only ten percent of people that are healed of their sin by the Lord truly thankful? Jesus Christ, One and only Son of the Eternal God, came into this world for one purpose and only His love for creation drove Him to that horrible cross. You may be thinking, "doesn't Ernie ever talk about anything else?" Yes I do, but repeatedly I am reminded of what He did and does for me and how so many of us take everything for granted. Does our ingratitude and indifference remind Him of the pain of those nails? This life is not about us, yet we so often live like we are the center of it all. Our prayers are give me, give me, give me. How much better if we concentrate on praising the One who made all things possible, how much better if we sought His will and not our own? A few years ago my wife came home from hours of Dr. appointments with her mother, fully aware that the long day had less to do with mom's health than with being given the opportunity to share the reality of Christ with those who crossed their path. If we trust Jesus as Savior we MUST trust Him as LORD of our lives. If He is not both, He is probably neither. As Lord of our lives He directs our every step. We come to see all things through HIS eyes rather than our own, and we "return" to give Him thanks and praise.

## Keep no record

**1 Cor 13:4-5 Love is patient, love is kind. It does not envy, it does not boast, it is not proud. It is not rude, it is not self-seeking, it is not easily angered, it keeps no record of wrongs.**

**Eph 4:2 Be completely humble and gentle; be patient, bearing with one another in love.**

**Rom 12:17 Do not repay anyone evil for evil. Be careful to do what is right in the eyes of everybody.**

All who have never been wronged please stand up. I'd be willing to bet that the vast majority of you are still sitting, for all of us have been hurt in life by at least one person. What really matters here is OUR RESPONSE to what happens to us. Awhile back a child ended up in a coma because a frozen piece of meat was thrown at someone else. Now this child, an innocent bystander, has to pay the price for someone else's anger. This presents a good picture of what can happen when we've been offended and lash back because we think, "I should never be hurt." That would be the ideal but it's not the case, for we live in a fallen sin-filled world, a world that says get over it or get even and make the other person hurt in return. How much better our own world would be if we could learn not to seek revenge but be humble, patient and bear with others, if we could forget past hurts and realize that we also have caused pain. Jesus said regarding forgiveness, **"I tell you, not seven times, but seventy-seven times."** (Matt 18:22) The KJV says, "until seventy times seven!" Either way, unlimited forgiveness on our part is required, just as God forgives us as many times as we fail (SIN). For our own well being we need to ERASE ALL RECORDS OF WRONGS and FORGIVE, lest HE hold OURS in remembrance. **"But if you do not forgive men their sins, your Father will not forgive your sins."** (Matt 6:15)

## When we walk with the LORD

**Prov 8:17 I love those who love me, and those who seek me find me.**

**John 14:21 "Whoever has my commands and obeys them, he is the one who loves me. He who loves me will be loved by my Father, and I too will love him and show myself to him."**

**Matt 6:33 "But seek first his kingdom and his righteousness, and all these things will be given to you as well."**

"I will love those who love Me." (Prov 8:17) Most of us understand that if we want to enjoy human love we have to get to know that other person. On the other hand, we seem to think we can walk an aisle, say a prayer and from then on enjoy God's love automatically. When prayers appear to go unanswered or troubles overwhelm us we want to blame Him, but the plain truth is that we are only as close to God as we want to be. Some see Him as a way to heaven some day, as a safety net (when all else fails) or as a mystical grandfather in the sky who will grant our every wish. What we fail to understand is that a relationship with God has one and only one purpose and that is to bring honor and glory to Him. Any one of us who thinks we can claim God's salvation then live a trouble-free life purely for our own enjoyment is in for a rude awakening. John said, **"We know that we have come to know him if we obey his commands. The man who says, "I know him," but does not do what he commands is a liar, and the truth is not in him. But if anyone obeys his word, God's love is truly made complete in him. This is how we know we are in him: Whoever claims to live in him must walk as Jesus did."** (1 John 2:3-6) Jesus' commands must be obeyed, but if we don't know Him through His WORD (The Bible) we cannot walk as He walked. If we are not walking a blameless (not sinless) life, we may not know Him at all.

*Just A Thought*

## Differing gifts and abilities!

**Rom 12:3-8 For by the grace given me I say to every one of you: Do not think of yourself more highly than you ought, but rather think of yourself with sober judgment, in accordance with the measure of faith God has given you. Just as each of us has one body with many members, and these members do not all have the same function, so in Christ we who are many form one body, and each member belongs to all the others. We have different gifts, according to the grace given us. If a man's gift is prophesying, let him use it in proportion to his faith. If it is serving, let him serve; if it is teaching, let him teach; if it is encouraging, let him encourage; if it is contributing to the needs of others, let him give generously; if it is leadership, let him govern diligently; if it is showing mercy, let him do it cheerfully.**

Maybe you've noticed that for some people praying for the needs of others comes easily. Other folks are quite at home behind the podium while many shudder at even the thought of standing in such a place. God made us all uniquely with differing talents and abilities. I read of the following incident that illustrates the way we parents sometimes think. A mother's four-year-old daughter attended her first performance of the Ice Capades. This young girl was so mesmerized that she didn't budge from her seat even during the intermission and watched intently while the ice was being cleaned and leveled. At the end of the show she exclaimed, "I know what I want to be when I grow up!" The mother immediately could see her daughter in skates and starring in the Ice Capades; but she was brought back to earth when the girl continued, "I want to be a Zamboni driver!" Many of us envision our kids or ourselves as "the star" when we are more talented to be the Zamboni driver. Within the church there is as great a need for janitors as elders and if we are using our God-given gifts it matters not the position. What does matter is if you or I are called and designed to clean toilets and can do it with a cheerful heart, we are fulfilling a ministry as important as the elder or pastor. Better to clean toilets joyfully than to pray with a bitter attitude. So let's stop complaining and fill the niche God has for us.

## A Friend of Sinners

**Luke 15:1-2 Now the tax collectors and "sinners" were all gathering around to hear him. But the Pharisees and the teachers of the law muttered, "This man welcomes sinners and eats with them."**

**Matt 9:10-11 While Jesus was having dinner at Matthew's house, many tax collectors and "sinners" came and ate with him and his disciples. When the Pharisees saw this, they asked his disciples, "Why does your teacher eat with tax collectors and 'sinners'?"**

**1 Tim 1:15 Here is a trustworthy saying that deserves full acceptance: Christ Jesus came into the world to save sinners-of whom I am the worst.**

**Matt 11:19 The Son of Man came eating and drinking, and they say, 'Here is a glutton and a drunkard, a friend of tax collectors and "sinners." ' But wisdom is proved right by her actions."**

I recently heard the statement that churches want growth but they want it on their own terms. They expect sinners to clean up their lives, put on the proper clothing and then start attending church with proper decorum and poise no less. In our fallen world that method has never worked nor ever will. Jesus came to the organized religion of that day and the fact is they wanted to stone Him, but Jesus said to them, **"I have shown you many great miracles from the Father. For which of these do you stone me?"** (John 10:32) Over and over He was the subject of negative press and everything else because He reached out to the lost people of His day. Ironically it was the religious that crucified Him. The greatest honor a church can receive is to be known as a friend of sinners. If sinners feel welcomed, loved, and cared for they will be open to hearing about the salvation Jesus has provided for them. No more can the church be effective in their community without direct, even dirty-hands, involvement with people than a doctor can mend the gunshot victim without getting his own hands bloody.

## Confess and go on!!!!

**Ps 51:4-13 Against You, You only, have I sinned and done what is evil in your sight, so that You are proved right when You speak and justified when You judge. Surely I was sinful at birth, sinful from the time my mother conceived me. Surely You desire truth in the inner parts; You teach me wisdom in the inmost place. Cleanse me with hyssop, and I will be clean; wash me, and I will be whiter than snow. Let me hear joy and gladness; let the bones You have crushed rejoice. Hide Your face from my sins and blot out all my iniquity. Create in me a pure heart, O God, and renew a steadfast spirit within me. Do not cast me from your presence or take your Holy Spirit from me. Restore to me the joy of Your salvation and grant me a willing spirit, to sustain me. Then I will teach transgressors Your ways, and sinners will turn back to You.**

David went for an innocent nighttime walk that turned out to be far from innocent. Upon spotting Bathsheba he liked what he saw and instead of turning and running home to one of his wives, he looked again. Enlisting help from his staff he proceeded to the sin of adultery and when his plot to blame her husband, Uriah, for her subsequent pregnancy failed, he arranged for his murder. What we do eventually catches up with us and at some point in time Nathan the prophet revealed to David his sin. There are those today who would like to put this mighty and repentant king on a shelf in cold storage, but look again at the last verse in our reading. **"Then I will teach transgressors Your ways, and sinners will turn back to You."** Those of us who have failed know only too well the ensuing pain and sorrow and we can be good teachers, warning others in the hope that they will avoid a similar situation. Do you want someone else who has fallen to experience the social or church-induced stigma you have felt from a sin that has been confessed and forgiven? I know I don't. It is you and I that must accept those who repent into the fold and allow God to use them in whatever way He chooses.

## Those in authority

**1 Tim 2:1 I urge, then, first of all, that requests, prayers, intercession and thanksgiving be made for everyone 2 for kings and all those in authority, that we may live peaceful and quiet lives in all godliness and holiness.**

I remember awhile back watching the news when members of the House of Representatives were voting for a non-binding resolution against steps being taken to put an end to the war in Iraq, Even commentators saw the political games being played and I was reminded again how much we need to be in prayer for our country. Church, if we do not spend more time on our knees, we may well lose the precious freedoms, including religion, that we take so for granted. When a grandma is arrested for sharing Christ, when kids are told they cannot mention Jesus, when evil is called good and good is called evil, we need to PRAY; Pray for ourselves, Pray for our Christian brothers and sisters, and especially Pray for all in authority over us. We are weak and we need God's help and guidance. The Lord told the Apostle Paul, **"My grace is sufficient for you, for my power is made perfect in weakness."** (2 Cor 12:9) When we come to realize how powerless we are and how strong we can become in God's strength, as individuals and as a nation, we will have taken the first step toward true freedom and joy. Because God's strength is made complete in our weaknesses, we can find the ability to pray and act in accordance with His will. If the state of our country makes your blood boil as it does mine please join me in prayer that as a nation we will repent and return to the Lord to know His power and peace. Anger does no good but great things can happen through prayer, releasing God to work in and through us. Let us remember our great leaders of yesteryear and pray that our nation will return to its roots, Judeo-Christian ethics and a society where we are free to be Christian, Moslem, or even agnostic or atheist. Don't forget, if the Moslem or atheist or anyone else has no freedom, neither do we.

## MODESTY????

**1 Tim 2:9-10 I also want women to dress modestly, with decency and propriety, not with braided hair or gold or pearls or expensive clothes, 10 but with good deeds, appropriate for women who profess to worship God.**

**1 Peter 3:3-4 Your beauty should not come from outward adornment, such as braided hair and the wearing of gold jewelry and fine clothes. 4 Instead, it should be that of your inner self, the unfading beauty of a gentle and quiet spirit, which is of great worth in God's sight.**

**Titus 2:3 Likewise, teach the older women to be reverent in the way they live, not to be slanderers or addicted to much wine, but to teach what is good.**

The world we live in has expectations of saved and lost people alike. Many men and women, unfortunately even Christians, are convinced that they have to have a perfect ten body and it's OK to show it off. It is quite easy for those of us who carry a few extra pounds to be modest, but in our "Victoria's NON-Secret" world the trim fall into Satan's trap of revealing as much skin as possible without being arrested. Awhile ago the paper pictured a Muslim lady in a swim suit that covered all but her feet and I wondered what it is that a false god has that would motivate such modesty. Why are not followers of Jesus Christ the Son of the only true God so motivated? Paul, Titus and Peter addressed this issue so it is nothing new, but today with the deluge of child porn, child abductions and sexual abuse wouldn't it be wise to take seriously the warnings of the Bible? One day on Oprah a lady with a rather large chest was complaining that men never look at her face. A man in the audience was brave enough to suggest that that might be happening because of the skintight sweater she was wearing, at least that day that draws full attention to her torso. Ladies AND gents, immodesty might be popular in a sin-filled world, but modesty brings the opportunity for the REAL YOU to be seen. That is what brings honor to our Jesus.

## Press On

**Phil 3:14 I press on toward the goal to win the prize for which God has called me heavenward in Christ Jesus.**

**2 Cor 4:17 For our light and momentary troubles are achieving for us an eternal glory that far outweighs them all. 18 So we fix our eyes not on what is seen, but on what is unseen. For what is seen is temporary, but what is unseen is eternal.**

**1 Thess 2:12 encouraging, comforting and urging you to live lives worthy of God, who calls you into his kingdom and glory.**

Imagine if you will, what would be the reaction of the fans and media alike if a runner in a mile event suddenly sat down on the side of the track for a rest. Maybe in a football game there has just been an interception and the carrier has a clear opportunity to make it safely into the end zone, but he stops for a break or takes time to look up into the bleachers to say hello to a friend. All of life is a race, sometimes feels like a rat race, but the Christian life is an amazing race that has the reward of living with God in His heaven. Too many of us, though, are like the athletes above, taking side trips, not keeping our eyes on our goal. A true sports fan might suggest that the above-mentioned be kicked off their teams. Personally, I'm glad that God's reserves judgment of us for Himself and does not give it to others, which means all the more that we must put forth every effort to live this Christian life with our eyes fixed on our Goal, Jesus, so that one day we can say like the Apostle Paul, **"I have fought the good fight, I have finished the race, I have kept the faith. Now there is in store for me the crown of righteousness, which the Lord, the righteous Judge, will award to me on that day-and not only to me, but also to all who have longed for his appearing.** (2 Tim 4:7 –8) and hear from our Lord, **"'Well done, my good servant!"** (Luke 19:17)

## Worse than an infidel?

**1 Tim 5:8 If anyone does not provide for his relatives, and especially for his immediate family, he has denied the faith and is worse than an unbeliever.**

**2 Cor 12:14 Now I am ready to visit you for the third time, and I will not be a burden to you, because what I want is not your possessions but you. After all, children should not have to save up for their parents, but parents for their children.**

Paul used some pretty tough language for a seldom-addressed subject when he said that if we do not provide especially for our immediate families we are worse than an unbeliever. The KJV translates the word infidel. Both words paint the portrait of one who is able to do some kind of work to provide for his family but refuses to do so. Some lay it on God by saying that this family is trusting the Lord and He will provide because their finances are dedicated to Him. Maybe so, but Jesus Himself spoke to this issue when He said, **"But you say that if a man says to his father or mother: 'Whatever help you might otherwise have received from me is Corban' (that is, a gift devoted to God)".** (Mark 7:11) Those to whom He was talking had selfish motives for not helping their families and put the blame on God. In other words, we're not to cheat our families by saying God is more important. Titus said, **"Our people must learn to devote themselves to doing what is good, in order that they may provide for daily necessities and not live unproductive lives."** (Titus 3:14) It is good and healthy to get out there, be productive and work for the necessities of life. We must certainly trust God for His provision for us, but we are also to be using the abilities He gave us to provide for those in our care. He entrusts us with precious ones who rely on us and we owe it to Him and them to meet their needs. If you have talents and abilities (who doesn't) and are not using them to care for your family, are you worse than an infidel? The Scripture says you are.

## You are not your own!

**1 Cor 6:19-20 Do you not know that your body is a temple of the Holy Spirit, who is in you, whom you have received from God? You are not your own; you were bought at a price. Therefore honor God with your body.**

**Rom 14:7-8 For none of us lives to himself alone and none of us dies to himself alone. 8 If we live, we live to the Lord; and if we die, we die to the Lord.**

**2 Cor 5:15 And he died for all, that those who live should no longer live for themselves but for him who died for them and was raised again.**

"Nobody's going to tell ME what to do." Familiar attitude? But the truth is if we want to know love, joy, peace and fulfillment we MUST LET GOD tell us what to do. I well remember looking forward to getting back to work after my back surgery but quickly found that was not gonna happen. The real crisis came the day I told the Lord I was willing to give up my insurance license. I struggled on two fronts, 1) I enjoyed my work and the Lord had richly blessed my sales in the past; now I would lose all hope of returning to the field and 2) I also would lose connection with my clients who meant more to me than their money. I had developed deep relationships with many and enjoyed helping them achieve certain financial goals as well as ministering to other needs. Finally I came to realize that the Lord would meet our financial needs and that He had another way for me to serve Him and help people, not necessarily with finances but with something far more important, eternal destinies. Maybe you are facing something similar. Recently I heard a young pastor say that the Lord had challenged him to think with his heart (obedience to HIM) instead of thinking with his head (I AM going to handle this). When God allows circumstances to come into our lives that change things, it is for our good and for His glory. The test may well be," Do you love Me enough to totally TRUST ME?" After all, YOU ARE NOT YOUR OWN.

## Forgive what?

**Col 3:13 Bear with each other and forgive whatever grievances you may have against one another. Forgive as the Lord forgave you. 14 And over all these virtues put on love, which binds them all together in perfect unity.**

**Matt 5:44 "But I tell you: Love your enemies and pray for those who persecute you,"**

**Matt 6:14 "For if you forgive men when they sin against you, your heavenly Father will also forgive you. 15 But if you do not forgive men their sins, your Father will not forgive your sins."**

**Mark 11:25 "And when you stand praying, if you hold anything against anyone, forgive him, so that your Father in heaven may forgive you your sins."**

At times we're tempted to harbor resentment toward someone who has really hurt us, mostly for the fact that they've never shown any hint of remorse or of feeling sorry for what they've done. After all, there are limits, or so we think. But read over the above verses once again. Do you see anything that says forgive only after they apologize? Fact is, they may never get around to that and so we're left stewing forever in our anger and pain. Jesus set the perfect example for us regarding this issue. He did not look down from that cruel cross and ask if the men who beat Him unmercifully and drove nails into Him were sorry. Rather He forgave them and looking to heaven prayed, **"Father, forgive them, for they do not know what they are doing."** (Luke 23:34) Without any doubt these people are responsible for what they did and one day will give an account, but at the time did they understand the full consequence of their actions? NO. Don't we sometimes hurt others without realizing what we have done? We even hurt ourselves. It's said that as many as 85% of people in mental facilities could leave if only they would forgive themselves. Setting all this aside, if and when I MAKE THE CHOICE to forgive I set my spirit free from tyranny and the life's

*Just A Thought*

destruction that comes from harboring unforgiveness AND best of all, God can then forgive MY sins. No wonder Jesus had so much to say on this subject.

## Your FIRST love!

**Rev 2:4 Yet I hold this against you: You have forsaken your first love.**

**Jer 2:2 "Go and proclaim in the hearing of Jerusalem: "'I remember the devotion of your youth, how as a bride you loved me and followed me through the desert, through a land not sown.**

**Matt 24:12-13 Because of the increase of wickedness, the love of most will grow cold, but he who stands firm to the end will be saved.**

Oh how we remember the times spent with that special someone. We just couldn't be together enough. The joy of young love, no matter ones age, is a force to be reckoned with. Work gets left undone and there are sleepless nights as we dream of being in the arms of the one we love. Our attention is drawn to some couples because their love for each other is obvious, even if they are ninety years old. A TV ad once showed a very elderly husband and wife walking hand in hand in a park. This inspired a younger couple passing by to do the same and sent out the message that the joy of young love need never fade. The same is true with our relationship with Jesus. Even as human love must be worked on so must our love for Him. The old line goes, "I told you I love you once and I will let you know if that ever changes" may bring a chuckle or two, but that is not the way to maintain a close relationship. Jesus told the church at Ephesus to, **"Remember the height from which you have fallen! Repent and do the things you did at first."** (Rev 2:5) He also said, **"And this gospel of the kingdom will be preached in the whole world as a testimony to all nations,"** (Matt 24:14) The salvation of lost souls rests squarely on those of us who accept the love of Christ and His salvation. We who do not adhere strongly to that first love not only harm ourselves, but we also bring harm to the whole of humanity.

## What will happen tomorrow?

**Prov 27:1 Do not boast about tomorrow, for you do not know what a day may bring forth. (**

**James 4:13-17 Now listen, you who say, "Today or tomorrow we will go to this or that city, spend a year there, carry on business and make money." Why, you do not even know what will happen tomorrow. What is your life? You are a mist that appears for a little while and then vanishes. Instead, you ought to say, "If it is the Lord's will, we will live and do this or that." As it is, you boast and brag. All such boasting is evil. Anyone, then, who knows the good he ought to do and doesn't do it, sins.**

So much of our lives are spent in making plans, "unchangeable" major ones, not to mention those that are relatively minor. We invest in our IRA or 401K expecting great returns and blame everybody from the government to God when things don't happen just as we thought they would. Herein lies the dilemma. WE plan it, so it has to be. The Bible warns us against doing this. God is the only one who knows what the future holds and we would always be better off consulting Him FIRST about our hopes and dreams. In doing so we would no doubt prevent many problems and much sorrow. Perhaps the hardest thing for us human beings to do is change our view of God from God to LORD. It is so easy to see and talk about God as some ethereal way-out-there being, but quite another to see Him as MY LORD, totally in charge of all my life. Peter tells us, **"But grow in the grace and knowledge of our Lord and Savior Jesus Christ. To him be glory both now and forever! Amen."** (2 Peter 3:18) So what it comes down to is this; is He simply God, maybe even God your Savior, OR is this God of all eternity YOUR LORD as well? The first may leave us confused, without direction and even angry while the second will bring us peace, joy and hope. Which is it for you?

## God means it for good!

**Gen 50:19-20 But Joseph said to them, "Don't be afraid. Am I in the place of God? You intended to harm me, but God intended it for good to accomplish what is now being done, the saving of many lives.**

**Luke 23:34 Jesus said, "Father, forgive them, for they do not know what they are doing."**

**Acts 3:17 "Now, brothers, I know that you acted in ignorance, as did your leaders.**

**1 Tim 1:13 Even though I was once a blasphemer and a persecutor and a violent man, I was shown mercy because I acted in ignorance and unbelief.**

Pain and hurt are so much a part of our day-to-day lives and can come from loved ones and friends or complete strangers. We never know when it will come knocking at our door. The time and means is not what is important here. What does matter is how we handle its impact on our lives. Joseph was betrayed by his family, his boss, and others he helped, yet he believed that God was ultimately in control. Jesus knew that the soldiers did not grasp at all what they had done to Him so He wanted them to be forgiven. Peter told the Jews that he knew they acted in ignorance and "the old Paul" truly believed he was doing right when he blasphemed God and persecuted followers of "The Way" and later acknowledged his wrong. When people hurt us there are two possibilities; they have acted ignorantly or maliciously. Either way we need to follow the Bible's exhortations to forgive, then look for the good that God will bring out of it all. Another reason to respond Biblically is that WE ALSO NEED FORGIVENESS for what we have done against Him and others. Never forget, **"For if you forgive men when they sin against you, your heavenly Father will also forgive you. But if you do not forgive men their sins, your Father will not forgive your sins."** (Matt 6:14-15)

## Sin is SIN

**1 John 1:9 If we confess our sins, he is faithful and just and will forgive us our sins and purify us from all unrighteousness.**

**Jer 33:8 I will cleanse them from all the sin they have committed against me and will forgive all their sins of rebellion against me.**

Some of us don't believe God is able to forgive certain sins; you know, the "big" ones, even though sizes exist only in the human mind. Usually there are two reasons we have this struggle. One is that Satan keeps reminding us that we have been guilty of that horrible offense. (Horrible yes, but still guilty? DEFINITELY NOT, if we have confessed it). The second is that other people want to keep us reminded and don't want us to be forgiven. Often this is because they cannot forgive themselves for something they've done, so they cannot bear the thought that forgiveness has been extended to us. God has given His word that **"If we confess our sin"** we will be forgiven. In fact He says through the Psalmist that, **"If the LORD delights in a man's way, He makes his steps firm; though he stumble, he will not fall, for the LORD upholds him with his hand."** (Ps 37:23) So let us consider doing two things; first, take God at His word. He has said it and that makes it true. Try reciting John 1:9 over and over until you get its truth clear in your mind. Next, pray hard for those who struggle with unforgiveness in their own lives. Satan likes to keep us in a prison of guilt for then we will be ineffective as a Christian. So just hand Satan a dose of truth and walk forward in the love of Jesus. If you have truly confessed your sin, whether large or small in human eyes, you are clean and He can use you for His glory.

## WORSHIP the LORD

**Ps 29:2 Ascribe to the LORD the glory due his name; worship the LORD in the splendor of his holiness.**

**Ps 27:4 One thing I ask of the LORD, this is what I seek: that I may dwell in the house of the LORD all the days of my life, to gaze upon the beauty of the LORD and to seek him in his temple.**

What exactly does it mean to worship God? For many this word WORSHIP refers to the time in a church service given to offering Him praise in music and testimony. Others believe that worship begins when the pastor starts to preach his sermon. The plain simple truth is that EVERYTHIG we think, say or do in life is for the purpose of pleasing God and is to be considered worship to Him. Matt Heard, Senior Pastor of Woodmen Valley Chapel in Colorado Springs defines worship in this way, *"Worship is my active all of life response to the worth of who God is and what He does."*. That about says it all. **"Jesus declared, "Believe me, woman, a time is coming when you will worship the Father neither on this mountain nor in Jerusalem. You Samaritans worship what you do not know; we worship what we do know, for salvation is from the Jews. Yet a time is coming and has now come when the true worshipers will worship the Father in spirit and truth, for they are the kind of worshipers the Father seeks. God is spirit, and his worshipers must worship in spirit and in truth."** (John 4:21-24) The very fact that Jesus left His eternal home to become one of us and suffered and died that He might offer us salvation should drive home to us that He MUST be the center of our lives. Simply put, our every breath in every second of life is to be a conscious act of worship to Him. Yes, it's about the music, the message, the prayer but it's also about our work our play and oh so much more. Are you worshipping?

## He WILL take care of you!

**Prov 3:31-35 Do not envy a violent man or choose any of his ways, for the LORD detests a perverse man but takes the upright into his confidence. The LORD's curse is on the house of the wicked, but he blesses the home of the righteous. He mocks proud mockers but gives grace to the humble. The wise inherit honor, but fools he holds up to shame.**

**Ps 91:9-11 If you make the Most High your dwelling even the LORD, who is my refuge—then no harm will befall you, no disaster will come near your tent. For he will command his angels concerning you to guard you in all your ways;**

The Lord is trustworthy, reliable, dependable and sure. We are often afraid of what the Lord may want of us if we give our all to Him and put Him in charge of everything so we resist Him. When we do that, though, we are really setting ourselves up for failure. We look around us and see what we think are successful, top-of-life folks while we are barely eking by, but we have to remember that it's not about these few years here on earth. We who name the name of Jesus as our Hope and Redeemer live in an eternal realm. It's true that we live right now in the moment here on earth, but our citizenship is in heaven and that means eternal life for us that will never end. We will move again to be with Him and be changed **"in the twinkling of an eye"** (1 Cor 15:52) in the future, but spiritually speaking we live there with Him now. It is better than anything else to know that this God of all eternity is my God, my salvation, my strength and my life and that far outweighs the fickleness of this crazy, evil world. To know God and His blessing is to live in the absolute and know real peace and joy.

## Keep a list?

**1 John 1:8 If we claim to be without sin, we deceive ourselves and the truth is not in us.**

**Rom 3:23 for all have sinned and fall short of the glory of God.**

It's apparent that for many in the Church there's this list of sins. If one can avoid doing what's on the list he or she is in good standing and can feel a sense of security before God. Usually included are the Ten Commandments, other admonitions from Scripture and additional ones that man has come up with. Knowing the rules and following them assures success, what's more it makes for an easy system because do's and don'ts can easily be measured. The problem, though, is that all this sounds very much like the rich young ruler. Jesus told him to keep the commandments and he responded with, **"Which ones?" Jesus replied, "'Do not murder, do not commit adultery, do not steal, do not give false testimony, honor your father and mother,' and 'love your neighbor as yourself, "All these I have kept," the young man said, "What do I still lack?"** (Matt 19:18-20) When Jesus then told him to sell all that he had and give to the poor, the man went away sorrowful, proving that he had not fully obeyed the law. **"When the young man heard this, he went away sad, because he had great wealth."** (Matt 10:22) In short, the guy coveted his possessions (tenth commandment) to the extent that they kept him from knowing God, "The law DID NOT and COULD NOT offer salvation; what's more it is impossible to evaluate our standing before God based on any list. The fact is that we do sin, even after salvation, and it is necessary for us to lay claim to that sin, confess it and receive God's forgiveness. And by the way, it is very easy to adhere to a list without giving any thought to God at all. In short, we are to obey God out of love for Him only and avoid the temptation to simply keep a list and feel smug about it.

## Pure religion pleases God

**James 1:26-27 If anyone considers himself religious and yet does not keep a tight rein on his tongue, he deceives himself and his religion is worthless. Religion that God our Father accepts as pure and faultless is this: to look after orphans and widows in their distress and to keep oneself from being polluted by the world.**

**Gal 2:6 As for those who seemed to be important-whatever they were makes no difference to me; God does not judge by external appearance; those men added nothing to my message.**

Many years ago I read a list of steps to gaining popularity in New York City. Interestingly enough, number one on the list was church attendance. That got me to thinking about why people go to church in the first place. It seems that many choose a particular church because superficially it appears to be the correct one to attend, but I'm afraid the sorry truth is that a lot of people "do church" for all the wrong reasons. James said that three things would evidence pure religion, a controlled tongue, caring for widows and orphans and keeping ones self from the stains of the world. Love from a pure heart is pleasing to God and Jesus said, **"But go and learn what this means: 'I desire mercy, not sacrifice.' For I have not come to call the righteous, but sinners."** (Matt 9:13) Merely attending church or keeping some list of rules will not get His attention or approval. Neither does religiosity and outward show of piety cut the mustard, BUT loving and serving the Lord does please Him and will bring rich rewards. So let us strive to know and follow God and His Word and serve others. That is pure religion.

## How do we reach the lost?

**1 Cor 9:20-23 To the Jews I became like a Jew, to win the Jews. To those under the law I became like one under the law (though I myself am not under the law), so as to win those under the law. To those not having the law I became like one not having the law (though I am not free from God's law but am under Christ's law), so as to win those not having the law. To the weak I became weak, to win the weak. I have become all things to all men so that by all possible means I might save some. I do all this for the sake of the gospel, that I may share in its blessings.**

**James 5:20 remember this: Whoever turns a sinner from the error of his way will save him from death and cover over a multitude of sins.**

World Magazine (10/20/05) ran an article about church closings. Interestingly enough, its view was that churches are dying from implosion rather than external pressure. Many are failing because they are set in sometimes long-standing ruts that forbid them to reach out with love to a lost and dying world. Many cannot understand why people aren't coming to their services, yet they're not able (or maybe not willing) to make the church relevant to today's culture. Some require a certain dress style or have other non-essential regulations as mandatory for attendance. Some complain that "if a person with body odor comes in they might smell up the seat"; whether taken literally or figuratively, it's considered that these folks are living a "wrong" lifestyle. In today's society we must do as the Apostle Paul did and allow Christ to become attractive to the lost THROUGH US. In no way does this suggest that we become like them in their sin or compromise the Gospel, BUT, dress, hairstyle, jewelry, tattoos etc. are not at all relevant to their salvation. Fish are not cleaned until caught and people may not ever come to Christ if they are kept outside our doors. Every day souls are dying and going to hell while the church remains a clueless cluster of saints making demands, their signs of "pure religion", that Jesus would never have imposed. Oh church, get your hands dirty and sincerely love the lost.

## Oh for the romance of yesteryear

**Rev 2:4 "Yet I hold this against you: You have forsaken your first love. 5 Remember the height from which you have fallen! Repent and do the things you did at first."**

**1 Thess 4:9 Now about brotherly love we do not need to write to you, for you yourselves have been taught by God to love each other. And in fact, you do love all the brothers throughout Macedonia. Yet we urge you, brothers, to do so more and more.**

Do you remember the first time you "fell in love"? You were pretty unhappy and out of sorts when you couldn't be near that special one. Maybe this was the one you married, perhaps many years ago. Do you still ache when you are apart or has that deep passion faded a bit (or a lot) over time? Oh you still love them, but now they're always around, sometimes under foot, and you've come to take them and your relationship for granted. We read in Revelation that that's what happened to the church in Ephesus. In the early days they loved Jesus soooo much, but now their love had waned. Like the spouse that yearns for the romance of courtship, Jesus is yearning for the same ardor and zeal in our relationship with Him that we felt in the beginning. Even more so than with our human lover, we need to keep the closeness and fire alive with Jesus. He is the One who laid down His life for us before we knew Him and it is He who has the light lit, watching for us to come home. By staying close to Him through prayer, studying His Word and countless other ways, we must do all we can to keep that same excitement alive that we had at first.

## Many Believed

**Ps 37:23 If the LORD delights in a man's way, He makes his steps firm.**

**Matt 19:17 "Why do you ask me about what is good?" Jesus replied. "There is only one who is good. *If you want to enter life, obey the commandments.*"**

Barnabas was a good man and many came to believe in Christ, so Luke tells us in the book of Acts. There is no greater compliment that can be paid to a person than it be said, "many came to believe because of him/her." How does one ever come to merit such a legacy? How does one get into a position before God as to earn His great favor? Jesus said that there was only one who was good and of course he was speaking of Himself. So how does Luke dare to write that Barnabas was a good man? What Luke is saying is that Barnabas was a man who lived the life of a true believer, adhering to the teachings of Christ. One day Jesus proved to a rich young ruler that he had not totally kept the commandments by making him see that he loved his riches and his present life more than he wanted eternal life. See (Matthew 19:16 – 25). Later the Apostle Paul wrote, **"The entire law is summed up in a single command: "Love your neighbor as yourself."** (Gal 5:14) The test of where we stand in living this Christian life is" Do you love your neighbor as your self?" Barnabas (which means encourager) did just that, so it could be said of him that he was good and that many came to know Christ because of the life he lived. Oh how I want that said of me. How about you?

## They devoted themselves to …

**Acts 5:42 Day after day, in the temple courts and from house to house, they never stopped teaching and proclaiming the good news that Jesus is the Christ.**

**Acts 4:18-20 Then they called them in again and commanded them not to speak or teach at all in the name of Jesus. But Peter and John replied, "Judge for yourselves whether it is right in God's sight to obey you rather than God. For we cannot help speaking about what we have seen and heard."**

It has been said that we need more of the Acts church in modern times. That sounds like a good idea to me for it would certainly help eliminate many church difficulties as well as promote the spreading of the Gospel. The thing about this church was, **"They devoted themselves to the apostles' teaching and to the fellowship, to the breaking of bread and to prayer."** (Acts 2:42) The Gospel was a way of life for them nonstop, not just a Sunday religion or a conscience salving ritual. Jesus was THE VERY CENTER of their lives; and yes, we do need a lot more of that. When we come together for worship it should be a celebration of our precious Lord, a time of encouragement and teaching so we then go out and make disciples. As we are living our ordinary daily lives, our devotion to Jesus should be so evident, simply by the way we live, that people see His truth and are drawn to Him. It is our responsibility, not an option, to be accountable to the Great Commission, Matt. 28:19-20. But if to us Christianity is nothing more than going to church on Sunday and that's it, we are sad examples of the Church. If we are devoted to Christ it will become second nature to live a life pleasing to Him. How about you? Are you fully devoted to Him?

## If you love Me!

**John 13:35 "By this all men will know that you are my disciples, if you love one another."**

**John 14:15 "If you love me, you will obey what I command.**

For some reason many who claim to belong to Jesus fail to follow Him closely. Is it a matter of not wanting to at all or is it an unwillingness to put forth the effort or both? We growl and snarl because our lives are overcrowded, stressed and filled with problems, but we refuse to allow the Lord to handle things and give us His peace and joy. Maybe we are too busy (if you're too busy for Him you are too busy). Maybe we are too lazy or maybe we just don't want Him interfering with our plans and expectations. After all if I obey Him I won't have the other "ten percent" to spend or I'd be in church instead of at a ball game. Well consider this: if Jesus had been too busy to leave heaven and come to earth and if He had been too preoccupied with His other assignments and agendas, He would never have gone to that cruel cross. What if He had not told the Father, **"Father, if you are willing, take this cup from me; yet not my will, but yours be done."**? Luke 22:42 Exit salvation, exit God's love for us and exit a future in heaven. Think about that if you are too busy for Him now and another question. Just why do you want to spend eternity with Him in His home? Is it possible that if we do not obey Him here, we never loved Him in the first place? If the later is true you are only fooling yourself into thinking you will go to heaven. Believing in Him requires loving Him, serving Him and sharing Him with family, friends and all people. Do you love Him, truly love Him?

## Pleasing to HIM!

**1 John 3:24 Those who obey his commands live in him, and he in them. And this is how we know that he lives in us: We know it by the Spirit he gave us.**

**John 14:21 Whoever has my commands and obeys them, he is the one who loves me. He who loves me will be loved by my Father, and I too will love him and show myself to him."**

**1 John 3:22 and receive from him anything we ask, because we obey his commands and do what pleases him.**

The way some of us act one might think that we as believers figure that God will never hold us accountable for the sins we commit. While it is true that He sees the sin of a Christian differently than that of the unbeliever He does see it. I believe there are two types of sin. One I see as accidental; you hit your hand instead of the nail and a word slips out. That is an accident. The other is when we KNOW that what we are involved in is sin and we willfully continue on that course, that sin is intentional. Perhaps a couple is living together or at least having sex outside marriage and they know it is wrong but refuse to make any changes. Another example is that of someone carrying a vengeful spirit who refuses to deal with their bad attitude. I was once told, "I know I should do differently, but I'm not ready". That is deliberately saying to God, "I don't care, it's my life and I'm going to do it". Well, maybe you'd better take another look at the verses for today. "Those who obey" are the ones who live in God and He in them. Those are the ones who love God and are loved by Him. And those are the ones whose prayers are answered. What about you? Oh and don't be surprised not if but when your children also live and act as if God doesn't exist.

## God's Word can be troubling

**Luke 1:29-35 Mary was greatly troubled at his words and wondered what kind of greeting this might be. But the angel said to her, "Do not be afraid, Mary, you have found favor with God. You will be with child and give birth to a son, and you are to give him the name Jesus. He will be great and will be called the Son of the Most High. The Lord God will give him the throne of his father David, and he will reign over the house of Jacob forever; his kingdom will never end." "How will this be," Mary asked the angel, "since I am a virgin?" The angel answered, "The Holy Spirit will come upon you, and the power of the Most High will overshadow you. So the holy one to be born will be called the Son of God.**

Imagine yourself a teenage girl around fourteen and an angel visits you. This alone would throw most of us into freak out time and the news he brings defies everything we know. Mary knew well the penalty for becoming pregnant prior to marriage (stoning). And what kind of girl who's in love gets pregnant by another man before she has even "known" her man? I'm sure she was a very average girl except for this; she was devoted to her God. She knew the law and kept it so well that God took notice and honored her with His Son, a tremendous honor because not every girl would get to be the mother of the Christ child. But it was not without cost. She would become one of "those girls" and she would cause her husband the pain of believing her to be unfaithful. Joseph could have chosen to have her stoned to death but he did not. Mary could have rejected this whole idea but chose to believe her God and now we have a Savior. Remember, that first Christmas was anything but the beautiful, joyful time we now present it to be. The King of kings was born of a virgin girl in a barn under a cloud of illegitimacy, eventually to die on a cross. Let us put Christ at the center of our Christmas, even if doing so makes us uncomfortable, as it did these special parents so long ago.

## Could I be causing my own problems?

**Hag 1:7-11** This is what the LORD Almighty says: "Give careful thought to your ways. Go up into the mountains and bring down timber and build the house, so that I may take pleasure in it and be honored," says the LORD. "You expected much, but see, it turned out to be little. What you brought home, I blew away. Why?" declares the LORD Almighty. "Because of my house, which remains a ruin, while each of you is busy with his own house. Therefore, because of you the heavens have withheld their dew and the earth its crops. I called for a drought on the fields and the mountains, on the grain, the new wine, the oil and whatever the ground produces, on men and cattle, and on the labor of your hands."

**Matt 10:37-39** "Anyone who loves his father or mother more than me is not worthy of me;"

Oh how we moan and groan when things seem to go south on us. How often we say, "How could God allow this to happen". But if we really dig into the Bible we will find that many times our problems are of our own making. When we refuse to live for the Lord and obey Him why should He not allow what we see as negatives in our lives? In Haggai's day people lacked money, oil, crops and rain and the whole reason was they had never gotten around to repairing the Temple. Their homes were all completed and were finished in fine paneling at that, but not God's Temple. Jesus said, **"Anyone who loves his father or mother more than me is not worthy of me"**. When we get all absorbed in our own lives and neglect the Lord, even as the Jews had forgotten the Temple, we set ourselves up for failure and trouble. When all else takes such priority that Jesus gets pushed aside we are truly unworthy of the Son of God who gave His very life for us. NOTHING was more important to Him than us, so how can ANYTHING be more important to us than Him?

## Not my way!!

**Luke 22:42 "Father, if you are willing, take this cup from me; yet not my will, but yours be done."**

**Ps 40:8 I desire to do your will, O my God; your law is within my heart."**

**Heb 10:5-7 Therefore, when Christ came into the world, he said: "Sacrifice and offering you did not desire, but a body you prepared for me; with burnt offerings and sin offerings you were not pleased. Then I said, 'Here I am-it is written about me in the scroll-I have come to do your will, O God.'"**

**James 4:1 What causes fights and quarrels among you? Don't they come from your desires that battle within you?**

When Jesus lived here on earth He was the one and only human being that had a right to demand His own way. Miraculously conceived and born of a virgin, He faced every temptation that we face; yet never once did He fail in any way. Certainly a man who lived such a pure life earned the privilege of doing what He wanted; but no, He conceded to the Father. He had a mission to accomplish and He knew that any deviation from the cross would mean disaster. Oh how much better our world would be if we were focused like Him. We waste so much time seeking our own agendas, running around to gain support for our point of view and waste time promoting "me". If that time was invested in prayer and concession to God's leading, we could know real peace and see Him work in powerful ways. James reminds us that spats within the body of Christ are caused by selfishness that diverts our focus from our real purpose. Let's work on HIS way, not our own.

## One Body

**Eph 4:20-24 You, however, did not come to know Christ that way. Surely you heard of him and were taught in him in accordance with the truth that is in Jesus. You were taught, with regard to your former way of life, to put off your old self, which is being corrupted by its deceitful desires; to be made new in the attitude of your minds; and to put on the new self, created to be like God in true righteousness and holiness.**

There's an old story that tells of three guys rescued from an island. As they sailed away the captain of the boat asked what were the three buildings on the beach. "Oh that's easy to explain; you see the first guy is of one denomination and the other two of another". So he then asked," Why three?" The answer was, these guys were unable to worship together so they built a First church and then a Second, both of their denom. The sad thing is that there are way too many of us refusing to unite together and even acknowledge that other believers exist. I once heard a pastor say, "I can't pray WITH or FOR anyone whose beliefs are not like mine". This isn't to say that we can't keep our distinctives, BUT, if we believe in One God, One Savior, the virgin birth and the sufficiency of the blood atonement of Christ for forgiveness of sin, WE ARE ONE in HIM. We can work together for His cause, the Gospel, without competition and disdain. It grieves God's heart when His family fights over trivial stupid stuff that in the whole scheme of things doesn't matter at all. We've got to bury the dumbness and start acting like children of the LIVING GOD? It's time to love and build up one another and join together in prayer and His work WHILE THERE IS TIME. I'm afraid some will be shocked when they find "others" of God's people in heaven. Jesus said, **"May they be brought to complete unity to let the world know that you sent me and have loved them even as you have loved me."** (John 17:23 NIV) It's all about Jesus, the world seeing our love and unity and then being drawn to Him. Come on Church; let us honor our Savior's prayer.

## We are the Victors

**Gen 3:15 And I will put enmity between you and the woman, and between your offspring and hers; He will crush your head, and you will strike his heel."**

**1 John 3:8 He who does what is sinful is of the devil, because the devil has been sinning from the beginning. The reason the Son of God appeared was to destroy the devil's work.**

The way some Christians act one might get the impression that they have no idea they are on the winning team. Unless and until we start standing up for God in our world we will never know His joy nor fulfill His purpose. The story was told of a young man who entered the Navy and his family feared for his safety once the other recruits found out he was a Christian. Upon his arrival home after basic training the first question he faced was, "How did it go? Just great", he replied. "They didn't tease and harass you about your being a Christian?" "No, they don't have any idea yet that's what I am". How about you and I? Do our friends and contacts know that we love God? We so often fear their response if we are "found out", but as for me, my greater fear is God's response if I deny Him. God said **"This is what the LORD Almighty says: "Give careful thought to your ways. Go up into the mountains and bring down timber and build the house, so that I may take pleasure in it and be honored," says the LORD. "You expected much, but see, it turned out to be little. What you brought home, I blew away. Why?" declares the LORD Almighty. "Because of my house, which remains a ruin, while each of you is busy with his own house. Therefore, because of you the heavens have withheld their dew and the earth its crops. I called for a drought on the fields and the mountains, on the grain, the new wine, the oil and whatever the ground produces, on men and cattle, and on the labor of your hands."** (Hag 1:7-11) In these days of unprecedented national and personal problems we need to let the world know as never before that we are children of the living loving God.

## "I AM a Sinner!

**1 John 1:8-10 If we claim to be without sin, we deceive ourselves and the truth is not in us. If we confess our sins, he is faithful and just and will forgive us our sins and purify us from all unrighteousness. If we claim we have not sinned, we make him out to be a liar and his word has no place in our lives.**

**1 Tim 1:16 But for that very reason I was shown mercy so that in me, the worst of sinners,**

Some born again people (at least by their claims) forget that they are still sinners by nature. The Apostle Paul, who wrote a major portion of the New Testament, admitted he was "the worst of sinners" and that two very different natures live within him. John said that if we claim to be without sin we are only fooling ourselves. Sad to say, we are ALL sinners. We are human beings born under the curse and that means that as long as we are here on this earth our defiled sin nature is still with us. Some days we do well and avoid at least the appearance of evil and some days we do not. But there are always bad attitudes, judgmental thoughts, bad temper at red lights and so on lurking around ready to jump out at any moment. The really good news is that once we have admitted we are sinners we receive His forgiveness. Having accepted Christ as Savior, we are part of the family of God and from that point on He looks at our sin through the shed blood of Jesus, which makes us clean. If Paul needed to own and confess his sin, I think I will do well to follow his example. "Thank You oh great and mighty God that You love me, You see Your Holy Son's payment for my sin, You are cleaning me up and beyond my sinning, You see my potential. Thank You in Jesus precious Name." Amen

## "Keep My Commands"

**John 14:21 "Whoever has my commands and obeys them, he is the one who loves me. He who loves me will be loved by my Father, and I too will love him and show myself to him."**

**John 15:10 "If you obey my commands, you will remain in my love, just as I have obeyed my Father's commands and remain in his love."**

As Jesus walked the paths of His Hebrew nation He had a fairly simple agenda. He came to earth to teach a few men and women how to live and then He died to give freedom to all who will believe. Well what were His commands? Just one was, **"Remain in me, and I will remain in you. No branch can bear fruit by itself; it must remain in the vine. Neither can you bear fruit unless you remain in me."** John 15:4 To remain in Him means to get to know Him more and more, day by day, moment by moment. HE is the source of all peace, joy and fullness of life. We all have family members who are stressed out and in turmoil because they haven't given in and let God become the center of everything. The need to do this applies to all of us, because none of us will find peace and completeness until we reach the point of putting Him in charge of every detail of our life. The only way we can even begin to do this is to build a strong relationship with Him. Two lovers can't stand to not be together as they get to know one another and even an hour apart seems like days. We allow our daily bread to be so important to us but ignore God and His food and still think we can enjoy the benefits of being a Christian. WRONG. The only way we can know all He has for us is to keep on keeping on with Him and learn His requirements, His commands and His ways. Are you even trying?

# FORGIVE

**Matt 18:26-30 "The servant fell on his knees before him. 'Be patient with me,' he begged, 'and I will pay back everything.' The servant's master took pity on him, canceled the debt and let him go. "But when that servant went out, he found one of his fellow servants who owed him a hundred denarii. He grabbed him and began to choke him. 'Pay back what you owe me!' he demanded. "His fellow servant fell to his knees and begged him, 'Be patient with me, and I will pay you back.' "But he refused. Instead, he went off and had the man thrown into prison until he could pay the debt.**

Recently on the web someone started a discussion about forgiving and forgetting. It reminded me of our scripture today and how Jesus often taught the great importance of forgiving. I wonder why some who claim the name "Christian" want to be forgiven, but at the same time they fail or even refuse to forgive. Perhaps it is because they have never committed what they consider to be the "real bad sins", or maybe the thought of forgiving others reminds them of something they stand guilty of which really "sets them off". Many people like to quote **Mal 2:16 "I hate divorce," says the LORD God of Israel, "and I hate a man's covering himself with violence as well as with his garment," says the LORD Almighty"**, and have no trouble condemning someone with this sin, but they fail to see the rest of that verse and others which tell us all the other things God lists, like gossip, slander, lying etc. Try doing a study sometime on what God does hate and I think you will be surprised. We are all sinners and as such we'd better remember what we have been forgiven and freely pass that forgiveness on to everyone else who needs it. A lady related to me a few days ago that she recently ran into someone she had not seen for some time who has gone through a divorce. After my friend gave her a hug and told her she loved her, the gal broke down and said that this was the only time she has been treated like this since her divorce. Many had "stoned" her, but no one had loved on her. Church, we had better start acting like Jesus if WE ourselves want to be forgiven Remember the rest of the parable in Matthew, **"In anger his master turned him over to the jailers to be tortured, until he should pay back all he owed"**. Matt 18:34 I sure don't want to be like that merciless servant, how about you?

# What's that in your hand?

**Exodus 4:2 Then the LORD said to him, "What is that in your hand?" "A staff," he replied.**

**Judges 15:15 Finding a fresh jawbone of a donkey, he grabbed it and struck down a thousand men.**

**Joshua 2:18 when we enter the land, you have tied this scarlet cord in the window through which you let us down, and unless you have brought your father and mother, your brothers and all your family into your house.**

**Acts 9:39 Peter went with them, and when he arrived he was taken upstairs to the room. All the widows stood around him, crying and showing him the robes and other clothing that Dorcas had made while she was still with them.**

People often say, "I can't do anything for the Lord" or "I don't have anything to give", but let us take another look at the verses above. Moses had a staff, Samson had the jawbone of a donkey, Rahab had a piece of red cord and Dorcas had a needle and thread. Each of these were faithful and made a great impact in their day with what God had given them. The staff became the tool God used to part the Red Sea and draw water from rocks, the jawbone was used to slay a thousand men, the red cord saved a family and many mourned the death of Dorcas for she had used her gift of sewing to help the poor. And don't forget David's little sling and what happened to Goliath. Gail Halverson, a US pilot during the Berlin airlift, had two sticks of gum. Longer story short, they were the start of Operation Little Vittles that resulted in the dropping of over three tons of candy to kids in Berlin. No matter how small or insignificant what we have may seem, it can be GREAT in the hands of God. The moment we humbly seek Him to work with our "needle", or "chunk of candy" He will bless others and us for His honor and glory.

## Do your job and love it

**Ps 90:17** May the favor of the Lord our God rest upon us; establish the work of our hands for us yes, establish the work of our hands.

**Prov 16:3** Commit to the LORD whatever you do, and your plans will succeed.

**2 Thess 2:16** May our Lord Jesus Christ himself and God our Father, who loved us and by his grace gave us eternal encouragement and good hope, 17 encourage your hearts and strengthen you in every good deed and word.

**Col 3:17** And whatever you do, whether in word or deed, do it all in the name of the Lord Jesus, giving thanks to God the Father through him.

"I hate my job, the boss is a pain, the conditions are horrible, and no one appreciates what I do". They tell us that a high percentage of Americans are dissatisfied in their careers. This may be true and there are those who might need to make a change, but there is something else to consider here. As Christians it is our responsibility to do our work, whatever it is, as unto the Lord. Imagine you are a waitress and Jesus is sitting at your table. Would you treat Him any differently than you do others? If your answer is yes, then you should reconsider how you are serving other people, be it in the workplace or wherever. One day Jesus borrowed Peter's boat and after using it He told Peter to go out into the deep water and lower the nets. Peter's response was, **"Master, we've worked hard all night and haven't caught anything. But because you say so, I will let down the nets."** (Luke 5:5) I do not hear a lot of enthusiasm, but I do hear a firm "OK". After so many fish were caught that help was needed to handle them all Peter said, **"Go away from me, Lord; I am a sinful man!"** (Luke 5:8) We should never assume that God will make us wealthy from our work, but if we do everything as unto Him we will be richly rewarded.

## Come aside and smell the roses

**Matt 14:23 After he had dismissed them, he went up on a mountainside by himself to pray. When evening came, he was there alone,**

**John 6:15 Jesus, knowing that they intended to come and make him king by force, withdrew again to a mountain by himself.**

**Luke 5:16 But Jesus often withdrew to lonely places and prayed.**

Somewhere along the line even Christians have fallen into the trap of thinking that busyness means everything. I must confess that if someone awakens me from a nap I'm prone to try to excuse the fact that I am resting. The truth is because of my constant pain I often need rest. There are times when all of us need to stop, get away from our work and "smell the roses", whatever that means for you. Even Jesus made it a regular part of His schedule to spend time alone to pray and rest. I once read of a pastor who said, "I never take a day off; the devil doesn't so neither do I". Another pastor responded, "Jesus DID take a day off now and then and I would rather pattern my life after Him than the devil any day". I read of yet another pastor who takes Monday off as his day of rest. He and his wife make it a habit to go for a walk without talking with one another until they stop for lunch. The object is to be able to silently concentrate on and enjoy God's creation together, then share what they individually heard from Him. Oh that more of us had the desire to take the time to rest but even more so to seek and hear from our Lord.

## Do not trample on the grace of God

**Matt 4:7 Jesus answered him, "It is also written: "Do not put the Lord your God to the test."**

**Ps 78:41 Again and again they put God to the test; they vexed the Holy One of Israel.**

**Acts 5:9 Peter said to her, "How could you agree to test the Spirit of the Lord? Look! The feet of the men who buried your husband are at the door, and they will carry you out also."**

**1 Cor 10:9 We should not test the Lord, as some of them did-and were killed by snakes.**

In Matt 4:5 it is recorded that Jesus was challenged by Satan to throw Himself down from the highest point of the temple. God has indeed promised to protect us, but to deliberately put ourselves in danger is to dare Him to keep His word. One commentator says this – *"The meaning is, thou shalt not try him; or, thou shalt not, by throwing thyself into voluntary and uncommanded dangers, appeal to God for protection, or trifle with the promises made to those who are thrown into danger by his providence. It is not true that the promise was meant to extend to those who wantonly provoke him and trifle with the promised help"* (Barnes notes) As I write this today my heart is breaking, hurting for people I know and love who are saying to God "I am going to live in sin and I know down the line You will forgive me." Some are having sex outside of marriage, some are refusing to forgive, some are getting high on drugs and alcohol etc. and the list could go on. I'm thinking now what part of repentance do they not understand. In case you are wondering, NO I am not living a perfect life, but when I do mess up (SIN) it breaks my heart; I confess it and ask God's forgiveness and help to not do it again. That is not the case for those I'm speaking of today. They appear to want their sin too much to do anything different. God help them and us to have HIS attitude toward our sin.

## Stand with the RIGHT, Jesus Christ

**Luke 9:58** Jesus replied, "Foxes have holes and birds of the air have nests, but the Son of Man has no place to lay his head."

**Luke 14:26-27** "If anyone comes to me and does not hate his father and mother, his wife and children, his brothers and sisters-yes, even his own life-he cannot be my disciple. And anyone who does not carry his cross and follow me cannot be my disciple."

**Luke 18:22-23** When Jesus heard this, he said to him, "You still lack one thing. Sell everything you have and give to the poor, and you will have treasure in heaven. Then come, follow me." When he heard this, he became very sad, because he was a man of great wealth

Many a teacher has used the story of the young ruler to make a case against having possessions. In one sense they may be correct, especially if possessions own us and not the reverse. I've always understood from this parable that Jesus was attempting to prove to the man that in reality he coveted his things. Now not all Christians are called to be poor and needy, but all are expected to follow the Lord first and foremost no matter their position in life. Abraham Lincoln once said, *"I am not bound to win, but I am bound to be true. I am not bound to succeed, but I am bound to live by the light that I have. I must stand with anybody that stands right, stand with him while he is right, and part with him when he goes wrong."* Jesus is always right and never wrong so we are to always stand for Him. Whether we have no home, as in His case, or whether we've been blessed with a mansion, whatever our circumstance, we are to live godly lives for Him and be grateful in all things.

## God will make a way

**Ps 55:22 Cast your cares on the LORD and he will sustain you; He will never let the righteous fall.**

**Ps 37:5 Commit your way to the LORD; trust in him and he will do this:**

**Matt 6:25 "Therefore I tell you, do not worry about your life, what you will eat or drink; or about your body, what you will wear. Is not life more important than food, and the body more important than clothes?"**

**Matt 11:28 "Come to me, all you who are weary and burdened, and I will give you rest."**

One of the reasons we don't see answers to our prayers is that we do not totally trust God to answer. Oh we know that He is God and He is all-powerful and down deep we even know HE CAN, but WILL HE? Consider – *"In 1853, the twenty-one-year-old Hudson Taylor sailed for China as an agent of a new mission society. He arrived in Shanghai the next spring and immediately began learning Chinese. Funds from home rarely arrived, but Taylor was determined to rely upon God for his every need, and he never appealed for money to his friends in England. Repeatedly he later told others, "Depend upon it. God's work, done in God's way, will never lack for supplies."(Christian History Institute)* Taylor had such great faith that he moved to China believing his God would supply what was needed. This same God is the God we worship today and He is just as dependable now as he was back then. The main reason we do not see God's hand is US. A missionary couple I know left the USA, reported for duty on a foreign field in total dependence on Him and He has met their every need. Too many of us want to see the bottom line before we dare make a move and I am sure that we restrain God's hand in doing so. Where there is sight faith becomes unimportant but FAITH and TRUST in GOD will move that mountain, in His time and in His way.

## Do you know God?

**Ps 86:11 Teach me your way, O LORD, and I will walk in your truth; give me an undivided heart, that I may fear your name.**

**Ps 25:4-5 Show me your ways, O LORD, teach me your paths; guide me in your truth and teach me, for you are God my Savior, and my hope is in you all day long.**

Think if you will about your understanding of rocket science; I'd say that most of us are lacking in this area. Now imagine yourself applying for the position of mission specialist on an upcoming flight to Mars. How would you answer the interviewer when asked about the technical aspects of such a flight? Suppose you are asked to explain the Orbiter Azimuth/Co-elevation System. I can hardly pronounce never mind explain it. The amazing thing is that folks think they can be Christians and know no more about Christ than they do about space flight. We so desperately need to spend time learning of God and His ways. Benjamin M. Ramsey's hymn, "Teach Me Thy Way, O Lord" says, *"Teach me Thy way, O Lord, teach me Thy way! Thy guiding grace afford, teach me Thy way! Help me to walk aright, more by faith, less by sight; Lead me with heavenly light, teach me Thy way!"* He goes on to write of sadness, doubts and eventually entering heaven, things we can only be prepared to face if God teaches us. HE is our salvation and light and we must KNOW HIM. We must know His Word and His ways, and not just in passing. Even as a spouse must know their mate, so must a Christian know the Father, Son and Holy Spirit. Do you?

# Why fight it?

**Acts 26:14b "Saul, Saul, why do you persecute me? It is hard for you to kick against the goads."**

**Prov 16:20 Whoever gives heed to instruction prospers, and blessed is he who trusts in the LORD.**

We all have an idea of what should and should not occur in our lives. Some things we view as blessings and others as curses. I may think something or someone is very good for me and brings value to my life, but God may not see it that way at all. He knows beforehand everything that will happen and remember He knew and even approved of the disastrous events in Job's life. As a matter of fact, God challenged Satan to take a look at Job. **Then the LORD said to Satan, "Have you considered my servant Job? There is no one on earth like him; he is blameless and upright, a man who fears God and shuns evil."** (Job 1:8) Job had the choice either to accept what was coming his way or fight it. Had he fought it, he would not have known the peace of God in it. Job trusted God even to the point of saying, **"Though he slay me, yet will I hope in him;** (Job 13:15). So what does this say to us? I believe it means that whatever comes along we would do well to stop our selfish arguing and allow God to be our portion and get us THROUGH the circumstance rather than OUT of it. How much easier it is if HE is really at the helm of our lives. God will not allow the enemy to destroy us, but we may well do that ourselves by kicking against what He has allowed. I would love the opportunity to fly with the NASA shuttle, but if I were so blessed I would definitely leave the driving to the trained pilot. So it should be in our lives. God is the trainer, the pilot and the One who knows the way, all wrapped up into one.

## Do you love as Jesus loved?

**John 13:34-35 "A new command I give you: Love one another. As I have loved you, so you must love one another. By this all men will know that you are my disciples, if you love one another."**

**Lev 19:18 "'Do not seek revenge or bear a grudge against one of your people, but love your neighbor as yourself. I am the LORD.**

It is usually easy to love someone who loves us in return, but how do we treat the one who is spiteful and hurtful? They are probably the ones who most need but are hardest to love. Jesus' command was to "love as I have loved you" and there is no better example of that than when the Lord, on the night He was betrayed, took water and a towel and deliberately went around the room washing the feet of each of His disciples. One fact to be considered here is that there were ten men who would fade into the woodwork before the evening was over, one man who would deny that he even knew Jesus and one man who would hand Him over to be crucified. Yet Jesus, the King of all kings, washed the feet of all twelve. Have we ever seen so powerful an example of love? He then said to them, **"You call me 'Teacher' and 'Lord,' and rightly so, for that is what I am. Now that I, your Lord and Teacher, have washed your feet, you also should wash one another's feet. I have set you an example that you should do as I have done for you."** (John 13:13-15) How does the church you attend rate in its love for people on a scale of one to ten? What are you doing to bump up that score?

## Full of grace and power

**Acts 6:8-10 Now Stephen, a man full of God's grace and power, did great wonders and miraculous signs among the people. Opposition arose, however, from members of the Synagogue of the Freedmen (as it was called) Jews of Cyrene and Alexandria as well as the provinces of Cilicia and Asia. These men began to argue with Stephen, but they could not stand up against his wisdom or the Spirit by whom he spoke.**

**Acts 7:55-56 But Stephen, full of the Holy Spirit, looked up to heaven and saw the glory of God, and Jesus standing at the right hand of God. "Look," he said, "I see heaven open and the Son of Man standing at the right hand of God."**

**1 Tim 3:13 Those who have served well gain an excellent standing and great assurance in their faith in Christ Jesus.**

I remember the morning that headlines were filled with the news of angry people who had mistakenly been told that men trapped in a mine in West Virginia had been found alive. Moments earlier these same people had been singing hymns and praising God, but now upon hearing that twelve of their own had indeed perished, their praises turned to cursing. I thought of these words of Stephen as he was being stoned to death following a mock trial, **"Lord Jesus, receive my spirit." Then he fell on his knees and cried out, "Lord, do not hold this sin against them."** (Acts 7:59-60) To understand how he could react as he did, we have to look at why they were stoning him in the first place. The fact is that he had been so filled with the power of God's Spirit that those who wanted to argue with him could not stand against his words. Certainly therein lies a lesson for us. If we desire and seek to be intimate with God, we will be given that same power and the ability to sing hymns even when our prayers are not answered the way we think they should be. One surviving family member later did give God honor even in her loss. I want to be that kind of Christian. Don't you?

## What is your gift?

**Acts 6:1 In those days when the number of disciples was increasing, the Grecian Jews among them complained against the Hebraic Jews because their widows were being overlooked in the daily distribution of food. 2 So the Twelve gathered all the disciples together and said, "It would not be right for us to neglect the ministry of the word of God in order to wait on tables.**

**Neh 6:3 so I sent messengers to them with this reply: "I am carrying on a great project and cannot go down. Why should the work stop while I leave it and go down to you?"**

For some reason over the years there has developed the idea that it is totally the pastor's job to do all the work of the local church. Nothing could be further from the truth. When the apostles saw the need to devote more time to the Word they appointed seven deacons that were to attend to the daily needs of the congregation so that they could spend more time in prayer, study and preaching. Does this mean the pastor should never call on folks? NO. But it does mean that we the congregation are responsible to know our gifts and be actively using them. The old saying "many hands make light work" is never truer than in the church. If each one is using the gift or gifts that the Holy Spirit has given him the church will be seeing fewer burned out pastors and more spiritual growth. On Sunday morning would you rather hear a sermon from a pastor who has invested much time in prayer and study, or one who has been out doing the work of the congregation? Nehemiah said, **"I am carrying on a great project and cannot go down. Why should the work stop while I leave it and go down to you?"** We need to let our pastors carry on their work while we carry on ours. They are responsible to give us the true Word of God and that is their "GREAT PROJECT".

## Church is where YOU GIVE

**Acts 2:44-47 All the believers were together and had everything in common. Selling their possessions and goods, they gave to anyone as he had need. Every day they continued to meet together in the temple courts. They broke bread in their homes and ate together with glad and sincere hearts, praising God and enjoying the favor of all the people. And the Lord added to their number daily those who were being saved.**

**Acts 4:32 All the believers were one in heart and mind. No one claimed that any of his possessions was his own, but they shared everything they had.**

Carefully reading the above verses shows us some truths we need to take to heart. In the early church two things stand out. First, everyone had all things in common and they gladly gave so that all could share in the joy of Jesus. It seems they were not required to give their every penny, though many did give all. In fact Peter told Ananias that he could have kept any part of his money and not lied about what he was keeping. Secondly, they devoted themselves to learning more about their great Savior and were so very hungry to know Him and be supportive of the body. It is safe to say that if we begin to attend church with these two objectives in mind we will see growth in the number of souls saved and ongoing spiritual growth as well. We need to attend in order to give our monies But most of all ourselves to God. AND we need to attend with the goal of learning more about Him. It is not acceptable to be a churchgoer only to be blessed or to get something from attending. Our Lord will bless us and we will see more of God's working in our lives if our aim is HIM. Sometimes people say, "I'm not going to a church unless the pastor calls on me or unless _____". Such excuses focus on me and what I can get and not on Jesus who must be the total object of our faith and worship. So let's forget about all our self-centered demands and follow the example of the early church. Let us focus on HIM.

## A "House of Prayer"

**Isa 56:7 these I will bring to my holy mountain and give them joy in my house of prayer. Their burnt offerings and sacrifices will be accepted on my altar; for my house will be called a house of prayer for all nations.**

**"Matt 21:13 "It is written," he said to them, "'My house will be called a house of prayer,' but you are making it a 'den of robbers.'"**

**John 4:21-24 Jesus declared, "Believe me, woman, a time is coming when you will worship the Father neither on this mountain nor in Jerusalem. You Samaritans worship what you do not know; we worship what we do know, for salvation is from the Jews. Yet a time is coming and has now come when the true worshipers will worship the Father in spirit and truth, for they are the kind of worshipers the Father seeks. God is spirit, and his worshipers must worship in spirit and in truth."**

There used to be a saying that went like this, "different strokes for different folks". The way some treat the church it would appear that in places this still holds true. People find all kinds of reasons for meeting together for church, but the Bible comes down hard on all uses of the Lord's house except one. Isaiah told the nation of Israel that if they honored God and His Sabbath He would bring them to Himself and accept their burnt offerings. Our beautiful churches, busy programs and all of our other trappings of religion can be good, but only if they are the PRODUCT OF our communion with God and not a REPLACEMENT FOR intimacy with the Holy One. The Apostle Paul makes clear God's will for us, **"I want men everywhere to lift up holy hands in prayer, without anger or disputing."** We need to focus on what GOD wants which is communication with Him (PRAYER) and we need to earnestly evaluate all other things. Oh and how many churches excel in the "anger or disputing" and fall short on the "spirit and truth"?

## What do we worship?

**Isa 55:1-2** "Come, all you who are thirsty, come to the waters; and you who have no money, come, buy and eat! Come, buy wine and milk without money and without cost. Why spend money on what is not bread, and your labor on what does not satisfy? Listen, listen to me, and eat what is good, and your soul will delight in the richest of fare.

**Ps 42:1-2** As the deer pants for streams of water, so my soul pants for you, O God. My soul thirsts for God, for the living God. When can I go and meet with God?

**Isa 46:6** Some pour out gold from their bags and weigh out silver on the scales; they hire a goldsmith to make it into a god, and they bow down and worship it.

All over our country men and women are driven to attain the "American Dream". Work, a means to an end, becomes an obsession and seemingly the only way to success, joy and satisfaction. Meanwhile children are at day care or they become "latchkey kids" and all too often literally cry for mom and dad's attention. Sad to say but for many, careers and the pursuit of achieving goals has become an object of worship. Isaiah asks, **"Why spend money on what is not bread, and your labor on what does not satisfy?"** God's word to us deserves our full attention and begs this question. Does your soul PANT for time with Him? **"The Spirit and the bride say, "Come!" And let him who hears say, "Come!" Whoever is thirsty, let him come; and whoever wishes, let him take the free gift of the water of life."** (Rev 22:17) Do you yearn for fulfillment, peace and happiness? Then come to the REAL SOURCE of that which will last and bring you all you truly crave.

## It takes an army

**Neh 4:19 Then I said to the nobles, the officials and the rest of the people, "The work is extensive and spread out, and we are widely separated from each other along the wall. 20 Wherever you hear the sound of the trumpet, join us there. Our God will fight for us!"**

**Ps 35:1 Contend, O LORD, with those who contend with me; fight against those who fight against me.**

**Deut 3:22 Do not be afraid of them; the LORD your God himself will fight for you."**

**Deut 20:4 For the LORD your God is the one who goes with you to fight for you against your enemies to give you victory."**

Maybe you are like many out there who struggle with some hidden (so you think) sin in your life. It could be an addiction like nicotine, alcohol, porn, sex or food, but you always seem to lose the fight. You know your health is at risk or you'd be just plain better off without _____., but you can't get a handle on it. Today's readings tell us the secret to winning these battles. Basically there are two principles set before us: 1) Nehemiah announced to the people that because they were wide spread along the wall, a trumpet would sound in the event of an enemy invasion, signaling everyone to rally at the point of attack and 2) when they would come together the Lord would do the fighting. So our solution is this. We need to do our part by obeying what He's asking of us, then draw together, share our needs in confidence and support one another as God does the fighting. He will win and be glorified, and we will be the better for it. Oh the wonderful joy of knowing that our battles belong to the Lord and we are VICTORS not victims.

## Let your yes be yes!

**Matt 5:37 Simply let your 'Yes' be 'Yes,' and your 'No,' 'No'; anything beyond this comes from the evil one.**

**James 5:12 Above all, my brothers, do not swear-not by heaven or by earth or by anything else. Let your "Yes" be yes, and your "No," no, or you will be condemned.**

**2 Cor 1:17 When I planned this, did I do it lightly? Or do I make my plans in a worldly manner so that in the same breath I say, "Yes, yes" and "No, no"?**

**Col 4:6 Let your conversation be always full of grace, seasoned with salt, so that you may know how to answer everyone.**

Some politicians have a habit of saying what they think the present audience wants to hear and there are times when we ourselves say or do what will appease the current situation. God is not that way at all and He expects us to follow His example. There are repeated warnings in Scripture about instability,.**"because he who doubts is like a wave of the sea, blown and tossed by the wind. That man should not think he will receive anything from the Lord; he is a double-minded man, unstable in all he does.** (James 1:6-8) **"Come near to God and he will come near to you. Wash your hands, you sinners, and purify your hearts, you double-minded."** (James 4:8) **"No one can serve two masters. Either he will hate the one and love the other, or he will be devoted to the one and despise the other.** (Matt 6:24) We can find ourselves in some pretty uncomfortable spots, but being on God's side is the safest place to be in the long haul. Jesus could have appeased the Pharisees, but then we would all be lost. There are those who say that they're quite discretionary, but though discretion may be an indication of wisdom, even wiser is the one who walks in integrity and is the same ALL the time.

## Through the fire anyone?

**Isa 43:2 When you pass through the waters, I will be with you; and when you pass through the rivers, they will not sweep over you. When you walk through the fire, you will not be burned; the flames will not set you ablaze.**

**Ps 66:10-12 For you, O God, tested us; you refined us like silver.**
**You brought us into prison and laid burdens on our backs.**
**You let men ride over our heads; we went through fire and water, but you brought us to a place of abundance.**

**Luke 21:12 "But before all this, they will lay hands on you and persecute you. They will deliver you to synagogues and prisons, and you will be brought before kings and governors, and all on account of my name.**

**1 Peter 4:12-13 Dear friends, do not be surprised at the painful trial you are suffering, as though something strange were happening to you. But rejoice that you participate in the sufferings of Christ, so that you may be overjoyed when his glory is revealed.**

"Oh God, just get me out of this mess". In a pinch Christians and non-believers alike make such statements; some even offer God a deal. "You solve this and I will serve you the rest of my life." Time and again God has provided the rescue knowing that the rescuee will not live up to their end. The fact is God has promised that WE WILL have trials and testings. Peter said, **"do not be surprised at the painful trial you are suffering"** For sure none of us want to go through hard times but they are good for us and the final outcome is what's most important, **"so that you may be overjoyed when his glory is revealed"** "Reality" shows on TV let us see people putting themselves into dangerous situations in hopes of gaining money and fame. But what God promises is joy and His presence when we endure what He allows in our lives. Do we trust God? That is the question. HE is the answer to everything, so let us act like we believe He is.

## Produce a crop

**Phil 1:6 being confident of this, that he who began a good work in you will carry it on to completion until the day of Christ Jesus.**

    As a farmer at heart I know the joy of plowing the ground and preparing it for seeding. Once the seeds are buried in that warm moist earth, the farmer waits with baited breath for the sprouts to emerge. Day after day he walks by the field and then "wow" the plants appear. He throws his shoulders back with a sense of pride for his work was not in vain. He knows that the fun has just begun for it is necessary to nurture the new plants and keep the weeds out of his field. He also must watch for disease and then at just the right time the harvest will come. That farmer reminds me of our God who literally jumps for joy when the seed of faith bursts into a sprout at the moment of salvation. **"I tell you that in the same way there will be more rejoicing in heaven over one sinner who repents than over ninety-nine righteous persons who do not need to repent"**. (Luke 15:7) Like the farmer, God knows that the sprout is not yet all it can or should be. He knows that He has to nurture and attend to this new convert to bring them to maturity and He will never leave that one alone to fend for themselves. WE need to constantly be weeded, fed, watered, treated for disease and given the sunshine of God's love, then be assured we will yield fruit if we allow Him to do His work in us. If the farmer's field or the gardener's plot were to refuse the necessary treatments, there would be no crop to harvest. Let us take a hint from the farmer and allow God to have His way in us.

## In a spirit of humility

**Gal 6:1 Brothers, if someone is caught in a sin, you who are spiritual should restore him gently. But watch yourself, or you also may be tempted**

**James 5:19 My brothers, if one of you should wander from the truth and someone should bring him back, 20 remember this: Whoever turns a sinner from the error of his way will save him from death and cover over a multitude of sins.**

**1 Cor 4:21 What do you prefer? Shall I come to you with a whip, or in love and with a gentle spirit?**

**1 Peter 3:15 But in your hearts set apart Christ as Lord. Always be prepared to give an answer to everyone who asks you to give the reason for the hope that you have. But do this with gentleness and respect,**

Scripture often admonishes us to be careful with our words and remember that we too are frail and prone to failure. That is indeed very good advice, but having said that there are times when we must in gentle, kind and loving ways address difficult issues. For sake of illustration let us consider the situation where someone has hurt you deeply, for instance a spouse seeking divorce or someone spreading malicious gossip about you. It hurts and we may want to carry anger for a long time. Friends want to be of help and so they support you by saying things like, "I understand" or "you have every right to be angry". They mean well, but they are wrong and so are we when we encourage another to continue carrying an unforgiving spirit. The better approach may be to very gently point them to what Jesus said **"For if you forgive men when they sin against you, your heavenly Father will also forgive you. But if you do not forgive men their sins, your Father will not forgive your sins."** (Matt 6:14-15) It's all about being allowing the Holy Spirit to direct us in ALL we say to other people and when necessary speaking the truth in kindness and with much love.

## Perfect Peace

**Isa 26:3 You will keep in perfect peace him whose mind is steadfast, because he trusts in you.**

**Ps 85:7-8 Show us your unfailing love, O LORD, and grant us your salvation. I will listen to what God the LORD will say; He promises peace to his people, His saints but let them not return to folly.**

**John 16:33 "I have told you these things, so that in me you may have peace. In this world you will have trouble. But take heart! I have overcome the world."**

**Phil 4:7 And the peace of God, which transcends all understanding, will guard your hearts and your minds in Christ Jesus.**

I once saw a cartoon that pictured a car with a set of landing wheels from an airplane protruding from the roof. Standing beside the car were two ladies and the one was saying, "George would never fly. He was afraid an airplane would kill him." This humorous illustration of the futility of worry and fretting reminds us of the fears that plague so many of us. Over and over in His Word God promises perfect peace to those who love Him. What we need to remember is that He is the same God when the cancer is cured as He is when the cancer results in death. He is the same God whether the bills are paid or whether they're not. He is the same God whether a family member rebels or whether they walk the narrow path. No matter what our trial or burden, He is still God and He offers total and perfect peace to those whose minds are stayed on Him. He remains the same; the only variable is us. **"He promises peace to his people, His saints, but let them not return to folly.** Hearts filled with fear and trust in ourselves equal folly, but trust in God, no matter what comes, equals peace.

## The letter kills, BUT the Spirit......

**2 Cor 3:6 He has made us competent as ministers of a new covenant-not of the letter but of the Spirit; for the letter kills, but the Spirit gives life.**

**Rom 3:20 Therefore no one will be declared righteous in his sight by observing the law; rather, through the law we become conscious of sin.**

**Gal 3:10 All who rely on observing the law are under a curse, for it is written: "Cursed is everyone who does not continue to do everything written in the Book of the Law." 11 Clearly no one is justified before God by the law, because, "The righteous will live by faith."**

Somehow we've been given the impression that God is this cosmic killjoy out there just waiting to drop the other shoe and "get us" for our sin. It's safe to say that there is partial truth in that, if all we're doing is trying to keep some set of rules and regulations. The Word says that the letter of the law kills. There is no redemption or restoration in the law, only condemnation because the law does no more than show us our sin without giving us the power to do anything about it. In short, it is impossible to keep any list perfectly. The rich young ruler proved so when he claimed to have kept the law from his youth, but in reality coveted his possessions. (Matthew 19:16) All God's commands, including The Ten, are the ultimate for us to live by, but it is only the Holy Spirit who can give us victory over sin and the power to keep them. And only by making Jesus LORD of our lives can we live a life pleasing to Him, demonstrating to others that though we aren't perfect, we are His. **"By their fruit you will recognize them."** (Matt 7:16) **"But the fruit of the Spirit is love, joy, peace, patience, kindness, goodness, faithfulness, gentleness and self-control. Against such things there is no law."** (Gal 5:22-23)

## Rightly Dividing

**2 Tim 2:15 Do your best to present yourself to God as one approved, a workman who does not need to be ashamed and who correctly handles the word of truth.**

**2 Peter 3:14 So then, dear friends, since you are looking forward to this, make every effort to be found spotless, blameless and at peace with Him.**

**2 Cor 5:9 So we make it our goal to please Him, whether we are at home in the body or away from it.**

**Matt 13:52 He said to them, "Therefore every teacher of the law who has been instructed about the kingdom of heaven is like the owner of a house who brings out of his storeroom new treasures as well as old."**

Ruthie (my precious wife) and I often watch the food network. It is quite amazing how one can take an inexpensive cut of meat and make a very tasty, dare I say beautiful, meal. Even a tough old flank steak can be sliced and garnished to be both appealing to the eye and very pleasing to the tongue. The Apostle Paul told his spiritual son, Timothy, to rightly divide or handle the Word of truth. We are in this world to share this Word from God with today's culture. We can by our talk and walk misrepresent the gospel and who God is or allow the Holy Spirit to give us the ability to present the Christian life in both a truthful AND appealing way that will draw men and women, boys and girls, to Him. We've all been given a sphere of influence and our lives influence people more than we realize. Our task is to bring honor and glory to the One who redeemed us and made us fit to come into God's holy presence; so let us rightly handle God's Word. That is both our privilege and responsibility.

# FREE

**John 8:34-36 Jesus replied, "I tell you the truth, everyone who sins is a slave to sin. Now a slave has no permanent place in the family, but a son belongs to it forever. So if the Son sets you free, you will be free indeed.**

**Luke 4:18 "The Spirit of the Lord is on me, because he has anointed me to preach good news to the poor. He has sent me to proclaim freedom for the prisoners and recovery of sight for the blind, to release the oppressed,"**

**John 8:31-32 To the Jews who had believed him, Jesus said, "If you hold to my teaching, you are really my disciples. Then you will know the truth, and the truth will set you free."**

**Ps 19:13 Keep your servant also from willful sins; may they not rule over me. Then will I be blameless, innocent of great transgression.**

Several years ago the news reported a story of a dog that showed up well over a thousand miles from home. Questions were asked as to how this could happen. The answer is simple; with freedom came free will and no restrictions. That was a good thing for a while but in time the dog found himself too far from home to get back alone. Sometimes in our Christian lives we can experience similar problems. David noted in Psalm nineteen that he needed God to keep him from drifting into willful or intentional sin. When we are free there is the danger of becoming wrapped up in our own wants and desires and that is the very reason we need to continually be building a close relationship with our Savior. He can give us His good freedom of safety, security and a real sense of His presence that will keep us from the traps of the not so good. This is real freedom, while everything else leads to a bondage to sinful habits. In what kind of freedom are you living?

## Let THIS mind be in you

**Phil 2:5-8 Your attitude should be the same as that of Christ Jesus: Who, being in very nature God, did not consider equality with God something to be grasped, but made Himself nothing, taking the very nature of a servant, being made in human likeness. And being found in appearance as a man, He humbled himself and became obedient to death,-even death on a cross!**

**Matt 11:29-30 "Take my yoke upon you and learn from me, for I am gentle and humble in heart, and you will find rest for your souls. For my yoke is easy and my burden is light."**

**Matt 20:28 "just as the Son of Man did not come to be served, but to serve, and to give his life as a ransom for many."**

In a monarchy it is understood that the eldest child of the current ruler will become the next sovereign. Christ being God the Son and the earthly born Son of Man was totally entitled to all the perks of sovereignty. From a personal standpoint He did not need to yield to death on a cross, but His love for us would not allow Him to take any route other than the mission He came to fulfill. His love, oh His love. How can we ever even think about holding on to our selfish ambitions, greediness, angers and all the other countless things in which we wallow? We use excuses like "I enjoy what I'm doing" (my sin), "I have a right to be angry" or "I deserve this goal". Aren't you glad Jesus did not use any such excuses to avoid the cross? I AM. *"...Actually, salvation without obedience is a self-contradicting impossibility."* A. W. Tozer

## So you think you can do it?

**Phil 4:8 Finally, brothers, whatever is true, whatever is noble, whatever is right, whatever is pure, whatever is lovely, whatever is admirable-if anything is excellent or praiseworthy-think about such things.**

**Rom 12:9 Love must be sincere. Hate what is evil; cling to what is good. 10 Be devoted to one another in brotherly love. Honor one another above yourselves.**

**Luke 16:15 He said to them, "You are the ones who justify yourselves in the eyes of men, but God knows your hearts. What is highly valued among men is detestable in God's sight.**

**Eph 6:14 Stand firm then, with the belt of truth buckled around your waist, with the breastplate of righteousness in place,**

So many things clamor for our attention; so many decisions have to be made. At times we're not quite sure which turn to take. There is a possibility, though, that much of the time we are like the guy in the TV ad who is driving around in the dessert looking for the lake so he can launch his boat. Trouble is, he refuses to turn on the navigation system because doesn't need help. (right!!) There are two reasons we refuse to turn to our navigator, God. One is pride –"I can handle it myself", or two – "I don't want to hear what He might tell me". If I really like going my own way and are of the opinion that no one is going to tell me how to live, I must be willing to live with the consequences. God does not tell us to focus on what is good, true, noble, etc. for no reason. He knows our human weaknesses and wants to protect us from the bondage and outcome of bad choices. As in the ad, if the guy would turn on his GPS he would soon learn where he went wrong and be able to set things right. So will we when we think on such things, reject evil, cling to good, and surrender totally to God.

## Rejoice? But you don't understand!

**Phil 4:4 Rejoice in the Lord always. I will say it again: Rejoice!**

**Rom 12:12 Be joyful in hope, patient in affliction, faithful in prayer.**

**Matt 5:12 "Rejoice and be glad, because great is your reward in heaven, for in the same way they persecuted the prophets who were before you."**

**Acts 5:41 The apostles left the Sanhedrin, rejoicing because they had been counted worthy of suffering disgrace for the Name.**

According to the dictionary rejoice means "to feel joy or great delight". Another idea is to gladden, which is defined as "to make glad". Somehow it makes little sense in our finite minds to ALWAYS rejoice. Face it; there are days when we just do not "feel" like being glad. The operative word here is "feel". While feelings are very real and very important they are not always that reliable. They are usually based upon what ever is going on at the moment and they fail to take in the big picture. One day I was having a conversation with someone who was a little down and they answered my "how are you?" with "well I'm still alive". I quickly replied, "well consider the options". Later, I did just that. If we know the Lord Jesus the options are limited to one and that is going home to be with Him. Now how bad is that? How can we rejoice in ALL things? By remembering that the outcome of anything that could happen to us here on earth is to see our precious Savior. When you consider the options they are not bad at all and they put everything in perspective.

# Sing Praise

**Ps 7:17 I will give thanks to the LORD because of his righteousness and will sing praise to the name of the LORD Most High.**

**Ps 51:14 Save me from bloodguilt, O God, the God who saves me, and my tongue will sing of your righteousness.**

**Ps 9:1-2 I will praise you, O LORD, with all my heart; I will tell of all your wonders. I will be glad and rejoice in you; I will sing praise to your name, O Most High.**

**Rom 15:10-11 Again, it says, "Rejoice, O Gentiles, with his people." And again, "Praise the Lord, all you Gentiles, and sing praises to him, all you peoples."**

"I don't feel like praising God. Everything in my life is falling apart. Friends have deserted me, I've lost my job, money is tight and a lot of things right now are just plain wrong." We've all been there and have wanted to cry out with David, **"How long, O LORD? Will you forget me forever? How long will you hide your face from me? How long must I wrestle with my thoughts and every day have sorrow in my heart? How long will my enemy triumph over me?"** (Ps 13:1-2) However, it would be good for us to read a couple verses later where he says, **"But I trust in your unfailing love; my heart rejoices in your salvation. I will sing to the LORD, for he has been good to me."** (Ps 13:5-6) God is good ALL THE TIME even when we think things couldn't get worse. We will do well to remember that HE is the source of our joy, peace and security and that the good first step in getting close to Him is to give Him honor, praise and thanksgiving. He is God and will never allow anything in our lives just for the fun of it. He loves us far too much for that. He is in control and He will work everything out in His time and in His way.

## "I came for the sinner"

**John 8:11 "No one, sir," she said. "Then neither do I condemn you," Jesus declared. "Go now and leave your life of sin."**

**John 3:17 "For God did not send his Son into the world to condemn the world, but to save the world through him."**

**Prov 28:13 He who conceals his sins does not prosper, but whoever confesses and renounces them finds mercy.**

**Luke 5:32 "I have not come to call the righteous, but sinners to repentance."**

A few years ago we at Daybreak began asking the Lord to reveal the sources of the oppression in our area so that we could pray more effectively. Just one of the things He showed us was that there are many in the local church that are only a part in name. They have no real concept of what it means to walk like Jesus. He came to reach the lost, but unfortunately there are those who are like the Pharisees and reject the grace He shows. Oh yes, they want growth in the church, but they want that growth on their own terms. New people who come through the door must meet certain criteria. When Jesus forgave the adulteress (John 8:11), when He went to the house of Zacchaeus (Luke 19:5) and when many other times He performed miracles, the Pharisees were infuriated. They did not really care to see such riff-raff experience the love of Christ. After all, they did not measure up. Yes, there are those who still hold that mindset. We need to put that away and open our arms to the Zacchaeus's, the adulterers, the drug users, and any other such sinners of our day. Then and only then will we as a church be doing the business of the church that God intends. After all sin is sin and man may add values, but GOD sees them all as jet black. Whether it be gossip or divorce and remarriage to Him they are the very same.

## Oh be careful little mouth

**Eph 5:4 Nor should there be obscenity, foolish talk or coarse joking, which are out of place, but rather thanksgiving.**

**Mark 7:22 greed, malice, deceit, lewdness, envy, slander, arrogance and folly. 23 All these evils come from inside and make a man 'unclean.'"**

**Eph 4:29 Do not let any unwholesome talk come out of your mouths, but only what is helpful for building others up according to their needs, that it may benefit those who listen.**

**James 3:9 With the tongue we praise our Lord and Father, and with it we curse men, who have been made in God's likeness. 10 Out of the same mouth come praise and cursing. My brothers, this should not be.**

We all have acquaintances, "friends", who try their best to attract us to their lifestyle. They mock and ridicule a God-honoring life and they think we're a wuss if we don't do what they do. They go through life totally unaware that they are headed straight toward hell and we are helping them get there if we join them in their sin. We laugh at their coarse jokes and take part in other destructive behaviors and in doing so unwittingly become an ally of Satan in the destruction of a soul that our Lord loves and died to redeem. As His people, we are new creations the instant we accept His gift of salvation and as such we need to listen to the words of the Apostle Paul **"Do not lie to each other, since you have taken off your old self with its practices and have put on the new self, which is being renewed in knowledge in the image of its Creator."** (Col 3:9-10) Dear Christian, there is a lot of truth in that little ditty, *"Oh be careful little eyes what you see, little ears what you hear* (and I add) *little mouth what you say, for the Father up above is looking down in love, so be careful ......."*, for their sake as well as yours.

## Jesus Only!

**Lev 20:26 You are to be holy to me because I, the LORD, am holy, and I have set you apart from the nations to be my own.**

**Ex 22:20 "Whoever sacrifices to any god other than the LORD must be destroyed.**

The world is full of people who for one reason or another cannot accept the fact that God is God, so they add other things into their mix. When confronting the Athenians, **"Paul then stood up in the meeting of the Areopagus and said: "Men of Athens! I see that in every way you are very religious. 23 For as I walked around and looked carefully at your objects of worship, I even found an altar with this inscription: TO AN UNKNOWN GOD"** (Acts 17:22-31) In their case they did know God so they wanted to make sure to cover all the bases. I fear that is the problem today; or if people do know Him, they do not trust Him so they include other things to make sure they will be all right in the end. God is a jealous God, not jealous OF us but rather FOR us. He wants our full assurance of His love, mercy and grace, but the only way that can be is if we MAKE HIM OUR ALL-IN-ALL. We do not need such things as superstitions, crystals, idols etc. that add up to being involved with what He hates. **"A man or woman who is a medium or spiritist among you must be put to death. You are to stone them; their blood will be on their own heads."** Lev 20:27) God gave His only Son to give us salvation, peace, joy and so much more; how dare we slap Him in the face by allowing other gods into our lives? If you have any things around that are contrary to Him it is time to clean house unless you want to incur the holy wrath of the Most Holy God. How about it? You may have excuses, like "it's my culture", but God sees only the sin that must be confessed and forsaken. **"You must not live according to the customs of the nations I am going to drive out before you. Because they did all these things, I abhorred them."** (Lev 20:23-24)

## Our citizenship is in heaven

**1 Cor 1:7 Therefore you do not lack any spiritual gift as you eagerly wait for our Lord Jesus Christ to be revealed.**

**Phil 3:20 But our citizenship is in heaven. And we eagerly await a Savior from there, the Lord Jesus Christ,**

**2 Tim 4:8 Now there is in store for me the crown of righteousness, which the Lord, the righteous Judge, will award to me on that day-and not only to me, but also to all who have longed for his appearing.**

**Jude 21 Keep yourselves in God's love as you wait for the mercy of our Lord Jesus Christ to bring you to eternal life.**

WAIT is definitely not one of our favorite words. We want everything now, better yet yesterday. There is a restaurant called "Timeless Destination" of which some have said, "that is about how long it takes to get your food". But it is one of those places where every meal is cooked to order and that does take time. If you are like me and appreciate a meal that is freshly cooked and the proof is its scrumptious taste, you realize that such a meal is well worth waiting for. Nearly two thousand years ago the disciples heard the angels announce **"This same Jesus, who has been taken from you into heaven, will come back in the same way you have seen him go into heaven."** (Acts 1:11) They fully believed that He could return in their day and that belief caused them to patiently live their lives looking for His return. The only difference between them and us should be the time gap. We think it has been a long time, but HE IS COMING and we need to eagerly look for Him. If we are Christians and know how the book of Revelation describes the events at that time we will not want anyone left behind. That alone should motivate us to live as He would have us live and while we wait do all we can to take others with us.

## Even unto death?!

**Phil 2:30 because he almost died for the work of Christ, risking his life to make up for the help you could not give me.**

**Matt 25:36 "I needed clothes and you clothed me, I was sick and you looked after me, I was in prison and you came to visit me."**

**Matt 25:38-40 When did we see you a stranger and invite you in, or needing clothes and clothe you? When did we see you sick or in prison and go to visit you?' "The King will reply, 'I tell you the truth, whatever you did for one of the least of these brothers of mine, you did for me.'**

When the Apostle Paul was yet Saul carrying out his vendetta against the church, he gave every ounce of energy for what he believed was right. After coming face to face with Jesus he refocused that same dedication to God. Now here in his letter to the Philippians he is giving Epaphroditus a commendation for going above and beyond the call of duty in his service to him. Epaphroditus had delivered a gift from the Philippian church to Paul and then stayed around to help meet his other needs. In so doing he became deathly sick and almost died. Epaphroditus knew what each of us need to know and practice and that is our service to God should have no bounds. We must be doing His work even if it places our lives in jeopardy. The only danger we need to worry about is that of NOT serving the Lord one hundred percent, for it is then that we are actually siding with the enemy. We can trust God no matter what. It may bring us trials and difficult times or even martyrdom but it is better for us to give our lives in service to Christ than to keep them for ourselves and serve Satan.

## My Shepherd

**Ps 23:1-6 The LORD is my shepherd, I shall not be in want. He makes me lie down in green pastures, He leads me beside quiet waters, He restores my soul. He guides me in paths of righteousness for His name's sake. Even though I walk through the valley of the shadow of death, I will fear no evil, for you are with me; your rod and your staff, they comfort me. You prepare a table before me in the presence of my enemies. You anoint my head with oil; my cup overflows. Surely goodness and love will follow me all the days of my life, and I will dwell in the house of the LORD forever.**

David knew the source of real joy and security and could lay claim to that ever- flowing spring because he had put his complete faith in his God. He was not perfect, but his heart was. He desired one thing above all else and that was to please God. He and all others who live with that purpose will be known as **His** and will demonstrate **"the fruit of the Spirit is love, joy, peace, patience, kindness, goodness, faithfulness, gentleness and self-control. Against such things there is no law. Those who belong to Christ Jesus have crucified the sinful nature with its passions and desires. Since we live by the Spirit, let us keep in step with the Spirit. Let us not become conceited, provoking and envying each other."** (Gal 5:22-26)

## Know freedom in Christ by obedience

**Phil 2:12-13 Therefore, my dear friends, as you have always obeyed not only in my presence, but now much more in my absence-continue to work out your salvation with fear and trembling, for it is God who works in you to will and to act according to his good purpose.**

**Phil 1:5-6 because of your partnership in the gospel from the first day until now, being confident of this, that he who began a good work in you will carry it on to completion until the day of Christ Jesus.**

**Rom 2:7 To those who by persistence in doing good seek glory, honor and immortality, he will give eternal life**

**Ps 119:120 My flesh trembles in fear of you; I stand in awe of your laws.**

Government has an annoying habit of reminding us often of our roads' speed limits. Personally I'm glad for cruise control because otherwise too much of the time I'd exceed that limit. Even with the cruise set I automatically check my speed when I see one of those irksome signs. Guilty conscience, I guess. All that said, speed limits are necessary for our good and obedience is the secret to a life of freedom. If I am within the speed limit I have the freedom of not having to worry about a trooper being around the next curve. Seeing those signs is not enough, though, we must act on them. If I am living within the guidelines of the Word of God I do not have to wonder if He will discipline me. There is a second and more important reason, though, for obedience. Our "fear" (respect for His awesomeness) and our recognition of His great sacrifice should cause us to WANT to do no less than be totally obedient to Him. Ray Boltz asked the question in his song, "Does He still feel the nails, every time I fail?". I don't know about you, but I sure don't want to cause my Lord and Savior further pain.

## Forgive, forgive, then forgive again

**Col 3:13-14 Bear with each other and forgive whatever grievances you may have against one another. Forgive as the Lord forgave you. And over all these virtues put on love, which binds them all together in perfect unity.**

**Matt 5:44 But I tell you: "Love your enemies and pray for those who persecute you,"**

**Matt 6:14-15 "For if you forgive men when they sin against you, your heavenly Father will also forgive you. But if you do not forgive men their sins, your Father will not forgive your sins."**

**Luke 23:34 Jesus said, "Father, forgive them, for they do not know what they are doing."**

Repeatedly the Bible addresses this whole issue of forgiveness so there must be a deep message here for us. The Greek word *charizomai*, translated "forgive", carries the idea of freely giving or granting forgiveness. It comes from the same root word *charis* meaning "grace". One reason for us to forgive is that unforgiveness is a bondage that Satan uses to keep us from being joyful and effective for God. Secondly, unforgiveness is an indication that I am still wrapped up in myself. I think that I am letting the offender "off" if I forgive. Well consider this; we don't get off that easily. If I sin by overeating, God will forgive but I will likely suffer a lifetime of medical problems. Thirdly, Christ on the cross forgave those who drove the nails through His body and there is no way that the desertion of a spouse; the abuse of a parent or any crime committed against us can come close to the killing of the Son of God. And last but not least, Jesus said, **"if you do not forgive men their sins, your Father will not forgive your sins"** (Matt 6:15) So, if you or I are holding on to any unforgiveness we need to follow Christ's example and be set free from the lies of Satan to serve our Lord. AND we should encourage others to do so as well.

## WHO tramples the Son of God under foot?

**Ps 81:10 I am the LORD your God, who brought you up out of Egypt. Open wide your mouth and I will fill it. 11 "But my people would not listen to me; Israel would not submit to me. 12 So I gave them over to their stubborn hearts to follow their own devices.**

**Deut 32:18 You deserted the Rock, who fathered you; you forgot the God who gave you birth.**

**Prov 1:30-33 since they would not accept my advice and spurned my rebuke, they will eat the fruit of their ways and be filled with the fruit of their schemes. For the waywardness of the simple will kill them, and the complacency of fools will destroy them; but whoever listens to me will live in safety and be at ease, without fear of harm."**

**Heb 10:29 How much more severely do you think a man deserves to be punished who has trampled the Son of God under foot, who has treated as an unholy thing the blood of the covenant that sanctified him, and who has insulted the Spirit of grace?**

It is hard to think that there are those who trample the Son of God, but before we sit in condemnation of only the most grievous of sinners, let us consider just what we're talking about. God's Word says how much more severely a man deserves to be punished who has treated as an unholy thing the blood of the covenant that sanctified him. When we lay claim to the salvation of God, namely say that we believe Jesus died and rose again to redeem our souls and say we have received His salvation, but do not change one thing about the way we live, WE are trampling on that sacred blood and insulting the Spirit of grace. God told the Jews, His chosen people, that because they would not listen to Him (pay attention and act upon what they had heard) He turned them over to their own stubborn hearts. He allowed them to follow their own devices and reap

*Just A Thought*

the fruit thereof. Oh friend, if you claim Him as Savior then I plead with you to begin to LIVE AS HE WOULD HAVE YOU LIVE.

## But I am not sure how to…..

**1 John 2:4** The man who says, "I know Him," but does not do what He commands is a liar, and the truth is not in him.

**Titus 1:16** They claim to know God, but by their actions they deny him…

**Luke 6:49** "The one who hears my words and does not put them into practice is like a man who built a house on the ground without a foundation. The moment the torrent struck that house, it collapsed and its destruction was complete."

**John 15:5** "I am the vine; you are the branches. If a man remains in me and I in him, he will bear much fruit; apart from me you can do nothing."

It is always a thrill to watch a tot take those first steps. They hang on to a finger so tightly to protect themselves from the fall they sense is coming, then the grip loosens as confidence develops and finally they get brave enough to take that first step alone; wow, they're off. Before long the parent who has been so encouraging finds they need to be slowing their youngster down a bit or at least wish they could. Many of us are unsure of how to get into a deeper walk with the Lord and we wonder how we can invest so much time in God when our days are full now. The answer is the same as for that toddler. Begin by taking baby steps. Read or memorize one real meaningful verse each day. Start with a short prayer of praising God, confessing sin, forgiving one who has offended you and thanking Him for His love. Move up to a daily devotional and longer prayer. Soon you will feel the Lord's increased presence and find that you have more time to do everything else. It will never be about the number of verses or the length of prayer, but the day will come when HE is the total focus of your life, which after all is the whole point anyway.

## Are You in the Light?

**Eph 5:8 For you were "once darkness, but now you are light in the Lord. Live as children of light**

**Isa 60:2 See, darkness covers the earth and thick darkness is over the peoples, but the LORD rises upon you and his glory appears over you.**

**1 Peter 2:9 But you are a chosen people, a royal priesthood, a holy nation, a people belonging to God, that you may declare the praises of him who called you out of darkness into his wonderful light.**

**Rev 22:5 There will be no more night. They will not need the light of a lamp or the light of the sun, for the Lord God will give them light. And they will reign for ever and ever.**

For some people the darkness of night is scary at the very least and they want a flashlight handy for even a short venture. I guess that's really not a bad idea since we do need some means of finding our way. The Apostle Paul makes it clear in today's lead verse that before we knew Christ we not only WALKED IN DARKNESS but we WERE DARKNESS. The original text here denotes darkness as being an evil system absolutely opposed to the light. That describes Satan's realm. Before coming to Jesus we were part of that evil world's system, but now we know the joy of living in the presence of THE LIGHT. There is a requirement, though, if we claim to be His. **"Whoever claims to live in him must walk as Jesus did."** (1 John 2:6) We must live a life that is loving, caring, forgiving, and the many other attributes that He possesses. In short, it is best to follow the advice of Jesus, **"So in everything, do to others what you would have them do to you, for this sums up the Law and the Prophets."** (Matt 7:12)

## The apple of HIS eye

**Ps 17:8 Keep me as the apple of your eye; hide me in the shadow of your wings**

**Ps 91:1 He who dwells in the shelter of the Most High will rest in the shadow of the Almighty.**

**Matt 23:37 "O Jerusalem, Jerusalem, you who kill the prophets and stone those sent to you, how often I have longed to gather your children together, as a hen gathers her chicks under her wings, but you were not willing."**

**John 17:11 "I will remain in the world no longer, but they are still in the world, and I am coming to you. Holy Father, protect them by the power of your name-the name you gave me-so that they may be one as we are one."**

Every girl, down deep every guy, longs to be the apple of someone's eye, to be loved, cared for and protected. The pupil is considered of greatest value to our physical eyes and they are what the lids and lashes guard from injury. So when we're the apple of ones eye we are given security and protection from harm. Anyone who owns, confesses, repents of their sin and accepts the forgiveness of Christ instantly becomes the apple of GOD'S eye with every access to peace, safety, and rest in the shadow of the Almighty. Jesus cried out to Jerusalem "how often I have longed to gather your children together, but you were not willing." Oh how big is that little word, "but". To reject God is to reject the presence of Almighty God and to give up the security of His arms. Sad to say, some parents know what it is like to ache to hold a wayward child once more. That is the type of ache in God's heart when we refuse the abundant life that He offers and choose to continue in our self-centered ways. WHY oh why do we settle for so little?

## HE is There

**Is 43:1-3 "Fear not, for I have redeemed you; I have summoned you by name; you are mine. When you pass through the waters, I will be with you; and when you pass through the rivers, they will not sweep over you. When you walk through the fire, you will not be burned; the flames will not set you ablaze. For I am the LORD, your God, the Holy One of Israel, your Savior;**

**Deut 31:6 Be strong and courageous. Do not be afraid or terrified because of them, for the LORD your God goes with you; he will never leave you nor forsake you."**

**Ps 23:4 Even though I walk through the valley of the shadow of death, I will fear no evil, for you are with me; your rod and your staff, they comfort me.**

There is an Old Danish proverb that says; "Life is not holding a good hand; Life is playing a poor hand well". While I'm not sure of the author's exact meaning, there is some truth here. We do not always have what we consider to be a good hand in life and some pretty difficult things come our way. I remember a few years ago I was struggling with something very hard when one day the Lord led me to the above Isaiah passage and He reminded me that I was safe and secure in Him. When we walk close to God and He is the center of everything, we learn over time that it matters not what comes our way because the KING of all eternity is with us. Sometimes our greatest need is more awareness and assurance of His presence. This can happen in several ways, but two very important ones are 1) invest more time with Him and 2) develop a deep intimate relationship with a group of believers for support and accountability. Nothing we have in this world can replace God and fellow Christians.

# Be holy for "I" am Holy

**Eph 5:1 Be imitators of God, therefore, as dearly loved children 2 and live a life of love, just as Christ loved us and gave himself up for us as a fragrant offering and sacrifice to God.**

**Lev 11:45 I am the LORD who brought you up out of Egypt to be your God; therefore be holy, because I am holy.**

**Luke 6:35 36 "But love your enemies, do good to them, and lend to them without expecting to get anything back. Then your reward will be great, and you will be sons of the Most High, because he is kind to the ungrateful and wicked. Be merciful, just as your Father is merciful."**

**1 Peter 1:14-16 As obedient children, do not conform to the evil desires you had when you lived in ignorance. But just as he who called you is holy, so be holy in all you do; for it is written: "Be holy, because I am holy."**

"Be holy" is the command, but just what does that mean? The dictionary offers the following in reference to God Himself; *"holy is an adjective meaning worthy of absolute devotion, sacred"*. We further learn that what being holy looks like in us is *"having a divine quality"*. Might I suggest that all this is saying that we should live worthy of the absolute devotion that Jesus had for us when He gave His life for us by being absolutely devoted to Him. If we have truly accepted Jesus as Savior we are "sacred" to Him, sacred meaning blessed, consecrated, hallowed and sanctified or set apart to Him. The first three are imputed or credited to us by God and the last, consecrated, is by our choice. From this day forward CHOOSE to respond to His holiness by living life fully consecrated to Him, because HE IS GOD and HE IS HOLY.

## FINISHED, Oh praise the Lord O my soul

**John 19:30 When He had received the drink, Jesus said, "It is finished." With that, He bowed His head and gave up His spirit.**

**Gen 3:15 "And I will put enmity between you and the woman, and between your offspring and hers; He will crush your head, and you will strike his heel."**

**John 4:34 "My food," said Jesus, "is to do the will of Him who sent me and to finish His work.**

**Heb 9:14 How much more, then, will the blood of Christ, who through the eternal Spirit offered himself unblemished to God, cleanse our consciences from acts that lead to death, so that we may serve the living God!**

As I think about two thousand years ago, the day we call "Good Friday", I wonder about some things, like, did the Pharisees really think they could get rid of this threat to their power base, did Satan really think he could get the Son of God permanently out of the way? Jesus taught the truth of the Kingdom. He set people free from sin and it's dominion. Souls were being changed then and even so more now, PRAISE GOD, and His enemies could not and can not tolerate such things. Little did they realize the truth of what they would accomplish that day. Little did they know that Jesus would FINISH the work He came to do and forever provide the freedom He had preached to all who would accept it. It was then that Satan learned the full meaning of God's declaration **"He will crush your head, and you will strike his heel."** Salvation was finished and three days later, oh three days later, He arose and lives forevermore! HALLELUJAH! PRAISE HIS HOLY NAME!

## Be glad for trials

**Rom 5:3 Not only so, but we also rejoice in our sufferings, because we know that suffering produces perseverance; 4 perseverance, character; and character, hope. 5 And hope does not disappoint us, because God has poured out his love into our hearts by the Holy Spirit, whom he has given us.**

**Matt 5:10-11 "Blessed are those who are persecuted because of righteousness, for theirs is the kingdom of heaven. "Blessed are you when people insult you, persecute you and falsely say all kinds of evil against you because of me."**

**James 1:2 Consider it pure joy, my brothers, whenever you face trials of many kinds,**

**Phil 1:20 I eagerly expect and hope that I will in no way be ashamed, but will have sufficient courage so that now as always Christ will be exalted in my body, whether by life or by death.**

Most people believe that anything which disturbs the ideal, should not be tolerated, or better yet, never occur in the first place. This is nothing new. The one closest to Job, **"His wife said to him, "Are you still holding on to your integrity? Curse God and die!"** (Job 2:9) In other words, "Job this is so bad, why not just give up?" Unfortunately that is what many of us do. But Job new better when **"He replied, "You are talking like a foolish woman. Shall we accept good from God, and not trouble?"** (Job 2:10). What a blessing it is when we are able to trust God and see that He is using the hard times to carry out His good purposes in our lives. He shapes and grows us for our good and gives us hope, a hope that is so much more than a "I hope such 'n such happens." This hope from God is the quiet and complete assurance that He is fully capable not only get us to the other side of the hard times, but to bring us through them with a strong witness to others of His grace and glory. All the way around, isn't it a good thing to endure our trials and sufferings patiently and with joy?

## He CAN be trusted

**Ps 103:11 For as high as the heavens are above the earth, so great is his love for those who fear him;**

**Ps 57:10 For great is your love, reaching to the heavens; your faithfulness reaches to the skies.**

**Is 55:9 "As the heavens are higher than the earth, so are my ways higher than your ways and my thoughts than your thoughts.**

**Luke 1:50 His mercy extends to those who fear him, from generation to generation.**

As children we were often confused by WHAT our parents did and WHY. Sometimes we asked what was going on, but the answer did not always help. So we decided, at least some of the time, "they are mom and dad so they must know what they are doing". Now as adults we find that we do not always understand life either. Nicodemus came to the Lord inquiring how a man could be saved. When Jesus said, "no one can enter the kingdom unless he is born again", he asked how that could be. (John 3). The point is, there are things we will never fully understand here in this life and it is better to be as we were as children and say, "God is God and He knows exactly what He is doing, period." It sounds too simplistic doesn't it, but consider this. How many of us know just what happens when we put the key in the ignition and head for town? Not many, however that doesn't keep us from making the trip, does it. We don't hesitate a second to trust a whole lot of things in our daily lives, like the chairs we sit in. Doesn't it then stand to reason that even more so, without any hesitation, our full faith and confidence should be in our God? For He is the same yesterday, today and forever and HE IS TRUSTWORTHY.

## HE sees ME

**Gen 16:13 She gave this name to the LORD who spoke to her: "You are the God who sees me," for she said, "I have now seen the One who sees me."**

**Ps 139:9 If I rise on the wings of the dawn, if I settle on the far side of the sea, 10 even there your hand will guide me, your right hand will hold me fast.**

**Job 34:21 "His eyes are on the ways of men; He sees their every step.**

**John 1:10 He was in the world, and though the world was made through him, the world did not recognize him. 11 He came to that which was his own, but his own did not receive him. 12 Yet to all who received him, to those who believed in his name, he gave the right to become children of God**

There's an old joke something like – "Why do famous people wear sunglasses outdoors? So they won't be recognized. Why do they wear them inside? So they will be." How great it is to know that with God we do not have to go to any such craziness to get His attention. His eye is on us every moment. Hagar was aware of this truth in the above verse when she received news from the angel of the Lord that she would bear a son and that her descendents would be too numerous to count. (Gen 16-13) So why do WE not "see Him" more often. John summed up the answer when he said, "He came unto His own, but His own did not recognize Him". Sometimes our eyes are blinded by our own ignorance. Like the Pharisees we expect God to appear in a way that we have conceived in our own minds, but at times He comes from "the other side of the tracks". He shows Himself in a way we do not expect so we think He has not shown up at all, but He has. "Thank You God for revealing Yourself to Your people. Oh help US to see You in every moment of our days so that we can in turn help OTHERS to see You. In Jesus precious name." Amen

## What Past?

**2 Cor 5:17 Therefore,** *if anyone is in Christ, he is a new creation; the old has gone,* **the new has come!**

**Rom 8:1 Therefore, there is now no condemnation for those who are in Christ Jesus,**

**Ps 51:10 Create in me a pure heart, O God, and renew a steadfast spirit within me.**

Oh how we seem to be prone to branding "used to be" on others. To say a person was once a test pilot, another a designer, etc. is fine, but to dig up past sins covered by the blood of Christ is a flat out sin on OUR part. Jesus forgave the woman taken in adultery then told her to go and leave her life of sin. The woman at the well became an instant missionary when He forgave her and the result was that many accepted Him as Savior. The Apostle Paul called those in Jesus "new creations"; John said, "Confess your sin and He will forgive and cleanse". (! John 1:9) If Jesus Christ makes a person new and clean how dare we hang on them a negative label? They are new and as such they have no past. Paul tells us **"Do you not know that the wicked will not inherit the kingdom of God? Do not be deceived: Neither the sexually immoral nor idolaters nor adulterers nor male prostitutes nor homosexual offenders nor thieves nor the greedy nor drunkards nor slanderers nor swindlers will inherit the kingdom of God. And that is what some of you were. But you were washed, you were sanctified, you were justified in the name of the Lord Jesus Christ and by the Spirit of our God".** (1 Cor 6:9-11) Whatever THEIR past, whatever OUR past, none of us have a past if we are in CHRIST.

## What does the WORD say?

**Heb 2:1 We must pay more careful attention, therefore, to what we have heard, so that we do not drift away.**

**Deut 4:23 Be careful not to forget the covenant of the LORD your God that he made with you; do not make for yourselves an idol in the form of anything the LORD your God has forbidden. 24 For the LORD your God is a consuming fire, a jealous God.**

**Luke 8:15 "But the seed on good soil stands for those with a noble and good heart, who hear the word, retain it, and by persevering produce a crop."**

**Heb 1:1 In the past God spoke to our forefathers through the prophets at many times and in various ways, 2 but in these last days he has spoken to us by his Son, whom he appointed heir of all things, and through whom he made the universe.**

In the past there were prophets who spoke for God but now in these last days we have the words of His Son. The Holy Spirit inspired the New Testament writers to record the teachings of Jesus and the challenge for us is that, **"We must pay more careful attention, therefore, to what we have heard."** We must put forth every effort to know God's words so that we do not let them slip away. Have you ever taken a Christmas trivia quiz? Usually they ask questions like, "How many wise men came to worship the baby Jesus?" We usually say three. Wrong. There were three gifts, but we are not told how many wisemen. Or "Who told Joseph and Mary to go to Bethlehem?" Actually it was not an angel, but Caesar whom God used to relay His plan, see Luke 2:1. Often we answer questions wrongly because we listen to the songs, carols, and lore and believe what other people think. We do not know what's in the WORD. Point is, to know what's true, we have to study and learn what the BIBLE says.

*Just A Thought*

## His words or ours?

**Matt 28:19-20 Therefore go and make disciples of all nations, baptizing them in the name of the Father and of the Son and of the Holy Spirit, and teaching them to obey everything I have commanded you. And surely I am with you always, to the very end of the age."**

**Matt 9:37-38 Then he said to his disciples, "The harvest is plentiful but the workers are few. Ask the Lord of the harvest, therefore, to send out workers into his harvest field."**

**Matt 22:37-40 Jesus replied: "'Love the Lord your God with all your heart and with all your soul and with all your mind.' This is the first and greatest commandment. 39 And the second is like it: 'Love your neighbor as yourself.' All the Law and the Prophets hang on these two commandments."**

Here at Daybreak we have been learning the importance of making God's Word clear to everyone no matter who they are. We've become more aware that sometimes the things we say have little or no meaning at all to those outside the church. If we are to be effective for our Lord we must use words and terms that are easily understood by today's culture. In light of that fact we revised our mission statement for the express purpose of making it more understandable. Originally it read – "To bring unity and strength In our world for the purpose of extending the Kingdom of God: We will, with the Holy Spirit's enabling seek to glorify God, become a discipling people, strive for unity, and assist in the establishment and growth of Christian LOVE." After several weeks of study and consideration we revised it to read – "We will love God with heart, soul and spirit, and everyone as ourselves. We will, with the Holy Spirit's help glorify God by becoming a church that teaches others to teach others. We will strive for unity through the love of Jesus Christ." "WE WILL LOVE GOD WITH HEART, SOUL AND SPIRIT, AND EVERYONE AS OURSELVES. WE WILL, WITH THE HOLY SPIRIT'S HELP GLORIFY GOD BY BECOMING A

CHURCH THAT TEACHES OTHERS TO TEACH OTHERS. WE WILL STRIVE FOR UNITY THROUGH THE LOVE OF JESUS CHRIST." Learning to communicate with others effectively and with love takes desire, time and effort but most of all the enabling of the Holy Spirit. Let's not just say so many words, but allow HIM to speak and do His work in and through us.

*Just A Thought*

## All roads .......

**Rom 3:4 Not at all! Let God be true, and every man a liar. As it is written: "So that you may be proved right when you speak and prevail when you judge."**

**Titus 1:2 a faith and knowledge resting on the hope of eternal life, which God, who does not lie, promised before the beginning of time,**

**Heb 6:18 God did this so that, by two unchangeable things in which it is impossible for God to lie,**

**Ps 62:9 Lowborn men are but a breath, the highborn are but a lie; if weighed on a balance, they are nothing; together they are only a breath.**

If you listen to the media at all you've heard of the many diet plans, one at every turn, which offer, "Lose that weight and lose it now!". One pill even goes so far as to say, "Eat all you want and watch that weight roll right away"; at least implying that you don't have to change your lifestyle at all. These and multitudes of other advertisements are proof of what the Scripture says, "men are liars." We all know that if you want to lose weight you DO have to change your life style by eating less and getting more exercise, etc. Similarly we hear of various ways to get to God without following HIS plan. People say, "After all, every religion is seeking the same God". Maybe some are honestly trying to find the true God while others follow gods of their imaginations, BUT anyone who is not lifting up Jesus Christ as THE WAY to God, is in gross error. Jesus said, "I am the way and the truth and the life. No one comes to the Father except through me." (John 14:6) Jesus is the ONLY WAY and no man is able to set such a standard but Him. ALL religions and ALL people will one day come face to face with this Jesus and the out come of that meeting will reveal whether they have accepted or rejected Him and His Truth, "I am The Way." Oh Christian, PRAY for those who are lost, LIVE so as to reach them for Jesus and when given the opportunity, SPEAK in love.

## Lift up holy hands

**1 Tim 2:8 I want men everywhere to lift up holy hands in prayer, without anger or disputing.**

**John 4:23-24 "Yet a time is coming and has now come when the true worshipers will worship the Father in spirit and truth, for they are the kind of worshipers the Father seeks. God is spirit, and his worshipers must worship in spirit and in truth."**

**Heb 10:22 let us draw near to God with a sincere heart in full assurance of faith, having our hearts sprinkled to cleanse us from a guilty conscience and having our bodies washed with pure water**

**James 1:6 But when he asks, he must believe and not doubt, because he who doubts is like a wave of the sea, blown and tossed by the wind.**

Martin Luther King Jr. had a dream that all men would be treated as equals. He knew that the same needs, desires, hopes and dreams are in all of us, no matter the color of skin. His was a correct dream and many years later America is still trying to move toward fulfilling his God-given vision. The Apostle Paul also had a dream. He desired that men everywhere would lift up holy hands in prayer to God and that this be done without anger and disputing. Simply put, God does not hear the prayers of the one who is angry and unforgiving. **"But if you do not forgive men their sins, your Father will not forgive your sins."** (Matt 6:15) What does it mean to have holy hands? Answer – confession of all known sin and true worship of God with sincerity in spirit and truth and full assurance that He will answer our prayers. If we meet these requirements our lifted hands will be holy ones that bring honor and glory to Jesus, our Lord and Savior. He does not ask for perfection but He does require a clean, pure and blameless heart.

## One Mediator, the man Christ Jesus

**1 Tim 2:5 For there is one God and one mediator between God and men, the man Christ Jesus,**

**Isa 44:6 "This is what the LORD says Israel's King and Redeemer, the LORD Almighty: I am the first and I am the last; apart from me there is no God.**

**John 1:14 The Word became flesh and made his dwelling among us. We have seen his glory, the glory of the One and Only, who came from the Father, full of grace and truth.**

**John 3:17 "For God did not send his Son into the world to condemn the world, but to save the world through him."**

When a problem arises between two parties be it union contracts, purchase of real estate or marital problems, etc, it is often necessary to bring in a mediator. A mediator is one who seeks to find common ground and bring difficulties to an end. Often, no make that usually, both parties have to make concessions in order for that to happen. When it comes to sinful man's relationship to God, though, there is the most serious dilemma. God is so pure, holy and righteous that He cannot yield in any way to lower the requirements for entering His Kingdom. Enter Jesus, the perfect mediator, the One who would give His own blood to pay the penalty for man's sin. His very name, Jesus (Yah-soos), comes from the Hebrew Yeshua meaning "He shall save". A shorter version of Yehoshua translates "Yahweh Is Salvation". That is exactly what Jesus accomplished through His own death, burial, and resurrection, and in so doing He guarantees to all who choose to believe on Him, a home in the Kingdom of God.

## What comes first?

**Matt 6:33 "But seek first his kingdom and his righteousness, and all these things will be given to you as well."**

**John 6:27 "Do not work for food that spoils, but for food that endures to eternal life, which the Son of Man will give you. On him God the Father has placed his seal of approval."**

**Hag 1:3 Then the word of the LORD came through the prophet Haggai: 4 "Is it a time for you yourselves to be living in your paneled houses, while this house remains a ruin?"**

**1 Kings 17:13 Elijah said to her, "Don't be afraid. Go home and do as you have said. But first make a small cake of bread for me from what you have and bring it to me, and then make something for yourself and your son.**

Is it possible that Christians sometimes have a totally wrong perspective on life? I believe the answer is yes. We so often think that God is some errand boy whose only purpose is to serve our needs and wants. When was the last time you heard someone testify, "I just praise the Lord for His presence in my life"? Usually we praise Him for getting us out of some tight spot or for healing Aunt Bessie's big toe. But put yourself in that poor widow woman's shoes. Elijah was asking her to go ahead and make bread and bring him the first cake. She had just finished telling him that she was preparing her final meal with the last of her flour and oil before she and her son would starve to death and now he's wants the bread she so desperately needs? We know the rest of the story, but she did not. She did, however, have complete trust in God, which enabled her to do as Elijah asked. She knew the value of being a servant. We are here to serve God, not Him serve us. Only when we get that straight in our minds and hearts CAN and WILL He provide that unfailing "bin of flour and bottle of oil" for us. Do you really want God's best? Then give Him His rightful position in your life.

## Watch your actions

**Acts 2:40 With many other words he warned them; and he pleaded with them, "Save yourselves from this corrupt generation."**

**Luke 21:36 "Be always on the watch, and pray that you may be able to escape all that is about to happen, and that you may be able to stand before the Son of Man."**

**2 Cor 5:20 We are therefore Christ's ambassadors, as though God were making his appeal through us. We implore you on Christ's behalf: Be reconciled to God.**

One day the things of this world, the things we cling to, will come to an end. **"Then I saw a new heaven and a new earth, for the first heaven and the first earth had passed away, and there was no longer any sea"** (Rev 21:1) They will all melt like butter and the wonderful possessions we hold on to will be gone. We who claim Christ need to refocus our desires and live our lives in light of Him and His return. The thing is, we spend so much time and energy on the here and now that we neglect the job we've been given of winning lost souls around us. When a person leaves this world there are only two options, heaven or hell, and we as Christians can make all the difference in the world to those who are not now seeking Him. Paul told Timothy, **"Watch your life and doctrine closely. Persevere in them, because if you do, you will save both yourself and your hearers."** That truth holds for us today. When we become part of an earthly organization we commit to do certain things and not to do others. Likewise there are expectations of us when we accept Christ as Lord and Savior. We are making a commitment to Him to live like we know and love God AND also to not sin against Him. What are people seeing in you? THEY ARE WATCHING.

## A badge of honor

**Matt 10:32-33 "Whoever acknowledges me before men, I will also acknowledge him before my Father in heaven. But whoever disowns me before men, I will disown him before my Father in heaven.**

**John 9:22-23 His parents said this because they were afraid of the Jews, for already the Jews had decided that anyone who acknowledged that Jesus was the Christ would be put out of the synagogue. That was why his parents said, "He is of age; ask him."**

**Rom 10:9 That if you confess with your mouth, "Jesus is Lord," and believe in your heart that God raised him from the dead, you will be saved.**

**2 Tim 1:8 So do not be ashamed to testify about our Lord, or ashamed of me his prisoner. But join with me in suffering for the gospel, by the power of God,**

A few years ago our granddaughter, Jackie, was named "Dairy Princess" for Tioga County PA. Now I am a normal grandpa and when given the chance I was quick to say, "that's my precious granddaughter". I would venture to say that all of us are tremendously proud in the accomplishments of those dear to us and a healthy pride is good. Likewise a healthy pride in our relationship to God is very good. When we have confessed and repented our sins and accepted the salvation of Jesus Christ, we become joint heirs with Him, **"So you are no longer a slave, but a son; and since you are a son, God has made you also an heir."** (Gal 4:7): We should wear this son ship of God as a badge of honor. In some countries admitting Christianity brings imprisonment and even death and those who truly know Him are most often accepting that possibility even without fear. Here in the USA some of us fear being made fun of or rejection by "friends" if we admit knowing Jesus. My brothers and sisters, this aught not to be. It's high time to demonstrate some backbone and openly acknowledge Christ.

## Meet together

**Heb 10:25 Let us not give up meeting together, as some are in the habit of doing, but let us encourage one another-and all the more as you see the Day approaching.**

**Matt 18:20 "For where two or three come together in my name, there am I with them."**

**Acts 2:42 They devoted themselves to the apostles' teaching and to the fellowship, to the breaking of bread and to prayer**

**1 Cor 5:4 When you are assembled in the name of our Lord Jesus and I am with you in spirit, and the power of our Lord Jesus is present,**

From what we are hearing, worship habits of people in the US are horrible and at one time it was reported that less than seventeen percent of us come together to worship God. It is no wonder there are so many weak and struggling Christians. The practice of meeting regularly with others of like faith helps provide us with what is needed to live victorious Christian lives. When we share time together in worship we gain strength, we receive encouragement, we experience accountability, and above all we are following the commands of God in His Word. The early church **"devoted themselves to the apostles' teaching and to the fellowship, to the breaking of bread and to prayer"** and as a result **"Everyone was filled with awe, and many wonders and miraculous signs were done by the apostles."** (Acts 2:43) I don't know about you, but I so long for God to powerfully show Himself among us today. I believe that if there was more devotion to Him on OUR part we would see just that, to say nothing of lost friends and family coming to Him if they were to see that He is as important to us as we say He is. If we take the above verses seriously there is nothing more vital to our Christian walk than worshiping together. NOTHING.

## "WORKOUT"

**Phil 2:12-13 Therefore, my dear friends, as you have always obeyed-not only in my presence, but now much more in my absence-continue to work out your salvation with fear and trembling, for it is God who works in you to will and to act according to his good purpose.**

**Matt 11:29 Take my yoke upon you and learn from me, for I am gentle and humble in heart, and you will find rest for your souls. 30 For my yoke is easy and my burden is light."**

**John 6:27 Do not work for food that spoils, but for food that endures to eternal life, which the Son of Man will give you. On him God the Father has placed his seal of approval."**

**Rom 2:7 To those who by persistence in doing good seek glory, honor and immortality, he will give eternal life.**

We once purchased an exercise machine and placed it in our home. Initially we didn't feel any effect from it, entirely understandable, because for various reasons it was awhile before we used it. There was a "from the factory" problem that needed repairing, about that time I had an occluded artery, Ruthie's dad started having problems that took her time and the list goes on. Sounds like a lot of excuses, but it reminds me of the reason we do not grow the way we should in our spiritual lives. Most of the time we lay it on our busy schedules, after all SOMETHING has to give, but unfortunately that "something" ends up being the wrong thing. Studies tell us that most Americans are overweight yet we still take time to eat; we are so busy but we have time for sports, hobbies, TV and in short we find enough time to do all the things we WANT to do. Why is it that the one who gets slighted is the Very One we so desperately need? We give God very little of ourselves or leave Him out of our lives altogether, yet we expect Him to answer all our prayers and our every whim at a moments' notice. Does that make any sense at all to you? If not, DO SOMETHING about it!

## Serve or be served?

**Matt 20:26** "Not so with you. Instead, whoever wants to become great among you must be your servant,"

**Matt 23:12** "For whoever exalts himself will be humbled, and whoever humbles himself will be exalted."

**Matt 25:44-45** "They also will answer, 'Lord, when did we see you hungry or thirsty or a stranger or needing clothes or sick or in prison, and did not help you?' "He will reply, 'I tell you the truth, whatever you did not do for one of the least of these, you did not do for me.'"

**Matt 6:33** "But seek first his kingdom and his righteousness, and all these things will be given to you as well."

Oh how we like to be served. The tip left on the table usually reflects whether we were satisfied with the service rendered. If the server did not smile just right, then little or no tip. That is not the attitude taught by our precious Lord. Jesus reminded His followers over and over that they and us are to be servants. He even lowered Himself to the point of washing their feet. Think about this, that just hours before Judas' unthinkable deed, Jesus knelt down and washed the feet of the one who He knew would betray Him. We find it hard to wash the feet of someone who loves us, never mind one who is about to be instrumental in our death. Personally, I believe THAT ACT of Jesus to be the most powerful illustration of being a true servant. But above and beyond that, He came here to serve us by the atoning work of the cross. He knew what sinners we would be and that we would resist Him, yet He went forward with joy to embrace that cruel death. How could He have loved us so? Doesn't such love demand our all and in turn giving our lives for others, even those who might betray us?

## The gates of hell shall not prevail

**Matt 16:16-18** Simon Peter answered, "You are the Christ, the Son of the living God." Jesus replied, "Blessed are you, Simon son of Jonah, for this was not revealed to you by man, but by my Father in heaven. And I tell you that you are Peter, and on this rock I will build my church, and the gates of Hades will not overcome it."

**Matt 27:54** When the centurion and those with him who were guarding Jesus saw the earthquake and all that had happened, they were terrified, and exclaimed, "Surely he was the Son of God!"

**John 11:27** "Yes, Lord," she told him, "I believe that you are the Christ, the Son of God, who was to come into the world."

Just a quick glimpse of the evening news will tell you that Satan is going full speed ahead in His attempts to harm and destroy all that God created and loves. As if that isn't enough, the Church seems to be too weak and splintered to take a solid stand for what is right and righteous. Some even approve of fighting for the right of those living in sin to be qualified as ministers of the Gospel and political correctness is the rule. Jesus Christ is LORD, He is, **"the way, the truth and the life"** (John 14:6), and strict adherence to that truth and to His example of how to live in a sin sick world is all that we are to seriously consider. Jesus won the battle, the war and everything else when He walked out of the tomb. Hell can unleash its total fury on the Church, but it can never destroy it. So why does the Church act so weakly? Can it be that God's people out of desire to please the world are not living close to the Lord, which allows Satan to gain a foothold in THEIR LIVES and thus THE CHURCH? Jesus said, **"Whoever acknowledges me before men, I will also acknowledge him before my Father in heaven. But whoever disowns me before men, I will disown him before my Father in heaven."** (Matt 10:32-33) While being politically correct may make us look good to the world, it generally flies in the face of everything the WORD teaches.

## His brothers and sisters

**Heb 2:11-12 Both the one who makes men holy and those who are made holy are of the same family. So Jesus is not ashamed to call them brothers. He says, "I will declare your name to my brothers; in the presence of the congregation I will sing your praises."**

**Matt 12:48-50 He replied to him, "Who is my mother, and who are my brothers?" Pointing to his disciples, he said, "Here are my mother and my brothers. For whoever does the will of my Father in heaven is my brother and sister and mother."**

**Matt 25:40 "The King will reply, 'I tell you the truth, whatever you did for one of the least of these brothers of mine, you did for me."**

Most of us are pretty ordinary people, but just imagine one day finding out that you are related to a famous athlete, star, politician or otherwise noted person. Taking this scenario further, imagine them giving you the privilege of being at their side at any time or place and on any occasion. No doubt many of us would feel special and very honored. By the same token we have to remember that the moment we fell at the cross and acknowledged and accepted Jesus' atonement for our sins, we became brothers and sisters to the Creator of all things, the "I AM" of all eternity, the One who gave His very blood to redeem us. If we would consider it a privilege to be called the brother or sister of some mortal, how much more so to be the chosen kin of God the Son. We are awesomely and wonderfully made and redeemed on top of that so we must honor this One who so honors us and show our gratitude by serving Him every moment of every day. He said, **"I tell you, whoever acknowledges me before men, the Son of Man will also acknowledge him before the angels of God. But he who disowns me before men will be disowned before the angels of God."** (Luke 12:8-9) Does He have reason to acknowledge YOU as His brother or sister?

## Worship Him in EVERYTHING!

**Rom 12:1-2 Therefore, I urge you, brothers, in view of God's mercy, to offer your bodies as living sacrifices, holy and pleasing to God-this is your spiritual act of worship. Do not conform any longer to the pattern of this world, but be transformed by the renewing of your mind. Then you will be able to test and approve what God's will is-his good, pleasing and perfect will.**

**Rom 6:13-14 Do not offer the parts of your body to sin, as instruments of wickedness, but rather offer yourselves to God, as those who have been brought from death to life; and offer the parts of your body to him as instruments of righteousness. 14 For sin shall not be your master, because you are not under law, but under grace.**

What is worship? Some would say; "the music part of a church service" for others it is "when the preacher has his say". The truth is that worship is what we do when we love God. Four folks showed up at Daybreak yesterday to worship God by cleaning. Paul reminded the Roman Christians that they were to "offer themselves as living sacrifices to the Lord". That is the clearest definition of worship I know. Everything I do, everything I say, everything I think, in other words every single thing in all of my very life IS TO BE WORSHIP of the One who made me, who loves me and who redeemed me out of Satan's cruel grip. If you or I were to stand trial for worshipping God, would there be enough evidence for a conviction? How can I do any less than worship God with the ALL of who I am and ever will be? After all, **"since you know that you will receive an inheritance from the Lord as a reward. It is the Lord Christ you are serving. Anyone who does wrong will be repaid for his wrong, and there is no favoritism."** (Col 3:24-25)

## LIVE like He Is Coming!

**Luke 12:40 "You also must be ready, because the Son of Man will come at an hour when you do not expect him."**

**Mark 13:33-37 "Be on guard! Be alert! You do not know when that time will come. It's like a man going away: He leaves his house and puts his servants in charge, each with his assigned task, and tells the one at the door to keep watch. "Therefore keep watch because you do not know when the owner of the house will come back-whether in the evening, or at midnight, or when the rooster crows, or at dawn. If he comes suddenly, do not let him find you sleeping. What I say to you, I say to everyone: 'Watch!'"**

Down through the years some people have been so sure of the time of Jesus' return that they have even set the date. Yes, HE IS COMING, maybe today, but the challenge to us is not the time but rather that we be prepared. The first step in that preparation is excitement and expectancy. If I were a gambling man I would bet that if most of us received a letter that someone was going to deliver us a check for five-million dollars sometime in the next ten days we would spread the word via telephone, email, Facebook or Twitter and we certainly would not leave the house until that person arrived. Why is it then that we aren't all that excited about the prospect of the return of the King of kings? For the most part we go on with "life as usual" when our ALL OF LIFE is to be focused on Him. Why is it that we want to someday live with God, but have no interest in life with Him now? Taking that one more step, why would God accept us into His heaven when we refuse to make Him the center of our lives here? Jesus said, **"If you love me, you will obey what I command"** (John 14:15). Does that mean that if I do not obey Him I do not love Him? YES. Just what would be your response if your spouse told you they love you but they preferred to live somewhere else? Something to think about; is that how you are treating God?

## Love your children, LOVE THEM

**Eph 6:4 Fathers, do not exasperate your children; instead, bring them up in the training and instruction of the Lord.**

**Deut 31:13 Their children, who do not know this law, must hear it and learn to fear the LORD your God as long as you live in the land you are crossing the Jordan to possess."**

**Ps 78:5 He decreed statutes for Jacob and established the law in Israel, which he commanded our forefathers to teach their children,**

**Prov 4:3-4 When I was a boy in my father's house, still tender, and an only child of my mother, he taught me and said, "Lay hold of my words with all your heart; keep my commands and you will live.**

On the Bill Cosby show several years ago there was a routine that ended with these words from Bill to his son, Theo; "I brought you into this world and I can take you out". This was the ending to a situation where Theo had been a real pest and Bill had good reason, humanly speaking, to make such an empty threat. We've all felt aggravated by our children, but it is at those times when we most need advise from the Lord. One problem out of many is that parents expect the younger generation to "do as I say, not as I do". We've all heard the example of a parent instructing their child to ALWAYS tell the truth. The phone rings, the child answers it, it's the boss wanting Dad and Dad tells his kid to tell him that he's sick, when he is not. Parents exasperate their families by living a double standard, one for their kids and another for themselves. Truth is, children learn FAR MORE from what we DO than from what we SAY. Examine your own life. Are your dishonest words and actions as a parent, past or present, staring you in the face? If so, confess them to God and repent AND if possible it's never too late to say to your children, spouse or anyone else, "I'm sorry; I was wrong". We parents can do no more important thing for our families than to live OUR lives openly, honestly and in such a way as to lead the next generation in the path of godliness.

## He will take care of you!

**Prov 3:31-35 Do not envy a violent man or choose any of his ways, for the LORD detests a perverse man but takes the upright into his confidence. The LORD's curse is on the house of the wicked, but he blesses the home of the righteous. He mocks proud mockers but gives grace to the humble. The wise inherit honor, but fools he holds up to shame.**

**Ps 91:9-11 If you make the Most High your dwelling even the LORD, who is my refuge—then no harm will befall you, no disaster will come near your tent. For he will command his angels concerning you to guard you in all your ways;**

The Lord is trustworthy, reliable, dependable and sure. We are often afraid of what the Lord may want of us if we give our all to Him and put Him in charge of everything so we resist Him. When we do that, though, we are really setting ourselves up for failure. We look around us and see what we think are successful, top-of-life folks while we are barely eking by, but we have to remember that it's not about these few years here on earth. We who name the name of Jesus as our Hope and Redeemer live in an eternal realm. It is true that we live right now in the moment here on earth, but our citizenship is in heaven and that means eternal life for us that will never end. We will move again to be with Him and be changed **"in the twinkling of an eye"** (1 Cor 15:52) in the future, but spiritually speaking we live there with Him now. It is better than anything else to know that this God of all eternity is my God, my salvation, my strength and my life and that assurance far outweighs the fickleness of this crazy, evil world. To know God and His blessing is to live in absolute peace and joy.

## Be Thankful

**Col 4:2 Devote yourselves to prayer, being watchful and thankful.**

**Col 2:7 rooted and built up in him, strengthened in the faith as you were taught, and overflowing with thankfulness.**

**Col 3:15 Let the peace of Christ rule in your hearts, since as members of one body you were called to peace. And be thankful.**

**Col 3:17 And whatever you do, whether in word or deed, do it all in the name of the Lord Jesus, giving thanks to God the Father through him.**

In just a few weeks we will be eating tons of turkey while having a great time with family and friends, probably watching a lot of football, too. Somewhere along the way even those of us who intend to celebrate true Thanksgiving have gotten swallowed up in the new name for the day, "turkey day". What a sad commentary that THANKSGIVING has become downgraded to merely a day of hoopla. In 1619 the settlers in Virginia celebrated their harvest with a festival and in 1621 the colony in New England invited their Indian friends to a celebration in order to give thanks to God for the bountiful crops that would sustain them through the winter ahead. In 1939 FDR declared the next to the last Thursday of November as Thanksgiving Day and it has been observed on that day ever since. The unfortunate part is that as a nation it seems we thank God less and less and lean more on our own abilities. If God were to remove our abilities we would soon find our dependence again on Him. May I suggest that those of us who know the Lord Jesus on a personal level make every effort to be thankful and when we're given opportunity let others know WHO provides for us. Jesus said, **"I am the vine; you are the branches. If a man remains in me and I in him, he will bear much fruit; apart from me you can do nothing."** (John 15:5) Nothing is more true so let us be thankful with our every breath for everything.

## Because He first loved

**Luke 2:11 Today in the town of David a Savior has been born to you; he is Christ the Lord.**

**Matt 1:21 She will give birth to a son, and you are to give him the name Jesus, because he will save his people from their sins."**

**Gal 4:4-5 But when the time had fully come, God sent his Son, born of a woman, born under law, to redeem those under law, that we might receive the full rights of sons.**

**1 John 4:14-16 And we have seen and testify that the Father has sent his Son to be the Savior of the world. If anyone acknowledges that Jesus is the Son of God, God lives in him and he in God. And so we know and rely on the love God has for us.**

From the very beginning when Eve and Adam sinned God promised to redeem His beloved creation in these words to Satan. **"And I will put enmity between you and the woman, and between your offspring and hers; He will crush your head, and you will strike His heel."** (Gen 3:15) John also reminded us of this truth when he said, **"We love because he first loved us."** (1 John 4:19) And the Apostle Paul told us, **"But God demonstrates his own love for us in this: While we were still sinners, Christ died for us."** (Rom 5:8) Love is what compelled God to send His precious Son to this vile earth for one purpose only, the redemption from sin of those He SO LOVED. Whether it be Christmas or Easter or other times of year we are to show this love to a world that doesn't have a clue. Amidst all the celebrations that center on Jesus, especially Christmas, most people are naively unaware that the God who created all that is loves them so much He sent His Son and that His cross casts it's ominous shadow across that blessed night. The world wants to paint both Christmas and Easter with strokes of beauty that please the eye, BUT the only beauty in a cold, smelly, barn and a blood stained cross is HIM. There are countless ways to give people Jesus. May our lives never fail to mirror HIS love and beauty.

## To the least of these…

**Matt 25:40 "The King will reply, 'I tell you the truth, whatever you did for one of the least of these brothers of mine, you did for me."**

**2 Sam 9:1 David asked, "Is there anyone still left of the house of Saul to whom I can show kindness for Jonathan's sake?"**

**Prov 14:31 He who oppresses the poor shows contempt for their Maker, but whoever is kind to the needy honors God.**

Jesus said, **"The poor you will always have with you, but you will not always have me."**

(Matt 26:11) There are those right among us who have dire needs. Our communities are rich with the poor, people who cannot pay their heat bills, buy food or get medical help. Ruthie and I have become great fans of Extreme Makeover Home Edition. All of us at times feel needy, but as we watch that show we have come to realize we don't have it so bad and that there are countless others who have it far worse than we can ever imagine. Carried to the extreme, there are even children dying here in the USA and more so around the world for lack of the most basic necessities, food and water. We who've been blessed have wonderful and awesome opportunities to minister to the hurting and the good news is that there is something you and I can do. At the very least we can volunteer our time to help another. We can pack a "Shoebox" for Operation Christmas Child, we can give even if it's a small amount to Christian organizations such as Operation Blessing, Samaritan's Purse or Life Today where every dollar goes a long way in giving such things as water and shoes to those who have none. We can offer a shoulder to cry on or just slow down long enough to give a "glass of cold water" to someone who needs it. That "glass" may be as little as an encouraging word or caring ear, but it will be priceless to the hurting soul. Will you, or better yet, ARE YOU obeying the Lord and reaching out to "ONE OF THE LEAST OF THESE" brothers of Christ.

## Good News

**Luke 2:8-14 And there were shepherds living out in the fields nearby, keeping watch over their flocks at night. An angel of the Lord appeared to them, and the glory of the Lord shone around them, and they were terrified. But the angel said to them, "Do not be afraid. I bring you good news of great joy that will be for all the people. Today in the town of David a Savior has been born to you; he is Christ the Lord. This will be a sign to you: You will find a baby wrapped in cloths and lying in a manger." Suddenly a great company of the heavenly host appeared with the angel, praising God and saying, "Glory to God in the highest, and on earth peace to men on whom his favor rests."**

Ever wonder how "shepherds" would react if angels were to make that same announcement today with science fiction becoming more popular than ever? In fact a soon-to-be released movie is already receiving great reviews for its remarkable special effects. But getting back to the thought, if this were to happen today, would people quickly jump up and rush to the manger or would they have a long discussion on what this was all about? Some eighty-five percent of Americans claim to be Christian, but at the same time abortion, homosexuality, and a multitude of other sinful practices are welcomed and even seen as "normal" ways of life. If we want to see America become the nation she once was we need to get back to the awe and wonder those men and boys had that night so long ago. Jesus has to become real and a positive byword in us and in our everyday actions, every moment of every day. If we really think the birth of Jesus is good news why is He not the absolute center of our lives? I know you have to earn a living, care for your home and family and have many other responsibilities, but when JESUS becomes the entire focus of your life, all other things fall into place and He lends peace and abilities beyond our comprehension. Sadly, many of us never will know that because we refuse to be sold out to THE GOOD NEWS.

## Belong to God? You CANNOT continue in sin!

**1 John 3:9 No one who is born of God will continue to sin, because God's seed remains in him; he cannot go on sinning, because he has been born of God.**

**1 John 2:29 If you know that he is righteous, you know that everyone who does what is right has been born of him.**

**1 John 5:18 We know that anyone born of God does not continue to sin; the one who was born of God keeps him safe, and the evil one cannot harm him.**

This can be a touchy subject but in short, we are not to continue to repeatedly and deliberately sin after we have confessed our sins and become God's child. Some will say "Well, I just can't change; there are financial concerns that are at stake" etc. But isn't the God who saved us from hell also able to tend to our day-to-day concerns "without my sinfully handling things myself"? John says, **"If you know that he is righteous, you know that everyone who does what is right has been born of him."** (1 John 2:29) If we do what is right we know we are born again, so it would follow that if we do not do right our salvation may be called into question. Consider the common practice today, even among Christians, of living together before marriage. Applying the truth of Scripture that sex outside of marriage is sin, those who cohabitate without being married are sinning. If they claim to know Jesus they should know that by doing so they are degrading God in the eyes of the world, and if they truly love Him they will not want to do that. I will not pronounce them unsaved, but their salvation might be in question. Or how about gossip, lying, porn, or you name it? John gives us the answer to winning the battle, **"for everyone born of God overcomes the world. This is the victory that has overcome the world, even our faith"** (1 John 5:4) No matter the sin, we can defeat it in the power of Jesus. So the question is, do we want to?

## Give to the LORD!!!!!

**Mark 12:42-44** But a poor widow came and put in two very small copper coins, worth only a fraction of a penny. Calling his disciples to him, Jesus said, "I tell you the truth, this poor widow has put more into the treasury than all the others. They all gave out of their wealth; but she, out of her poverty, put in everything-all she had to live on."

**Matt 10:42** "And if anyone gives even a cup of cold water to one of these little ones because he is my disciple, I tell you the truth, he will certainly not lose his reward."

"I would love to give to the Lord, BUT I just don't have any extra." Ever heard anyone say that or maybe you have? Truth of the matter is, we can't afford NOT to give. A lady once gave this testimony, "I put my last ten dollars in the church's collection plate and shortly after arriving home someone stopped by unexpectedly to pay the thousand dollars they owed us." At the time her husband was away on business and no other money would be forthcoming, but in faith she gave anyway and God met their needs just as she believed He would. The widow in Mark gave her last two coins and was given Jesus' full attention as well as honored by millions of people down through the years. There is not one of us who cannot afford at least to give a glass of cold water. When I was young my parents made a practice of sharing our meal with anyone who happened to be with us at the time, and even though we never had a lot, I do know we never went hungry. Dad would do work for neighbors including those who could not afford to pay him, never expecting them to. And even as he lay dying in a nursing home those memories brought him joy. Often the problem is our attitude when we do give. If we give just to get back or if we give out of compulsion (being forced to), we cannot expect any blessing from the Lord. Give, give and give again, but do it with one thought in mind; that is to be good stewards of what we've been loaned and to honor the One who gave His all.

## "They devoted themselves"

**Acts 2:42-43 They devoted themselves to the apostles' teaching and to the fellowship, to the breaking of bread and to prayer. Everyone was filled with awe, and many wonders and miraculous signs were done by the apostles**

**John 8:31-32 To the Jews who had believed him, Jesus said, "If you hold to my teaching, you are really my disciples. Then you will know the truth, and the truth will set you free."**

**Acts 11:23-24 When he arrived and saw the evidence of the grace of God, he was glad and encouraged them all to remain true to the Lord with all their hearts. He was a good man, full of the Holy Spirit and faith, and a great number of people were brought to the Lord.**

**Eph 2:20 built on the foundation of the apostles and prophets, with Christ Jesus himself as the chief cornerstone**

The early church grew by proverbial leaps and bounds. Makes us wish that were true today, doesn't it? Maybe the reason we don't see God working like this more often is because we are not as totally focused on Him and the spreading of His Good News as they were. Luke tells us in Acts, **"They devoted themselves to the apostles' teaching and to the fellowship, to the breaking of bread and to prayer."** How many of us have to dust off our Bible on Sunday morning, that is if and when we find it? We are faithful to carry God's Word on "The Lord's Day", but to many Christians it is little more than an adornment, sitting around to look good. The Bible, meant to be our guidebook to this life, needs to be the focus of our day, every day. If we would be as devoted to the Word, to fellowship, to breaking bread, (remembering Christ's death) and to prayer, we would soon see God work, many people coming to Christ and growing in Him. What the world must see is that He is real in those who claim Him.

## Anger Destroys

**Jonah 4:9 But God said to Jonah, "Do you have a right to be angry about the vine?"**
**"I do," he said. "I am angry enough to die."**

**Gen 4:6 Then the LORD said to Cain, "Why are you angry? Why is your face downcast? If you do what is right, will you not be accepted?**

**Job 18:4 You who tear yourself to pieces in your anger,**

"I'm so mad I could just chew nails; what's more I'm so upset my heart hurts." Even what we say in our times of anger defines the truth of the Word. Being that irate is going to hurt; it greatly stresses our heart, pushes our blood pressure through the roof and causes multitudes of other problems, physically, emotionally and spiritually. Anger is self destructive at it's very best. Because of Jonah's disobedience to God by refusing to preach to the Ninevites he found himself in the belly of a big fish and ultimately wanted to die. Take a look at why he was so angry. **"When God saw what they did and how they turned from their evil ways, he had compassion and did not bring upon them the destruction he had threatened. But Jonah was greatly displeased and became angry. He prayed to the LORD, "O LORD, is this not what I said when I was still at home? That is why I was so quick to flee to Tarshish. I knew that you are a gracious and compassionate God, slow to anger and abounding in love, a God who relents from sending calamity."** (Jonah 3:10-4:2) Jonah's intense dislike for the Ninevites because he knew God would ultimately forgive them began to destroy him. It does the same to us today. When we are angry with people and unforgiving toward them WE are the ones being harmed, harmed in every possible way by our own doing. And think about it, when we are upset isn't it usually because we are not getting our own way? God told Cain that if he did the right thing he would be accepted and the same applies to us.

## They labor in vain

**Ps 127:1-5 Unless the LORD builds the house, its builders labor in vain. Unless the LORD watches over the city, the watchmen stand guard in vain. In vain you rise early and stay up late, toiling for food to eat-for he grants sleep to those he loves. Sons are a heritage from the LORD, children a reward from him. Like arrows in the hands of a warrior are sons born in one's youth. Blessed is the man whose quiver is full of them. They will not be put to shame when they contend with their enemies in the gate.**

Today we celebrate the independence of our nation. Two hundred and thirty three years ago the founders put their all on the line and the United States of America was born. Benjamin Franklin stated, "In the beginning of the contest with Great Britain, when we were in sensible danger we had daily prayer in the room for divine protection. Our prayers sir were heard and they were graciously answered. All of us who engaged in the struggle must have observed frequent instances of a superintending Providence in our favor...And have we now forgotten that powerful Friend? Or do we imagine that we no longer need His assistance?..." Franklin said this and much more that we need to hear and take heed to for he knew that God had blessed the efforts to found this free nation. Many today who would like nothing better than to destroy Her and as Christians we have a God-given responsibility; **"I urge, then, first of all, that requests, prayers, intercession and thanksgiving be made for everyone for kings and all those in authority, that we may live peaceful and quiet lives in all godliness and holiness."** (1 Tim 2:1-2) If we would enjoy the benefits of freedom we must honor the call of Scripture. Never has the USA and a president needed more prayer than right now. So if you want to really celebrate this Independence Day then give praise, honor and obedience to the One who established our beautiful nation. Oh and note in Ps 127:3-5 the rewards of that obedience.

## Life Lessons

**Matt 6:31-34 "So do not worry, saying, 'What shall we eat?' or 'What shall we drink?' or 'What shall we wear?' For the pagans run after all these things, and your heavenly Father knows that you need them. But seek first his kingdom and his righteousness, and all these things will be given to you as well. Therefore do not worry about tomorrow, for tomorrow will worry about itself. Each day has enough trouble of its own."**

**Prov 26:27 If a man digs a pit, he will fall into it; if a man rolls a stone, it will roll back on him.**

One evening during a fellowship time at Daybreak the thought crossed my mind of how many times we learn Biblical truths without their being directly taught to us so I asked others in our group to be thinking of a story to share having to do with life lessons they have learned. Meanwhile I started out by relating one from my dad. One Sunday when I was about eight years old (yes, I can remember that far back) a man that owed Dad some money came to church one Sunday. As the morning progressed I began to wonder why he hadn't reminded the man of his debit and asked him about it when we got home. Dad quickly explained that his "dunning" the guy in God's house might well have kept the man from ever coming back to church again. He then went on to say that even if he never got paid, the guy's spiritual life was more important than the money. Knowingly or not, Dad taught me that day the meaning of seeking first the Kingdom. Another story came from a lady about how as a kid someone had hurt her sister. To get even she chopped a hole in some thin ice hoping the girl would fall in the cold water. Oops, though in the end it backfired on them when her sister fell in and suffered the pain she had planned to inflict on another. Sounds like the Proverb above was taught long ago to these young girls. Can YOU remember just such a time in your life? If so, would you be willing to share your story and give me permission to pass it on without disclosing your identity? Your testimony may well encourage someone else. THANK YOU

## Glad to KNOW HIM?

**John 4:28 Then, leaving her water jar, the woman went back to the town and said to the people, 29 "Come, see a man who told me everything I ever did. Could this be the Christ?" 30 They came out of the town and made their way toward him.**

Turn on your imagination for a minute and think about the woman at the well. She left her water jar and ran back to town to tell everyone — "Come, see a man who told me everything I ever did." That couldn't have been too bad, right? But ah, look at what Jesus told her, **"You are right when you say you have no husband. The fact is, you have had five husbands, and the man you now have is not your husband. What you have just said is quite true."** Now I am sure that if Samaria was anything like wherever I've lived, everyone was well aware of her numerous marriages plus the fact that she was now just shacking up with a guy, yet she was excited to tell them all about Jesus. Why? True forgiveness and restoration to God follows real ownership of our sin and repentance and produces the kind of joy and gladness this woman now experienced. No longer did the bond of sin cause her to be under the bondage of guilt and its pain. That is what real freedom does and the same can be true for us, **"It is for freedom that Christ has set us free. Stand firm, then, and do not let yourselves be burdened again by a yoke of slavery"**. (Gal. 5:1) When we are free we no longer live in fear of God and we want to share His good news. Oh, and one more thing, OUR PAST does not have to render us ineffective for God, only if we let it. Proof of that is what happened to the woman's neighbors, **"Many of the Samaritans from that town believed in him because of the woman's testimony, "He told me everything I ever did."** (John 4:39) Now do thou likewise; go tell and live in freedom.

## Come aside and get some rest

**Mark 6:31 Then, because so many people were coming and going that they did not even have a chance to eat, he said to them, "Come with me by yourselves to a quiet place and get some rest."**

**Luke 9:10 When the apostles returned, they reported to Jesus what they had done. Then he took them with him and they withdrew by themselves to a town called Bethsaida,**

"Get some rest". That was Jesus' order to His disciples when they had been hard at work, learning from Him and applying what they had learned. Jesus knew the value and need of quiet time away from work and He Himself made this His practice, **"Very early in the morning, while it was still dark, Jesus got up, left the house and went off to a solitary place, where he prayed."** (Mark 1:35) I don't know how early "very early" is, but I do know that Jesus regularly spent time alone with His Father and did what He had to do in order for that to happen. I have heard of Christians who think that rest is a sign of weakness, but if the Lord Jesus knew its importance we'd better know it too. I'm learning more and more that even when working on a less stressful project in the house it is amazing how much a short time of quiet rest and prayer will change my productivity as well as my attitude. Please DO NOT ever yield to the temptation of thinking that busyness is a sign of holiness because the enemy knows that if he can keep us busy and tired we will be ineffective for God. But DO pursue the habits of our Lord; get needed rest and invest time in getting to know Him and the Father better.

# FLEE

**1 Tim 6:11 But you, man of God, flee from all this, and pursue righteousness, godliness, faith, love, endurance and gentleness**

**1 Cor 6:18 Flee from sexual immorality, 1 Cor 10:14 Therefore, my dear friends, flee from idolatry, 2 Tim 2:22 Flee the evil desires of youth,**

**Matt 5:19 "Anyone who breaks one of the least of these commandments and teaches others to do the same will be called least in the kingdom of heaven,"**

If you observe how a beaver fells a tree you will note that he carefully and methodically gnaws his way around and around it until there is but a very small diameter of tree left. That small bit will not support the whole and down comes the tree. Little temptations we yield to do the same thing to us. As anything that is not God's best chips away at us bit by bit, a little here a little there, we soon are weakened to the point that we will crash and burn. Paul admonishes Timothy this, **"But godliness with contentment is great gain. For we brought nothing into the world, and we can take nothing out of it. But if we have food and clothing, we will be content with that. People who want to get rich fall into temptation and a trap and into many foolish and harmful desires that plunge men into ruin and destruction. For the love of money is a root of all kinds of evil. Some people, eager for money, have wandered from the faith and pierced themselves with many griefs."** (1 Tim 6:6-10) These words regarding contentment added to his admonitions in the verses above teach us how to escape the snares of sin. The Apostle Paul does not stop with the advice to flee and thankfully told Timothy and us to **"pursue righteousness, godliness, faith, love, endurance and gentleness."** You see it is easier to FLEE FROM something if we have in mind something to FLEE TO. How about your goals? Have any?

## A soft answer, a soft word

**Prov 15:1 A gentle answer turns away wrath, but a harsh word stirs up anger.**

**Prov 25:15 Through patience a ruler can be persuaded, and a gentle tongue can break a bone.**

**Prov 10:12 Hatred stirs up dissension, but love covers over all wrongs.**

**Prov 15:18 A hot-tempered man stirs up dissension, but a patient man calms a quarrel.**

My do we ever need to heed these words. It is the soft answer that usually can totally defuse situations and solve many of our day-to-day problems. On the other hand, when we speak and react harshly we only stir up disputes. Usually when we fail to answer softly it is because we are seeking to be the winner. We think the position of "winner" is awarded to the one who has the last word, but the fact is the winner of an argument is not always the winner. For instance, many people who now find themselves divorced "won" every argument with their former mate. The problem is they may think they won the fights, but in reality they lost their lover; so did they really win? **Solomon also said, "It is to a man's honor to avoid strife, but every fool is quick to quarrel."** (Prov 20:3) I remember hearing my dad say, "It takes more of a man to hold his tongue than it does to throw that punch or say that goading word". The Word is filled with great insight on this and we can do no better than to listen to the wisdom of our God. How many of us could lower our blood pressure and ease the strain on our hearts if we could only learn these lessons. What is more important then, winning a momentary victory or being like our Lord Jesus? He lost the battle that fateful day, but ultimately won total victory over the enemy once and for all. I want on that team, how about you?

# SELF!

**Phil 2:3-4 Do nothing out of selfish ambition or vain conceit, but in humility consider others better than yourselves.**

**Prov 13:10 Pride only breeds quarrels, but wisdom is found in those who take advice.**

**1 Cor 3:3 You are still worldly. For since there is jealousy and quarreling among you, are you not worldly? Are you not acting like mere men?**

**Matt 18:3 "I tell you the truth, unless you change and become like little children, you will never enter the kingdom of heaven."**

"I have a right to this. I've worked hard to get where I am so I deserve to be looked up to." Sad as it is, attitudes like this are prevalent in the church. In the world we expect there to be those who would step on their own mother to get ahead, but not in the church. God has given each and every one of us gifts and talents to accomplish certain things. **"There are different kinds of gifts, but the same Spirit. There are different kinds of service, but the same Lord. There are different kinds of working, but the same God works all of them in all men."** (1 Cor 12:4-6) The one who cleans the toilets and mops the floor is just as important to the overall ministry of the church as the deacon, elder or pastor. Those who attempt to exalt themselves because they are in what may be considered a higher position need to remember that they've been placed there by God and their gift for ministry is from Him. Jesus was the perfect example of such humility, **"And being found in appearance as a man, He humbled Himself and became obedient to death even death on a cross!"** (Phil 2:8) Jesus was and is God but He laid aside His "right" to demand recognition. So where do we get the idea to be any different? That's easy, it comes from the sin within us.

## THIRSTY?

**Ps 42:2 My soul thirsts for God, for the living God. When can I go and meet with God?**

**Ps 63:1 O God, you are my God, earnestly I seek you; my soul thirsts for you, my body longs for you, in a dry and weary land where there is no water.**

**John 7:37 On the last and greatest day of the Feast, Jesus stood and said in a loud voice, "If anyone is thirsty, let him come to me and drink. 38 Whoever believes in me, as the Scripture has said, streams of living water will flow from within him."**

When we are thirsty it doesn't take long for us to look for something like coffee, tea, a soda or bottled water. Thirst causes our mouths to dry out and creates this overall feeling of the need for a drink. On a hot summer day it's even more important to take in liquids in order to avoid serious health problems, even though we may not feel thirsty. Someone told me a few days ago about a loved one who was experiencing some of the symptoms of dehydration. As expected this person wound up in the hospital with an IV to replace lost fluid. Our spiritual lives suffer in much the same way when we do not "thirst" for the Word of God. Jesus promised, **"Blessed are those who hunger and thirst for righteousness, for they will be filled."** (Matt 5:6) If we do not have a genuine thirst, which in turn is quenched, our souls will quickly dehydrate. Real thirst will not be satisfied with a brief reading of a verse or two and a short wish list prayer. Earnest thirst seeks an ongoing intimacy with our Lord. It seeks to KNOW HIM and will GIVE HIM TIME to not only hear us but also respond to us. Prayer is a conversation with God and among other things a thirst for Him will allow Him to bless us with His close abiding presence. Are you genuinely thirsty?

## Does your spouse know LOVE?

**1 Cor 13:4-8a Love is patient, love is kind. It does not envy, it does not boast, it is not proud. It is not rude, it is not self-seeking, it is not easily angered, it keeps no record of wrongs. Love does not delight in evil but rejoices with the truth. It always protects, always trusts, always hopes, always perseveres. Love never fails.**

The Apostle Paul is a man who did not buy the pat answers we now days like to hear. It's easy to sound real and Christian-like, BUT "sounding" and "being" are often a universe apart. Look at our reading, phrase by phrase, in a question form as if your husband or wife were answering about you. "Love is patient"; would your mate say this of you? "Love is kind"; again what would he/she say about you? "It does not envy"; are you overly possessive of him/her? "It does not boast"; would your spouse say you talk more about yourself than them? "It is not proud"; do you often remind your loved one that you are right? "It is not rude or self seeking"; do you treat your wife/hubby well for their benefit or yours? "It is not easily angered and keeps no record of wrongs"; do you get either hysterical or historical? "Love does not delight in evil but loves truth"; do you? "It always protects, always trusts, always hopes and always perseveres. Love never fails"; does your spouse, who is your companion, your mate, your lover, believe this about you? **"Hatred stirs up dissension, but love covers over all wrongs. (Prov 10:12) "What a man desires is unfailing love; better to be poor than a liar." (Prov 19:22) "God opposes the proud but gives grace to the humble."** (James 4:6) Do these verses describe you?

## Our Choice

**John 16:33 "I have told you these things, so that in me you may have peace. In this world you will have trouble. But take heart! I have overcome the world."**

**Acts 14:22 strengthening the disciples and encouraging them to remain true to the faith. "We must go through many hardships to enter the kingdom of God,"**

**2 Tim 3:12 In fact, everyone who wants to live a godly life in Christ Jesus will be persecuted,**

**Heb 11:24-25 By faith Moses, when he had grown up, refused to be known as the son of Pharaoh's daughter. He chose to be mistreated along with the people of God rather than to enjoy the pleasures of sin for a short time.**

Most of us are well acquainted with the phrase "the patience of Job". Job was a man of very long ago who was sold out to God. He was true to his God no matter what came his way and justifiably God was proud of him, "Then the LORD said to Satan, **"Have you considered my servant Job? There is no one on earth like him; he is blameless and upright, a man who fears God and shuns evil."** (Job 1:8) To my way of thinking that is a compliment worth seeking. We often waste time pursuing the praise of this world, but to hear God say "That's My kid" is the ultimate. Jesus told us we would have problems in this life but that He overcame them by His death and resurrection. There is no persecution, torment or pain that was not utterly destroyed the day He walked out of that tomb and He did all this for us so that we could enjoy Him now and for eternity. Hallelujah What A Savior! Now we can live life abundantly and to the fullest amidst our temporary troubles, victorious through the power He gives us. Trials will either make us bitter or better (one letter makes the difference). What will it be? A miserable life or one of joy? The choice is ours.

## JESUS, only HE is the way

**John 14:6-7 Jesus answered, "I am the way and the truth and the life. No one comes to the Father except through me. If you really knew me, you would know my Father as well. From now on, you do know him and have seen him."**

**Acts 4:12 Salvation is found in no one else, for there is no other name under heaven given to men by which we must be saved."**

**Rom 5:2 through whom we have gained access by faith into this grace in which we now stand. And we rejoice in the hope of the glory of God.**

**Eph 2:18 For through him we both have access to the Father by one Spirit.**

What a sad commentary that even some so called Christians would suggest that there might be yet another way to God other than through His Son. Awhile back I heard a "Christian" speaker say, "a loving God would never send anyone to hell". How far we who supposedly know and love Jesus can get off track. Point one is that a person's destiny is not determined by God's will, but by their own choice in rejecting His offer of love in His Word. Those who would suggest that there are other ways into His presence have been duped into believing another gospel, not The Gospel of Christ. Jesus made it clear when He said to His disciples, **"I am the way"**. Those of us who have understood and accepted that statement have a great responsibility to share in some way the love of Jesus with everyone God brings across our path. If you knew someone who would give a million dollars to anyone who asked for it, I'm sure you would spread that news to close friends or relatives and hopefully first of all someone in need. Why not share all the more the GOSPEL, the very Good News that anyone who asks for it can have eternal life? No earthly value can be placed on knowing God, while all a million dollars might do is make life here on earth even more complicated. Now is there really any comparison?

## If we faint not!!!!

**Gal 6:9 Let us not become weary in doing good, for at the proper time we will reap a harvest if we do not give up.**

**1 Cor 15:58 Therefore, my dear brothers, stand firm. Let nothing move you. Always give yourselves fully to the work of the Lord, because you know that your labor in the Lord is not in vain.**

**1 Peter 2:15 For it is God's will that by doing good you should silence the ignorant talk of foolish men.**

**1 Peter 3:17 It is better, if it is God's will, to suffer for doing good than for doing evil.**

Awhile back we watched a drama on television in which a girl in her teens was kidnapped and escaped, then walked some distance before being found. At one point she almost quit and was about to lie down to die but something spurred her to keep on going. At that point she walked about fifteen feet more and collapsed on the side of the road. This makes me wonder how many Christians cave in to the enemy and give up on living for Jesus when they are only inches away from full victory in Him. Missionaries have toiled for years and years before they see their first convert. They could have given up, gone home and reported that a certain people group are just plain lost, but they kept on going and God showed them fruit, more fruit, and much fruit because they believed Him and not the lies of Satan. Have you and I struggled with a habit or addiction only to concede and continue on in defeat with our problem? We do not need to live like that. We have to remember that many others wage battles similar to ours AND God is fully able to rescue us, **"No temptation has seized you except what is common to man. And God is faithful; he will not let you be tempted beyond what you can bear. But when you are tempted, he will also provide a way out so that you can stand up under it."** (1 Cor 10:13) PUSH ON my friend, for you may well be on the verge of victory if only you will persevere.

## Trust, Trust, Trust

**John 16:33 "I have told you these things, so that in me you may have peace. In this world you will have trouble. But take heart! I have overcome the world."**

**Phil 4:7 And the peace of God, which transcends all understanding, will guard your hearts and your minds in Christ Jesus.**

**John 14:1 "Do not let your hearts be troubled. Trust in God; trust also in me.**

So many things happen day to day that threaten our peace and security. Homes are robbed, kids are abused, drugs etc. threaten the safety of our communities and on it goes. What is most upsetting is that Christians fall into the trap of fear. Not that we should not use good sense and be sure our doors are locked, park in well lit areas and take other precautions, but beyond that we have no reason to fear anything that comes our way. Sin and sinful events have no power to harm us in an eternal sense and testimonies abound proving that God has our well being in hand. People have found themselves even in the custody of murderers and God has protected them. Some time ago a lady told of being carjacked, of sharing the Lord with her abductor and of hearing him drive away as she prepared to meet Jesus face to face. But instead of killing her, the guy drove off because God was protecting this lady. "Oh Lord Jesus, we praise You that YOU have overcome the world and we confess our moaning and grumbling. Lord, strengthen us that we may live as if we really believe that You have overcome the world. In Jesus precious name."
Amen

## All Roads

**Luke 21:17-18 "All men will hate you because of me. But not a hair of your head will perish. 19 By standing firm you will gain life."**

**Matt 24:8-9 "All these are the beginning of birth pains. Then you will be handed over to be persecuted and put to death, and you will be hated by all nations because of me."**

**John 7:7 "The world cannot hate you, but it hates me because I testify that what it does is evil."**

**John 17:14 "I have given them your word and the world has hated them, for they are not of the world any more than I am of the world."**

Many people who hold to today's world view instead of God's truth come to the point of watering down that truth; even Christians (so called anyway) are guilty of this in their fear of the world and it's hatred of Christ and His followers. Most of the time they say, "Doesn't every road lead to the same God?" Yes indeed, all roads do lead to God and to His judgment, but it is the outcome of that meeting that is of utmost importance. All mankind will stand before the God of the universe and every knee will bow before His Son, but only those who have accepted and acted upon the claims of Jesus Christ, **"I am the way and the truth and the life. No one comes to the Father except through me"** (John 14:6) will enter into the presence of God in His heaven. Their names will be found in the book of life, **but, if anyone's name was not found written in the book of life, he was thrown into the lake of fire.** (Rev 20:15) Even though the road that many travel will lead them to the God of all gods, they still will be cast into the lake of fire because they have chosen not to accept the way He has clearly prescribed in His Word. It is never more important than now that we Christians begin living as if JESUS IS THE WAY. We will never win souls to Christ by assuring them in their error. Political correctness may ease our temporal minds and make us look good to the world, but it will never be effective for the cause of the Gospel.

*Just A Thought*

## A nation in need

**2 Chron 7:14 if my people, who are called by my name, will humble themselves and pray and seek my face and turn from their wicked ways, then will I hear from heaven and will forgive their sin and will heal their land.**

Recently there have been some staggering statistics, but one of the most alarming is that nearly seventy per-cent of "Christians" believe there is more than one way to salvation, even though Jesus Himself said, **"I am the way and the truth and the life. No one comes to the Father except through me. If you really knew me, you would know my Father as well. From now on, you do know him and have seen him."** (John 14:6-7) Also alarming is that many people are willing to overlook blatant unconfessed sin and abortion and the like are excused. Our founding fathers built the constitution upon solid Biblical principles and doctrines, but those very principles have been bent and twisted to the point of nearly being broken. For instance, **The Constitution of the United States of America Amendment 1** - Freedom of Religion, Press, Expression. Ratified 12/15/1791. *Congress shall make no law respecting an establishment of religion, or prohibiting the free exercise thereof; or abridging the freedom of speech, or of the press; or the right of the people peaceably to assemble, and to petition the Government for a redress of grievances.* Those who hate the USA can do so and have the constitutional right to express their opinions just as well as Christian Americans. BUT today many churches are being persecuted for speaking the truth. In a nutshell, our country is in need of revival (Christians acting like Christians). Evangelist Gypsy Smith was once asked how to start a revival. He answered: *"Go home, lock yourself in your room, kneel down in the middle of your floor. Draw a chalk mark all around yourself and ask God to start the revival inside that chalk mark. When He has answered your prayer, the revival will be on."* Will you join with me today and "get into that closet"? Is not this the greatest thing we can do for "THE UNITED STATES OF AMERICA", land of the free and home of the brave?

## Christianity – a life of ease. NOT

**Job 1:20-22 At this, Job got up and tore his robe and shaved his head. Then he fell to the ground in worship and said: "Naked I came from my mother's womb, and naked I will depart. The LORD gave and the LORD has taken away; may the name of the LORD be praised." In all this, Job did not sin by charging God with wrongdoing.**

**Job 2:7-8 So Satan went out from the presence of the LORD and afflicted Job with painful sores from the soles of his feet to the top of his head. Then Job took a piece of broken pottery and scraped himself with it as he sat among the ashes.**

**Matt 27:33-35 They came to a place called Golgotha (which means The Place of the Skull). There they offered Jesus wine to drink, mixed with gall; but after tasting it, he refused to drink it. When they had crucified him, they divided up his clothes by casting lots**

Politically correct has now for some time been the rule of the day. Reality is that political correctness reigns and TRUTH has little to do with a lot of folks, including many in the media. I wonder what these people think of those of us who would rather hear the truth than be told what they believe will not offend. In the church there is also "a school of correctness" that says if one gives their life to God they will enjoy a life of ease. They will, or should, never have financial problems, family upheavals, sickness or any other hardships. I wonder what these people would have said to Job who lost everything he had, including his children. If a Christian is never to suffer pain nor sorrow how does one explain the pain Christ endured? No way can we accept such teachings. If the founder of our faith suffered, it is an insult to Him to suggest that we should not. He is God and when we suffer for Him our complete hope and trust can be in Him and His wisdom for our situation. Job said, **"Though he slay me, yet will I hope in Him;"** (Job 13:15) Now there is a statement worth standing on.

## Today is the day!

**2 Cor 6:2 For he says, "In the time of my favor I heard you, and in the day of salvation I helped you." I tell you, now is the time of God's favor, now is the day of salvation.**

**Luke 4:18-19 "The Spirit of the Lord is on me, because he has anointed me to preach good news to the poor. He has sent me to proclaim freedom for the prisoners and recovery of sight for the blind, to release the oppressed, to proclaim the year of the Lord's favor."**

Many people think, "I have lots of time, after all I'm young". I read the obits every day and it is amazing how many listed there are less than forty years old. Paul told his audience that NOW is the time of salvation. Today may well be the only chance one has to accept this great gift and the assurance of a future home in God's heaven. Jesus proclaimed, **"For the Son of Man came to seek and to save what was lost."** (Luke 19:10) Men and women are often unaware that they are lost. They are oblivious to the fact that without Christ they can never hope to get to heaven. If you walk down the street and ask fifty people where they want to go when they die at least forty-nine responses will be "heaven". When asked if they think they will actually get there, most people will say, "I hope so". The problem is that many think they can somehow earn that privilege. If you and I have accepted God's forgiveness of our sin through the death of His Son, we owe it to Him and to our fellow man to live as if we truly do love this Savior so that they may know Him, too. If you do not know Jesus, I have to warn you that tomorrow may be too late. Come to Him TODAY and begin living the life He has for you of indescribable joy, peace and security.

# The "LIGHT"

**1 John 1:5-7 This is the message we have heard from him and declare to you: God is light; in him there is no darkness at all. If we claim to have fellowship with him yet walk in the darkness, we lie and do not live by the truth. But if we walk in the light, as he is in the light, we have fellowship with one another, and the blood of Jesus, his Son, purifies us from all sin.**

**John 8:12 When Jesus spoke again to the people, he said, "I am the light of the world. Whoever follows me will never walk in darkness, but will have the light of life."**

Many times Christians walk around as if in a daze. They have a decision to make and are not quite sure how to make it. Maybe the reason for this is not that they don't know what to do, but that they are reluctant to follow the way God is leading. Jesus promised, **"I am the light of the world. Whoever follows me will never walk in darkness, but will have the light of life."** If we truly are walking in His light we can be sure that He will meet our every need and supply every bit of wisdom and strength to accomplish what He has for us. I remember when I was in one of those times. I had struggled with a sinus infection for months before coming to the realization that the source of my problem was the dust from our wood stove. At that point my dilemma had to do mostly with the cost of heating only with gas; however, if I really believe what I have just written, I needn't fear, right? How often do we hurt ourselves because we do not quite trust "THE Light"? Isn't it time to live what we say we believe? When we say we are in the LIGHT we must live like we are. Our decisions are to be based upon God and His will and desires, not our own.

## "Consecrate yourselves" – be blessed

**Josh 3:5 Joshua told the people, "Consecrate yourselves, for tomorrow the LORD will do amazing things among you."**

**Lev 20:7-8 "'Consecrate yourselves and be holy, because I am the LORD your God. 8 Keep my decrees and follow them. I am the LORD, who makes you holy.**

**John 17:19 "For them I sanctify myself, that they too may be truly sanctified."**

Time and again the Word tells us that the Israelites were instructed to consecrate themselves, for tomorrow God was going to bless them. This was not a one-time deal, but they had to continually renew their commitment to Him. Then came Jesus who sanctified (consecrated, fully gave) Himself to be our atonement that WE, too, may be truly sanctified. (John 17:19) In doing so He knew that He would have to give His very being and even bear the rejection of the Father to be able to accomplish His work in US. A few years ago a missionary mother told that her young daughter became sick at a time when her husband was away. Getting help "out in the bush" was virtually impossible and she fought with God for the girl's recovery, but to no avail. Finally, giving her daughter to Him she told God that even should He take her home to heaven it would be all right. Immediately her daughter began getting better. The point is that many of the things that harass us are our own fault and if we could or would just "consecrate" ourselves ENTIRELY to Him all would be well, no matter the outcome. Do you, do I, want total peace? Then we must GIVE HIM OUR EVERYTHNG with no reservations, no ifs, ands, or buts. I am asking myself today if that is my heart's deepest desire. Will you join me? If we want to see Him work in our lives we have no choice.

## In Remembrance

**1 Cor 11:23-26 For I received from the Lord what I also passed on to you: The Lord Jesus, on the night he was betrayed, took bread, and when he had given thanks, he broke it and said, "This is my body, which is for you; do this in remembrance of me." In the same way, after supper he took the cup, saying, "This cup is the new covenant in my blood; do this, whenever you drink it, in remembrance of me." For whenever you eat this bread and drink this cup, you proclaim the Lord's death until he comes.**

**Isa 26:8 Yes, LORD, walking in the way of your laws, we wait for you; your name and renown are the desire of our hearts.**

Having lived through the Viet Nam era I still remember Barry Sadler's "Ballad of the Green Beret" in which he drew a picture in song of what being a green beret was all about. **"Fighting soldiers from the sky, Fearless men who jump and die, Men who mean just what they say, The brave men of the Green Beret, Silver wings upon their chest, These are men, America's best, One hundred men we'll test today, But only three win the Green Beret, Trained to live, off nature's land, Trained in combat, hand to hand, Men who fight by night and day, Courage deep, from the Green Beret"** What devotion and resolve. Oh that we Christians would be Green Berets for our Savior. He spread His arms and watched as evil men drove nails through His hands and feet, raised that cross and dropped it into the hole in the ground. His love for them and for us compelled Him to look to heaven and say, **"Father, forgive them, for they do not know what they are doing."** (Luke 23:34) Sadler's song tells us that one hundred would test, but only three would win the honor. Oh that ALL of us, "the whole one hundred", would be honored to be "Green Berets for the Lord Jesus Christ". Oh that NOTHING would be more important than serving Him. Do YOU remember His sacrifice by the way you live for Him?

## As you would have them....

**Matt 7:12 "So in everything, do to others what you would have them do to you, for this sums up the Law and the Prophets."**

**Rom 13:8-10 Let no debt remain outstanding, except the continuing debt to love one another, for he who loves his fellowman has fulfilled the law. The commandments, "Do not commit adultery," "Do not murder," "Do not steal," "Do not covet," and whatever other commandment there may be, are summed up in this one rule: "Love your neighbor as yourself." Love does no harm to its neighbor. Therefore love is the fulfillment of the law.**

**Luke 6:31 "Do to others as you would have them do to you."**

When talking with people do you ever really listen to what they say? Some feel it is necessary to add a descriptive term when referring to someone else, like bi- racial, black, Hispanic, ex-convict, fat, been divorced or any one of dozens of other designations that can be taken negatively. At times it's for clarification or meant as a compliment but often not, because we have less than pure motives. Jesus asks us, no make that COMMANDS us, to "do unto others as we want them to do unto us". Skin colors are "only skin deep" and beyond that every person on the planet is the same. The race issue, along with one's past history etc., has no place in what we think of others. If you and I want to claim that we love people we need to always be on our guard to treat everyone as we desire to be treated. Kids abuse other kids who are the least bit different from them in the same way that they see parents treat their peers. If adults, in particular Christian adults, would be obedient to the Word we would see an amazing change in our kids. An attitude of respect and love would soon prevail and Jesus would be honored by our obedience. Churches would become places of love and a powerful impact in their communities, safe havens for any and all. AND many more lost sinners would come to know Jesus Christ. Wouldn't that be awesome!

*Just A Thought*

## No Difference

**Gal 2:11-13 When Peter came to Antioch, I opposed him to his face, because he was clearly in the wrong. Before certain men came from James, he used to eat with the Gentiles. But when they arrived, he began to draw back and separate himself from the Gentiles because he was afraid of those who belonged to the circumcision group. The other Jews joined him in his hypocrisy, so that by their hypocrisy even Barnabas was led astray.**

**James 2:1-4 My brothers, as believers in our glorious Lord Jesus Christ, don't show favoritism. Suppose a man comes into your meeting wearing a gold ring and fine clothes, and a poor man in shabby clothes also comes in. If you show special attention to the man wearing fine clothes and say, "Here's a good seat for you," but say to the poor man, "You stand there" or "Sit on the floor by my feet," have you not discriminated among yourselves and become judges with evil thoughts?**

There are people today who have the same problem of discrimination that plagued Peter. They elevate or devalue others based on personal preferences, personality, race, religion, financial state or some other designation. Peter had been eating with Gentiles (that's us) and enjoying himself and them, but along came someone he knew to be a little racist and immediately he withdrew from his Gentile friends. Jonah also had this problem, **"But Jonah was greatly displeased and became angry. He prayed to the LORD, "O LORD, is this not what I said when I was still at home? That is why I was so quick to flee to Tarshish. I knew that you are a gracious and compassionate God, slow to anger and abounding in love, a God who relents from sending calamity."** (Jonah 4:1-2) Very quickly the Apostle Paul told Peter just how wrong he was and God pointed out to Jonah his error. **"Have you any right to be angry?"** (Jonah 4:4) We may not always agree with what others believe or do, but God created all of us equal. Jesus died to redeem all people, no exceptions; therefore we have no choice but to show everyone His love. What's more, ALL born again CHRISTians are our brothers. That church down the road is not just some ethnic church. If they truly worship Jesus Christ they are part of us and us them.

## Holy, Holy, Holy is the Lord

**Is 6:1-3 In the year that King Uzziah died, I saw the Lord seated on a throne, high and exalted, and the train of his robe filled the temple. Above him were seraphs, each with six wings: With two wings they covered their faces, with two they covered their feet, and with two they were flying. And they were calling to one another: "Holy, holy, holy is the LORD Almighty; the whole earth is full of his glory."**

Many of us long for the Lord change our world. Among other things we want a little of His heaven here on earth. It appears, though, that we think HE should do it all. We have such a limited view of who God is and how He works that we fail to realize that having Him act here on earth requires US to act. We need a reminder of just how "holy, holy, holy" He is and that this holiness signifies His extreme purity. He is so holy by nature that what would be a small sin to us is a major one to Him. Such holiness also calls for our highest praise like that of King David, **"Be exalted, O God, above the heavens; let your glory be over all the earth."** (Ps 57:11) **"My heart is steadfast, O God, my heart is steadfast; I will sing and make music. Awake, my soul! Awake, harp and lyre! I will awaken the dawn. I will praise you, O Lord, among the nations; I will sing of you among the peoples. For great is your love, reaching to the heavens; your faithfulness reaches to the skies".** (Ps 57:7-10) The psalmist steadfastly chose to bring praise to his God. Jesus told His disciples and us, **"Therefore go (as you live your life) and make disciples of all nations, baptizing them in the name of the Father and of the Son and of the Holy Spirit, 20 and teaching them to obey everything I have commanded you. And surely I am with you always, to the very end of the age."** (Matt 28:19-20) The question we have to ask ourselves is this, "am I consciously choosing to 'praisefully' live my life for Him or am I hoping to get by with little or no effort?" Do you and I have the intestinal fortitude (guts) to live an example of Him before the world even when it could be hard or embarrassing?

## Worthy is the Lamb

**Rev 5:1-9 Then I saw in the right hand of him who sat on the throne a scroll with writing on both sides and sealed with seven seals. And I saw a mighty angel proclaiming in a loud voice, "Who is worthy to break the seals and open the scroll?" But no one in heaven or on earth or under the earth could open the scroll or even look inside it. Then I saw a Lamb, looking as if it had been slain, standing in the center of the throne, encircled by the four living creatures and the elders. He had seven horns and seven eyes, which are the seven spirits of God sent out into all the earth. And when he had taken it, the four living creatures and the twenty-four elders fell down before the Lamb. Each one had a harp and they were holding golden bowls full of incense, which are the prayers of the saints. And they sang a new song: "You are worthy to take the scroll and to open its seals, because you were slain, and with your blood you purchased men for God...**

**Rev 4:11 "You are worthy, our Lord and God, to receive glory and honor and power,**

This same Jesus who was born in a stable, grew to be a carpenter and was crucified and rose again is the One who is worthy. Worthy to open the seals of judgment and worthy to receive all glory, honor and praise. He is the One who deserves our all. God the Father himself has assigned His Son, Jesus, such honor, **"Therefore God exalted him to the highest place and gave him the name that is above every name, that at the name of Jesus every knee should bow, in heaven and on earth and under the earth, and every tongue confess that Jesus Christ is Lord, to the glory of God the Father."** (Phil 2:9-11) On that day everyone, even the proudest and most defiant; will confess who He really is. How much more blessed it is to bow now and sing, "He's MY Lord, He's MY Lord, He is risen from the dead and He's MY Lord". Is He YOUR LORD?

## Thank You ???

**1 Thess 5:18 give thanks in all circumstances, for this is God's will for you in Christ Jesus.**

**Job 1:21 and said: "Naked I came from my mother's womb, and naked I will depart. The LORD gave and the LORD has taken away; may the name of the LORD be praised."**

**Ps 34:1 I will extol the LORD at all times; his praise will always be on my lips.**

**Heb 13:15 Through Jesus, therefore, let us continually offer to God a sacrifice of praise-the fruit of lips that confess his name.**

IN ALL THINGS GIVE THANKS. This is God's command, not just a suggestion or an optional reaction, but in ALL things give thanks. In our instant and self-pleasing society we expect everything to be right now and good, according to our definition of the word. Whether we chow down at McDonalds or dine at a fine dinner restaurant we want to wait no longer than "thirty seconds" for our food. It'd better be just the way we ordered it and it'd better taste great. All of this adds up to making it hard for us to be thankful for those things we consider less than the ideal. God was proud of His servant, Job, **"Then the LORD said to Satan, "Have you considered my servant Job? There is no one on earth like him; he is blameless and upright, a man who fears God and shuns evil."** (Job 1:8), yet He allowed Satan to run Job through the proverbial mill. Certainly if any one of us ever had the right to a pity party and be somewhat less than thankful, it would be this man, Job. But not so. In fact later he said, **"Though he slay me, yet will I hope in him;"** (Job 13:15) Truly a patient man, yes, but more than that Job was a man of integrity and faith. He knew the secret of "Kingdom living" here an earth. He knew that God deserved his thanks even when things were not going according to plan, his plan. Does that describe us?

## To Prepare A Place

**John 14:1-4 "Do not let your hearts be troubled. Trust in God; trust also in me. In my Father's house are many rooms; if it were not so, I would have told you. I am going there to prepare a place for you. And if I go and prepare a place for you, I will come back and take you to be with me that you also may be where I am. You know the way to the place where I am going."**

**John 17:24 "Father, I want those you have given me to be with me where I am, and to see my glory, the glory you have given me because you loved me before the creation of the world".**

This week we are celebrating the birth in human form of the Son of God. This was His first trip from His heavenly home to the place selected to be the home of mankind. Unfortunately we humans, created by Him, failed to live up to God's standards. Think for a moment of Jesus getting down on His knees, scraping the soil into the shape of a human being then performing CPR by breathing life into that mass. Oh the love of our awesome Savior! BUT, as people do, they went on to come up with a "better way". That act of sin threw all humanity into the chaos we have yet today. Just to think that the Lord Jesus knew at creation that He was going to have to die to redeem the very ones He created. **"Father, I want those you have given me to be with me where I am"** How could He love us so? May I be so bold as to strongly suggest it is time (more than time) to make Christmas more about this great and awesome Savior and less about the gifts we lust after only to return them a few days later. HIS GIFT is so much greater and so much more fulfilling than any earthly possession. He's gone to prepare a home with Him in heaven. So how about it?

## Worship and Wholeness

**Heb 10:25 Let us not give up meeting together, as some are in the habit of doing, but let us encourage one another-and all the more as you see the Day approaching.**

**Matt 18:19-20 "Again, I tell you that if two of you on earth agree about anything you ask for, it will be done for you by my Father in heaven. For where two or three come together in my name, there am I with them."**

**Acts 2:42 They devoted themselves to the apostles' teaching and to the fellowship, to the breaking of bread and to prayer.**

**1 Cor 5:4 When you are assembled in the name of our Lord Jesus and I am with you in spirit, and the power of our Lord Jesus is present,**

Some people adamantly proclaim, "I do not need anybody. I can take care of my own life." This is simply not true, for we all need others with whom to share our lives. In a famous passage from "For Whom The Bell Tolls" John Donne made a powerful statement "...No man is an island, entire of itself; every man is a piece of the continent, a part of the main." The Apostle Paul puts it another way — **The body is a unit, though it is made up of many parts; and though all its parts are many, they form one body. So it is with Christ. For we were all baptized by one Spirit into one body-whether Jews or Greeks, slave or free-and we were all given the one Spirit to drink.** (1 Cor 12:12-13) The truth that we learn from both of these authors is that when we fail to come together for worship we are cheating three entities. OURSELVES, for we deprive ourselves of support from the rest of the body. OTHERS, for we are not giving other people as well as ourselves the opportunity to be a complete body. And we are cheating JESUS CHRIST, for He is the One who gave His all that His body of believers might be whole. Furthermore, we are His bride, He is our bridegroom and HE after all is the whole reason we come together anyway.

## Real Richness

**Luke 9:58 Jesus replied, "Foxes have holes and birds of the air have nests, but the Son of Man has no place to lay his head."**

**Luke 18:22-23 When Jesus heard this, he said to him, "You still lack one thing. Sell everything you have and give to the poor, and you will have treasure in heaven. Then come, follow me." When he heard this, he became very sad, because he was a man of great wealth.**

For many years now there has been a teaching in the church that Jesus is the way to riches, comfort, and a soft life. Jesus never taught that nor did He compromise His message to attract anyone who was walking away from Him. He just gave the cold hard facts, then said it is your decision. In our reading today He told one guy **"the Son of man doesn't even have a home."** To the young ruler he said, **"sell everything"**. The Apostle Paul told Timothy, **Do your best to present yourself to God as one approved, a workman who does not need to be ashamed and who correctly handles the word of truth.** (2 Tim 2:15) Other translations use the words study, strive and work hard to do your best. Truth is the Christian life is not supposed to be totally easy. Jesus left heaven to have no home and to die. How can we expect to be so much better off than He was? People are leaving the church today. Many exit because they've been given a false hope for the "good life" and that just isn't reality. Perhaps we need to tell them that yes, this life will be hard, BUT Jesus will be there with you through every hard step. The real choice for all of us is this, do we want to face life alone or with the love and support of the Savior and His TRUE church, one that is filled with love and compassion and the Source of real life, peace, richness, comfort and fullness?

# Where is your focus?

**Hag 1:3 Then the word of the LORD came through the prophet Haggai: 4 "Is it a time for you yourselves to be living in your paneled houses, while this house remains a ruin?"**

**Phil 2:21 For everyone looks out for his own interests, not those of Jesus Christ.**

**Matt 6:33 "But seek first his kingdom and his righteousness, and all these things will be given to you as well."**

How often it's been said, "I have to get this and this done and I won't be happy until I do". Usually the things "needed doing" are very self-centered and have little to do with our spiritual welfare. In the day of Haggai the focus of the Israelites was on nice homes with fancy wood paneling while the Temple lay in ruins. Oh they had their excuses, but it came down to selfishness. It was costing them dearly, planting much yet yielding small crops, eating yet not being filled, drinking but still thirsty, wearing clothing but still cold, too much month at the end of the funds etc. (Haggai 1:4-5) The problem here was not the housing, the crop, nor the needs, but the failure to have the correct priorities. David penned these words, **"I will not enter my house or go to my bed, I will allow no sleep to my eyes, no slumber to my eyelids, till I find a place for the LORD, a dwelling for the Mighty One of Jacob."** (Ps 132:3-5) Is it possible that we suffer and lack today because we also have lost our focus? I think the answer to that is yes. Jesus told us to seek His kingdom first and our other needs would be met. Try asking yourself every day, "have I invested time alone with the Lord today?" If the answer is "no" then do something about the situation immediately, if not sooner, and experience the blessing of being with the One who loved you so much He died in your place. THEN all other things will come together. Where would WE be if He had said, "I am just too busy today."?

## Where does my help come from?

**Ps 121:1 I lift up my eyes to the hills where does my help come from?**

**Dan 4:34 At the end of that time, I, Nebuchadnezzar, raised my eyes toward heaven, and my sanity was restored. Then I praised the Most High; I honored and glorified him who lives forever.**

**Luke 9:16 Taking the five loaves and the two fish and looking up to heaven, he gave thanks and broke them. Then he gave them to the disciples to set before the people. 17 They all ate and were satisfied, and the disciples picked up twelve basketfuls of broken pieces that were left over.**

**John 17:1 After Jesus said this, he looked toward heaven and prayed: "Father, the time has come. Glorify your Son, that your Son may glorify you"**

Oh how glad we are when the Lord rescues us from a tough spot and how upset we sometimes get when He doesn't answer our prayers the way we want Him to. Think about the verses above. It took many trials for King David to know the source of his help and Nebuchadnezzar had to lose his sanity before he realized the same. Jesus trusted His Father and prayed thanking Him for multiplying the bread and fish to feed five thousand men plus women and children. Notice the twelve baskets of leftovers, one for each disciple who beforehand had wondered where they would get enough food for the crowd. And finally, Jesus was willing and even eager to give His life to glorify His Father. In all of these events it comes through loud and clear that GOD has to be the focus of all that we are and it is necessary to be one hundred percent for Him, even to the point of sacrificing our lives. Could it be that when I don't see or feel the Lord's help or His working in my life, that the problem is not Him, but me?

## I just knew you would forgive them!

**Jonah 4:1-2 But Jonah was greatly displeased and became angry. He prayed to the LORD, "O LORD, is this not what I said when I was still at home? That is why I was so quick to flee to Tarshish. I knew that you are a gracious and compassionate God, slow to anger and abounding in love, a God who relents from sending calamity.**

Jonah had a slight attitude problem. He ran from the Lord and the command He had been given to preach to the people of Nineveh and headed to Tarshish instead, all because he did not like, to put it mildly, those awful Ninevites. Makes me wonder if there are people today that we might consider Ninevites, perhaps one who hurt you badly or one who has certain "horrible" sins in their past. I suppose there are many reasons that we can find in our petty minds to deprive certain people of our forgiveness and God's. The truth is that God created them just as he did us and He loves us all equally. He gave Jonah an object lesson by providing a vine that grew to give him shelter from the hot sun, but when God also gave a worm to destroy the vine Jonah became very angry at the discomfort he once again suffered. God then reminded him that he should be far more concerned about the people of Nineveh who needed redemption than a simple vine. I wonder if some of the hardships we endure are brought on by our failure to forgive and our lack of desire that God forgive. Some of us are of the opinion that certain sinners should burn in hell, but God's word teaches us that even OUR slightest impurity is worthy of the same. Consequences of sin vary but God does not rank sin as we do. With Him a word of gossip is just as much sin as the molestation of a child. The only person who does not deserve hell is the one who has come before God in confession and humility of spirit with the determination to leave their sin behind. Having done that we need to remember from whence we've come and start loving as God loves.

## Can't Afford It!

**Mark 16:15-17 He said to them, "Go into all the world and preach the good news to all creation. Whoever believes and is baptized will be saved, but whoever does not believe will be condemned."**

**Matt 28:19-20 "Therefore go and make disciples of all nations, baptizing them in the name of the Father and of the Son and of the Holy Spirit, and teaching them to obey everything I have commanded you. And surely I am with you always, to the very end of the age."**

**Luke 5:31-32 Jesus answered them, "It is not the healthy who need a doctor, but the sick. I have not come to call the righteous, but sinners to repentance."**

A gentleman once said to me, "the church could afford this attitude at one time." The attitude he spoke of was that of legalistic superiority in the church, the thought being that those who had committed "certain sins" could be banned from serving in the church even though their sin had been forgiven. Late in life that man came to realize that this idea was both wrong and the very opposite of what Jesus did when He was here. Jesus came to bring forgiveness to ANY and ALL repented sin, for ANY and ALL people. Once forgiven, sin no longer exists. Perhaps in the business world some things can be afforded, but in the church ANYTHING that holds a shadow of the past over ANYONE is not affordable. I wonder how many people are in hell today because the church "could afford to make them inferior"? NO sin is unforgivable (except denying the Holy Spirit) and NO church can afford to think that people God wants to use for His Kingdom are expendable. Peter denied the Lord totally, was forgiven by God and three thousand souls came to Christ in one day. Acts 2 The woman taken in adultery was forgiven and literally lifted up by Jesus Himself. Matthew 8 The woman at the well living with a man outside of marriage repented and many believed. John 4. David committed adultery and murder, repented and went on to teach sinners God's ways. Psalm 51 WHATEVER THE SIN, if it is repented, God will forgive and that one is then a brand new person with no past, only a bright future and a home with Jesus Christ in His glory.

## Love God? Love you neighbor.

**1 John 4:19-21** We love because he first loved us. If anyone says, "I love God," yet hates his brother, he is a liar. For anyone who does not love his brother, whom he has seen, cannot love God, whom he has not seen. And he has given us this command: Whoever loves God must also love his brother.

**1 John 2:4-6** The man who says, "I know him," but does not do what he commands is a liar, and the truth is not in him. But if anyone obeys his word, God's love is truly made complete in him. This is how we know we are in him: Whoever claims to live in him must walk as Jesus did.

**1 John 4:12** No one has ever seen God; but if we love one another, God lives in us and his love is made complete in us.

**Luke 10:29** But he wanted to justify himself, so he asked Jesus, "And who is my neighbor?"

Did you ever notice that when someone wants to justify themselves he or she starts asking questions? In the parable of the Good Samaritan the question was **"And who is my neighbor?"** Why is it so hard to accept the fact that if we claim Jesus Christ we must love as He did? No questions, no stalling and no excuses, just do it. Jesus loved us so much that He willingly gave His life for our salvation. Ray Boltz asked *"Does He still feel the nails Every time I fail? Can He hear the crowd cry "Crucify" again? Am I causing Him pain? Then I know I've got to change. I just can't bear the thought of hurting Him."* I don't know if His hands literally hurt, but I am sure it does cause Him pain and brings a tear when I do not do as He would have me do. Someone once said when confronted with the world's desperate need of Christ's love and ours, "well our church has a committee to take care of things like that." Jesus tells us to LOVE. If we want Jesus to work in our midst we must be willing to get our hands dirty and do His work, starting with loving all people, even the unlovable.

## To Obey or not to Obey

**Matt 21:28-31 "What do you think? There was a man who had two sons. He went to the first and said, 'Son, go and work today in the vineyard.' "'I will not,' he answered, but later he changed his mind and went. "Then the father went to the other son and said the same thing. He answered, 'I will, sir,' but he did not go. "Which of the two did what his father wanted?"**

**Titus 1:16 They claim to know God, but by their actions they deny him. They are detestable, disobedient and unfit for doing anything good.**

**Matt 7:21-23 "Not everyone who says to me, 'Lord, Lord,' will enter the kingdom of heaven, but only he who does the will of my Father who is in heaven. Many will say to me on that day, 'Lord, Lord, did we not prophesy in your name, and in your name drive out demons and perform many miracles?' Then I will tell them plainly, 'I never knew you. Away from me, you evildoers!'**

Which is the better, to have disobeyed then repent or to only pretend to obey? Which is really obedience? Some will say, "that's a no-brainer." Well, it is just that. A few years ago I was trying to witness to a young man who made the following comment. "I don't know much about religion, but I do know that it's more than going to church on Sunday and living like hell the rest of the week." He was wiser than he knew. Jesus expects us to be obedient and He would rather we refuse and come to repentance than to see us pretend to obey and live our lives for ourselves. Any sinner who will earnestly be sorry for his sin will be welcomed into the arms of Jesus and be held so lovingly, but that one who outwardly appears to know Christ and does not live His life will only know His judgment. There will be those who pretend at Christianity who will hear **"away from me I never knew you"**; simply attending church and playing the role will not lead one to His Kingdom. HE gave His all so how can we do any less? Simply put, we can't, if we expect to hear Him say "well done".

*Just A Thought*

## Straining against the Oars!

**Mark 6:48 He saw the disciples straining at the oars, because the wind was against them.**

**Matt 14:22-24 Immediately Jesus made the disciples get into the boat and go on ahead of him to the other side, while he dismissed the crowd. After he had dismissed them, he went up on a mountainside by himself to pray. When evening came, he was there alone, but the boat was already a considerable distance from land, buffeted by the waves because the wind was against it.**

**John 6:16-19 When evening came, his disciples went down to the lake, where they got into a boat and set off across the lake for Capernaum. By now it was dark, and Jesus had not yet joined them. A strong wind was blowing and the waters grew rough. When they had rowed three or three and a half miles,**

Jesus sent the disciples on a mission; the only thing was the wind and waves opposed them greatly. Sounds like our lives some days, huh? The interesting thing is that they did not turn back, even though it would have made good sense to do so. What an example to us. Jesus said, **"I have told you these things, so that in me you may have peace. In this world you will have trouble. But take heart! I have overcome the world."** (John 16:33) If any of you have never had any problems of any kind, please let me know how you do that. Sometimes we encounter heaps of trouble and there are things that even set us back on our ears. We are tempted to cash in and run, and maybe have, but Jesus doesn't give us orders then forget us. Those sailors that night would have been totally correct in men's eyes to turn tail and scurry to shore, but the Master asked something of them and they were not about to let Him down. As they struggled to carry on, the Lord came on the scene, **Jesus approaching the boat, walking on the water; and they were terrified. But he said to them, "It is I; don't be afraid." Then they were willing to take him into the boat, and immediately the boat reached the shore where they were heading.** (John 6:19-21) Immediately upon bringing Him on board they arrived at their destination. How often have we fallen short just one second to soon?

*Just A Thought*

## What do you WANT to know?

**Phil 3:8 What is more, I consider everything a loss compared to the surpassing greatness of knowing Christ Jesus my Lord, for whose sake I have lost all things. I consider them rubbish that I may gain Christ.**

**Rom 8:18 I consider that our present sufferings are not worth comparing with the glory that will be revealed in us.**

**1 Cor 2:2 For I resolved to know nothing while I was with you except Jesus Christ and him crucified.**

The Apostle Paul stated that he was resolved not to know anything except Jesus. He did not want to know the daily dirt or gossip about the Corinthian people. All he wanted to know was Christ. How about us, what do we want to know? Some folks claim they cannot remember Bible verses etc., their memory just does not work that well, but try asking them about baseball, football, or some other area of interest, and they will tell you every game their team ever won or lost and why. They can recite every stat on their favorite players and will spend their last dollar to get into a game. They will ignore spouse, family, friends, and anyone else who may try to interrupt that all-important game on ESPN. Still other people are glad to share with you all the gossip they've heard on everyone else in the world, except their own of course. The fact is we retain in our minds or invest from our checkbooks whatever we really want to. Our inability to memorize scripture, to tithe, to be hospitable or to live out any other Christian attribute all has to do with our desire, or lack thereof, to love, know and be like Jesus Christ. What is your resolve?

## A Good Name

**Prov 22:1 A good name is more desirable than great riches; to be esteemed is better than silver or gold.**

**Eccl 7:1 A good name is better than fine perfume,**

**Luke 10:20 "However, do not rejoice that the spirits submit to you, but rejoice that your names are written in heaven."**

It's sad but so true that it comes naturally for our human nature to seek after money and fame, sometimes at any cost. We've all seen people say or do most anything to be noticed and in so doing forfeit the value of their name. The Bible tells us that a GOOD name is to be highly desired. Why? Simply put, it is the name that we will remember for the good a person has done during their lifetime. The names of George Washington and Abraham Lincoln immediately remind us of attributes such as honesty and patriotism. Both men are famous and will always be remembered for the efforts they put forth to improve the welfare of America and her people. Personally I believe there is no higher tribute that can be given to a man or woman than to be known as "one who loves the Lord Jesus". They will be remembered because they invested their lives in the lives of others. Their focus is on life with God, family and their world compared to the usual, "me, myself and I". Recognition and a name remembered may result however one lives, but the name of the self-centered will conjure up thoughts of a not so good person, one who would "step on their own mother" to get ahead. Jesus said we should rejoice that the God of the universe knows and loves us individually, far better than anyone else we could seek to impress. Are we living with the sole purpose of bringing honor and glory to Him? If we are, our name is written in "His book" and our GOOD NAME will follow us during our life here, as well as long after we're gone.

## The Lord hates WHAT?

**Prov 6:16-19 There are six things the LORD hates, seven that are detestable to him: haughty eyes, a lying tongue, hands that shed innocent blood, a heart that devises wicked schemes, feet that are quick to rush into evil, a false witness who pours out lies and a man who stirs up dissension among brothers.**

**Prov 8:13 To fear the LORD is to hate evil; I hate pride and arrogance, evil behavior and perverse speech.**

**Prov 12:22 The LORD detests lying lips, but he delights in men who are truthful.**

**Prov 16:5 The LORD detests all the proud of heart. Be sure of this: They will not go unpunished.**

It is always interesting to me to compare what God hates, as stated in His Word, with the usual list we hear from men. While it is true that God does hate adultery, murder and the like, included also are a whole lot of other things that we mere human beings think are not so bad. The book of Proverbs is full of truth that we would often like to overlook. Read the above verses once again; there is a good possibility you will be surprised at what you find. Our local radio station, The Family Life Network, occasionally airs a skit in which a simple prayer request ultimately becomes a scathing pack of lies, that if true would cause great damage to the one needing prayer. The Lord hates gossip, a false witness, lying, slander and stirring up trouble. The sins that we want to slough off are every bit as offensive to Him as those we consider to be the biggies. Oh, how every one of us needs to take a reality check of our lives in light of God's Word. Guard your hearts friends, **"For out of the overflow of the heart the mouth speaks. The good man brings good things out of the good stored up in him, and the evil man brings evil things out of the evil stored up in him. But I tell you that men will have to give account on the day of judgment for every careless word**

**they have spoken. For by your words you will be acquitted, and by your words you will be condemned."** (Matt 12:34-37)

## How could He love me so?

**Heb 4:16 Let us then approach the throne of grace with confidence, so that we may receive mercy and find grace to help us in our time of need.**

**Is 55:6 Seek the LORD while he may be found; call on him while he is near. 7 Let the wicked forsake his way and the evil man his thoughts. Let him turn to the LORD, and he will have mercy on him, and to our God, for he will freely pardon.**

Oh the love of our great God, He who spared not His only Son but delivered Him up for us all that we might know His grace and mercy. Do you ever wonder how He could so love us? Every day He shows us care and kindness. He causes the rain to fall on the unjust as well as the just. He allows good to things to happen to every kind of people and He does not destroy those who so adamantly oppose Him. What kind of mercy is that? His own people and those who do not know Him walk side by side each day, both enjoying His world. Many are not even aware of His many blessings. The time will come, though, when the "Gentle Shepherd" will no longer be so merciful. He will separate the saved from the unsaved and deal with each in justice and righteousness, **"When the Son of Man comes in his glory, and all the angels with him, he will sit on his throne in heavenly glory. All the nations will be gathered before him, and he will separate the people one from another as a shepherd separates the sheep from the goats. He will put the sheep on his right and the goats on his left. "Then the King will say to those on his right, 'Come, you who are blessed by my Father; take your inheritance, the kingdom prepared for you since the creation of the world."** (Matt 25:31-34) **"Then he will say to those on his left, 'Depart from me, you who are cursed, into the eternal fire prepared for the devil and his angels."** (Matt 25:41) "Gentle Shepherd", yes, BUT so much more. He is also the "GREAT JUDGE". He will not extend His mercy forever.

## "Come to ME"

**Matt 11:28-30** "Come to me, all you who are weary and burdened, and I will give you rest. Take my yoke upon you and learn from me, for I am gentle and humble in heart, and you will find rest for your souls. For my yoke is easy and my burden is light."

**Is 55:1-3** "Come, all you who are thirsty, come to the waters; and you who have no money, come, buy and eat! Come, buy wine and milk without money and without cost. Why spend money on what is not bread, and your labor on what does not satisfy? Listen, listen to me, and eat what is good, and your soul will delight in the richest of fare. Give ear and come to me; hear me, that your soul may live. I will make an everlasting covenant with you, my faithful love promised to David.

"I'm so angry, confused and upset. Nothing ever goes right. I can't win for losing. Things are such a mess and I have no idea what I'm going to do". We all have our pity parties and say stuff like this far more often than we realize. How our Savior must ache when he hears us rant and rave because we fail to see that He died to give us peace and is waiting patiently in the wings to wrap His loving arms around us if we will just slow down a moment and let Him. There is every needed supply available in abundance without cost or strings attached if we will just COME. We were playing the "Ungame" one night at a fellowship time. I drew this question, "What sermon do you think Jesus would preach if He were to come to your church this week?" I answered, "He would probably start out by asking, 'Why do you stay so far from me? I have so much for you if you will just come near'?" When will we realize that by our defiant independence and failure to just COME, He hurts and we lose?

## Isn't belief in God enough?

**James 2:19 You believe that there is one God. Good! Even the demons believe that-and shudder.**

**Matt 8:29 "What do you want with us, Son of God?" they shouted. "Have you come here to torture us before the appointed time?"**

**Mark 3:11 Whenever the evil spirits saw him, they fell down before him and cried out, "You are the Son of God."**

We've all heard people say, "I believe in God", and they may even go on to claim that they have read the Bible many times. That may be true but the question needs to be asked, "Do you have a personal relationship with Jesus Christ?". That is a valid question because even demons know all ABOUT God and believe who He is, but their knowledge cannot save them any more than our knowledge with no saving faith can save us. Demons are very resourceful and do a good job of convincing people that knowing ABOUT the Lord is enough, that church attendance is even a good thing and a sure sign of one's position before God, but don't take this religion thing too far. Demons talk people into believing that evil things are not really all that bad and that some evils actually have good purposes. Examples of this are horoscopes, extra sensory perception and other things used for Satan's purposes, but listen to what God says – **"Let no one be found among you who sacrifices his son or daughter in the fire, who practices divination or sorcery, interprets omens, engages in witchcraft, or casts spells, or who is a medium or spiritist or who consults the dead. Anyone who does these things is detestable to the LORD, (Deut 18:10-12)** No one can simply believe **about** God and know their Bible yet practice such evil and truly be saved. And those who buy into the lies of Satan and his demons are just as lost as they are. Only a personal relationship with Jesus Christ offers salvation.

## Trust God and give with the right motive

**Mal 3:8-10 "Will a man rob God? Yet you rob me. "But you ask, 'How do we rob you?' "In tithes and offerings. You are under a curse the whole nation of you because you are robbing me. Bring the whole tithe into the storehouse, that there may be food in my house. Test me in this," says the LORD Almighty, "and see if I will not throw open the floodgates of heaven and pour out so much blessing that you will not have room enough for it.**

How much do we Christians love God? One indicator is whether or not we return to Him a portion of what He has given to us. In Malachi God accused the people of robbing Him by not giving tithes and offerings, a tithe meaning one-tenth of what is earned and offerings, monies above and beyond the tithe. Some would ask if the tithe is based on gross or net and they would pose any number of other questions to maybe muddy the question or justify their particular position. But whether based on the gross or net is of no importance. What is important here is the condition of our hearts. If we truly love God we will want to give to Him out of love and obedience, not just our money, but our hearts, time and our very lives. Jesus told the Pharisees that they gave the tenth all right even to the herbs of the garden, but forgot about "justice and love of God". In regard to tithing, many professing Christians in America do not tithe at all and the average has been reported less than four percent. I believe that fact alone indicates a lack of love and appreciation for God and beyond that a lack of trust in His ability to meet our needs. God offered a challenge when He said, **"Test me in this, and see if I will not throw open the floodgates of heaven and pour out so much blessing that you will not have room enough for it."** James says, **"When you ask, you do not receive, because you ask with wrong motives, that you may spend what you get on your pleasures."** (James 4:3) Test the motive of your own heart. Not only WHAT we do but WHY we do it is the proof of the pudding. So, are you giving to God, and if so, why?

## BELONGING

**Gal 5:24 Those who belong to Christ Jesus have crucified the sinful nature with its passions and desires.**

**Rom 8:9 You, however, are controlled not by the sinful nature but by the Spirit, if the Spirit of God lives in you. And if anyone does not have the Spirit of Christ, he does not belong to Christ.**

**Gal 5:16 So I say, live by the Spirit, and you will not gratify the desires of the sinful nature. 17 For the sinful nature desires what is contrary to the Spirit, and the Spirit what is contrary to the sinful nature. They are in conflict with each other, so that you do not do what you want. 18 But if you are led by the Spirit, you are not under law.**

If you belong to Christ you are a different person. The old passions and lusts go away. Though temptations may arise, these things are to no longer control your thoughts and actions. If the world's desires that you once had, it's toys and non-Christlike activities and attitudes, still have a strong appeal to you, you may want to get alone with Jesus and make sure of your relationship with Him. Jesus taught that there will even be those who **think** they are His who will not enter His kingdom. **Many will say to me on that day, 'Lord, Lord, did we not prophesy in your name, and in your name drive out demons and perform many miracles?' Then I will tell them plainly, 'I never knew you. Away from me, you evildoers!'"** (Matt 7:22-23) I once knew of a sixty-seven year old man who came to the altar after forty years of church ministry, including service as deacon and Sunday school superintendent. Afterward he made this statement "I've been in this church for forty years and yet if I had died before tonight I would have spent eternity in hell." "Oh Lord, help us today to examine exactly where we are and confess those things that hinder our position in You." Amen

*Just A Thought*

## CLEAN– what part of clean confuses you?

**1 John 1:9 If we confess our sins, he is faithful and just and will forgive us our sins and purify us from all unrighteousness.**

**Ps 51:2 Wash away all my iniquity and cleanse me from my sin.**

**1 Cor 6:11 And that is what some of you were. But you were washed, you were sanctified, you were justified in the name of the Lord Jesus Christ and by the Spirit of our God.**

**Titus 2:14 who gave himself for us to redeem us from all wickedness and to purify for himself a people that are his very own, eager to do what is good.**

I Cor. 6:9 &10 says that the wicked, including the sexually immoral, idolaters, adulterers, prostitutes, homosexuals, thieves, greedy, drunkards, slanderers and swindlers will not inherit God's kingdom AND that some of you use to do those things. BUT NOW you've been washed, made holy and justified and according to I John 1:9 you've been forgiven and purified from all (ALL) unrighteousness. What part of ALL is so hard to grasp? Jesus told the woman taken in adultery — **"Then neither do I condemn you," Jesus declared. "Go now and leave your life of sin."** (John 8:11) Who of us does not have something in our lives, past or present, that we want to forget and wish others would, too? We all do, but sometimes there are people, along with Satan and his cohorts, who do not want you and I to live in the joy of God's grace and forgiveness. If Jesus Christ has forgiven a sin because we've taken ownership of that sin and confessed it to Him, it is no more. When Jesus forgives He forgives, period. You and I are brand new creatures and there is not even a hint of the old stain. Sin does carry consequences but our sin is gone, so be like the woman at the well and joyfully share your message of God's forgiveness. **"Then, leaving her water jar, the woman went back to the town and said to the people, "Come, see a man who told me everything I ever did. Could this be the Christ?"** (John 4:28-29) We all know people who need to hear the

Good News we've experienced and it is our privilege and responsibility to tell them.

## God is not the movies

**Mal 3:8 "Will a man rob God? Yet you rob me. "But you ask, 'How do we rob you?' "In tithes and offerings.**

**Prov 3:9-10 Honor the LORD with your wealth, with the firstfruits of all your crops; then your barns will be filled to overflowing, and your vats will brim over with new wine.**

Once in a while I tell a waitress I just don't understand why she expects me to give her money before I leave a restaurant just because I ate their food. This usually gets a laugh or a "yeah right". When we go to a movie, play or concert we pay the fee to get in. The way some of us treat God you would think He is just such an attraction. "I didn't get to church this week so I have a few extra bucks to play with." God owns everything. Our tithes and offerings are not an entrance fee to church but they are what God asks of us. They also show our worship and obedience to the God we say we love and appreciate. To do less tells Him that we really don't trust Him and prefer to work out our own problems. Furthermore, we are to give God the FIRST FRUITS (right off the top) of what He gives us so that our barns will be full to overflowing. Can the opposite be true? Could we be experiencing unmet needs because we have been robbing God? God said through Haggai, **"Now this is what the LORD Almighty says: "Give careful thought to your ways. You have planted much, but have harvested little. You eat, but never have enough. You drink, but never have your fill. You put on clothes, but are not warm. You earn wages, only to put them in a purse with holes in it."** (Hag 1:5-6) and we read in Malachi, **"Bring the whole tithe into the storehouse, that there may be food in my house. Test me in this,"** says the LORD Almighty, **"and see if I will not throw open the floodgates of heaven and pour out so much blessing that you will not have room enough for it"** (Mal 3:10). Will we stop treating God and our tithes like the movies and give Him the real honor he deserves?

## Heart for God, Friend of God

**Acts 13:22 After removing Saul, he made David their king. He testified concerning him: 'I have found David son of Jesse a man after my own heart; he will do everything I want him to do.'**

**1 Kings 15:3 He committed all the sins his father had done before him; his heart was not fully devoted to the LORD his God, as the heart of David his forefather had been.**

**1 Kings 15:5 For David had done what was right in the eyes of the LORD and had not failed to keep any of the LORD's commands all the days of his life-except in the case of Uriah the Hittite.**

**James 2:23 And the scripture was fulfilled that says, "Abraham believed God, and it was credited to him as righteousness," and he was called God's friend.**

What a blessing it is when a son or daughter is obedient and a double blessing if they sincerely apologize when they do mess up. A parent feels especially close to that child, not that the others are not loved, but the compliant child is a breath of fresh air. God called David "a man after my own heart". David was one hundred percent human for sure and as such he sinned, but the difference was that he took responsibility for his sin, confessed it, enjoyed God's presence and lived with his heart "fully devoted" to his God. Listen to his confession, **"For I know my transgressions, and my sin is always before me. Against You, You only, have I sinned and done what is evil in your sight, so that You are proved right when You speak and justified when You judge. Surely I was sinful at birth, sinful from the time my mother conceived me.** (Ps 51:3-5) David was a man after God's own heart and Abraham was a friend of God because they both believed in their heavenly Father, truly repented of and confessed their sins and strived to live pleasing to God. Can such be said of us?

## Savior and Judge

**Rom 2:16 This will take place on the day when God will judge men's secrets through Jesus Christ, as my gospel declares.**

**John 5:22 "Moreover, the Father judges no one, but has entrusted all judgment to the Son,"**

**Acts 10:42 He commanded us to preach to the people and to testify that he is the one whom God appointed as judge of the living and the dead.**

**Acts 17:31 For he has set a day when he will judge the world with justice by the man he has appointed. He has given proof of this to all men by raising him from the dead."**

We may know the District Justice in our area and even be friends, but when a traffic ticket comes along we do not look forward to appearing before that friend. Jesus is preached and presented as our loving Savior, which He is, but He is also the great Judge of all mankind. Jesus, the gentle Shepherd who holds the rescued lamb in His arms, is also the final judge who will call all men to account for the actions of their lives. **"Then I saw a great white throne and Him who was seated on it. Earth and sky fled from his presence, and there was no place for them."** (Rev 20:11) If earth and sky will flee from His presence, it is safe to say that this is an all-powerful judge before whom EVERYTHING will pass. He will look into the "Book of Life" and whoever's name is not found there will be cast into hell. **"If anyone's name was not found written in the book of life, he was thrown into the lake of fire."** Rev 20:15. All this will be done by that same Gentle Lamb. Our Savior never was, nor will He ever be, a powerless God who just let's things slide. He is the Gentle Shepherd, yes, but oooh so much more.

## IS He your King of kings?

**Rom 10:10 For it is with your heart that you believe and are justified, and it is with your mouth that you confess and are saved.**

**Rom 10:9 That if you confess with your mouth, "Jesus is Lord," and believe in your heart that God raised him from the dead, you will be saved.**

**1 John 4:15 If anyone acknowledges that Jesus is the Son of God, God lives in him and he in God.**

Did you ever see or enjoy something that impressed you so much you talked about it for days? We all have things happen in our lives that we're passionate about and anxious to share with others, the good and at times the not so good. In fact some people even like to relate over and over the details of their latest surgery. But think about this; Jesus Christ died, arose and returned to heaven so that we can one day live with Him. Have you accepted His wonderful gift of eternal life? If so have you shared this, your life's greatest event, with someone else? You and I should be so excited about Him that we desire above all else to tell others what God has done. Jesus said, **"If anyone is ashamed of me and my words in this adulterous and sinful generation, the Son of Man will be ashamed of him when he comes in his Father's glory with the holy angels."** (Mark 8:38) If we are truly His and have the promise of eternal life with the very God of all creation, the King of kings and the Lord of lords, what do we have to be ashamed of? And in light of eternity shouldn't we be spending less of our time investing in this life and put forth more effort into our life with Jesus so that others can know Him?

## Does Jesus care?

**1 Peter 5:7 Cast all your anxiety on him because he cares for you.**

**Ps 37:5 Commit your way to the LORD; trust in him and he will do this:**

**Matt 6:25 "Therefore I tell you, do not worry about your life, what you will eat or drink; or about your body, what you will wear. Is not life more important than food, and the body more important than clothes?"**

"I just don't know what I'm going to do. The mortgage is due and payday is not for days. I've had a bad cold, the kids are being less than perfect and I am lonely." You get the idea. We all have those days when the world seems to be closing in on us but it's how we handle them that will make the difference. This morning in my devotions I was led to the words of the old hymn "Does Jesus Care" by Frank Graef. *"Does Jesus care when my heart is pained too deeply for mirth or song, As the burdens press, and the cares distress And the way grows weary and long? Oh yes, He cares, I know He cares, His heart is touched with my grief; When the days are weary, the long nights dreary, I know my Savior cares."* What we need to remember is that HE DOES CARE and is just waiting for us to say, "I know You care, Jesus, please take care of this situation." As long as we keep trying to solve things on our own without Him His hands are tied. Many believing wives bear a very special "care" and Peter addressed their problem saying that when they refuse to nag, live godly lives and submit to their unbelieving husbands, God can bring loved one to Him. **"Wives, in the same way be submissive to your husbands so that, if any of them do not believe the word, they may be won over without words by the behavior of their wives"** (1 Peter 3:1) Oh how this and many other issues could be resolved if we patiently and quietly let Christ shine through us. Cast all your care upon Him, do not worry about tomorrow, commit your way to Him and you will find rest.

## The birth of death

**Ps 7:14 He who is pregnant with evil and conceives trouble gives birth to disillusionment.**

**Job 15:35 They conceive trouble and give birth to evil; their womb fashions deceit."**

**Is 33:11 You conceive chaff, you give birth to straw; your breath is a fire that consumes you.**

**James 1:15 Then, after desire has conceived, it gives birth to sin; and sin, when it is full-grown, gives birth to death.**

From the beginning of time Satan has duped mankind into sin and death. He said to Eve, **"You will not surely die,"** (Gen 3:4). The interesting part is that in verse one of Gen. 3 he got her attention by planting a doubt in her mind and she sealed her future and ours by replying to him. The enemy must be denied access to our minds at the very onset. He is a great debater and will talk us down if given half a chance. He will use "friends" to encourage us into sin with lies such as "just one____ won't hurt anything". A guy will say to a girl "if you love me you will _____". David saw Bathsheba, and that in and of itself was not necessarily wrong, but he gazed (kept looking) upon her and acted on his desires. Oh how many people are disillusioned by the appeal of sin. It is the seemingly innocent simple tastes of the dark side that give birth to death. Those who are caught in sinful lifestyles want company and will destroy anyone else they can draw in. James says, **"Submit yourselves, then, to God. Resist the devil, and he will flee from you. Come near to God and he will come near to you. Wash your hands, you sinners, and purify your hearts, you double-minded."** (James 4:7) Victory comes from submitting to God and resisting Satan, giving no attention to him. When ALL that we are and ALL that we do is given to God we are truly free to live lives of joy in Him and will never taste spiritual death.

## The source of beauty

**1 Peter 3:3-4** Your beauty should not come from outward adornment, such as braided hair and the wearing of gold jewelry and fine clothes. Instead, it should be that of your inner self, the unfading beauty of a gentle and quiet spirit, which is of great worth in God's sight.

**1 Tim 2:9** I also want women to dress modestly, with decency and propriety, not with braided hair or gold or pearls or expensive clothes, 10 but with good deeds, appropriate for women who profess to worship God.

**Ps 51:6** Surely you desire truth in the inner parts; you teach me wisdom in the inmost place.

**Rom 7:22** For in my inner being I delight in God's law;

There is a practice especially among ladies, sometimes men, to look in every mirror they pass by. First a look, then a pat on the hair, then they walk on. Now before anyone gives in to the temptation to do me in, let me say that the call here for inner beauty goes for men as well as women. Many an person who looks good in a mirror is far from good looking by the world's standards but beauty that can only be measured in a mirror is not beauty at all. Beauty is opening the door for your wife, making your mate feel loved, being courteous on the highway, loving lost people and showing kindness in countless other ways. It is the gentle heart, the humble spirit and the Christ-like soul that is truly beautiful. Beauty is living each day as Jesus desires us to. Even those who are poor according to the world's standards can be rich when they open their doors and arms to others in need. That is true beauty. **How beautiful on the mountains are the feet of those who bring good news, who proclaim peace, who bring good tidings, who proclaim salvation, who say to Zion, "Your God reigns!"** (Is 52:7) How about that; our feet are even beautiful as we spread the Gospel. Wouldn't you rather have that kind of beauty than be "the fairest of all"?

## "You never know"

**1 Cor 10:31 So whether you eat or drink or whatever you do, do it all for the glory of God**

**Prov 3:6 in all your ways acknowledge him, and he will make your paths straight.**

**John 5:23 "that all may honor the Son just as they honor the Father. He who does not honor the Son does not honor the Father, who sent him.**

We've all heard the phrase "you never know", but I want to offer a new twist on it. A lady one day called to tell me that twenty some years ago she provided free kid-sitting to a single father who was having trouble finding adequate care for his daughters while he worked. She offered to help and would make the girls breakfast, see them off on the bus each day, then give them a snack after school and a place to stay until daddy picked them up. During this time God gave her opportunities to take them to church including a church party, which they really enjoyed. Back to the present, all these years later one of the girls now all grown up tracked down our friend and called her just to say "thank you". She has since come to know Jesus and was so grateful for that brief window of care in her life. Jesus said, **"And if anyone gives even a cup of cold water to one of these little ones because he is my disciple, I tell you the truth, he will certainly not lose his reward."** (Matt 10:42) We do not realize how each and every action of ours will affect the life of another, whether for good or bad. This lady is oh so glad and greatly blessed because she offered some kindness to two little girls when they needed it. How about us? Are we planting seeds of love for Jesus Christ?

## Exercise, exercise, exercise

**Josh 1:8 Do not let this Book of the Law depart from your mouth; meditate on it day and night, so that you may be careful to do everything written in it. Then you will be prosperous and successful.**

**Deut 5:29 Oh, that their hearts would be inclined to fear me and keep all my commands always, so that it might go well with them and their children forever!**

**Matt 7:21 "Not everyone who says to me, 'Lord, Lord,' will enter the kingdom of heaven, but only he who does the will of my Father who is in heaven"**

We live in a day when Bible studies abound and oh how encouraging it is to know that folks want to learn more about the Word of God. But spiritually speaking, it is possible and far too easy to become the proverbial "couch potato". Just as with the food we consume every day, if we only take it in and do not get on the move or put it into practice we will become over weight and lethargic. Yes, it's absolutely necessary that we know all we can of God's Word, BUT if all we do is fill our brains with information, we will have failed Him, ourselves and other people. A perfectly tuned car with a full tank of gas left setting in the driveway is not of any benefit. If we are full of the Word yet do not let it flow through us to make a difference in lives, we waste that precious spiritual food. There are lost souls out there who may never hear, there are God's people out there, including pastors, worn to a frazzle and they need US to exercise and share what we know. Jesus said, **"Therefore everyone who hears these words of mine and puts them into practice is like a wise man who built his house on the rock"**. (Matt 7:24) Start being wise; build your house on the rock by putting into practice what you've learned.

## Intermittent Explosive Disorder

**Prov 10:19 When words are many, sin is not absent, but he who holds his tongue is wise.**

**Prov 12:18 Reckless words pierce like a sword, but the tongue of the wise brings healing.**

**Prov 16:24 Pleasant words are a honeycomb, sweet to the soul and healing to the bones.**

**Prov 17:27 A man of knowledge uses words with restraint, and a man of understanding is even-tempered.**

Man has a way of justifying sin and we live in a day of "Syndromes", "Disorders" etc. on which to blame our problems (oftentimes SIN). Awhile back we heard of a the newly diagnosed "IED" related to anger called "Intermittent Explosive Disorder". However, God in His Word calls on us to guard our tongues and Solomon offers the above verses to encourage careful use of words. I remember twenty-five years ago or so my son got our tractor stuck, and I do mean stuck, by accidentally driving into a real soft spot in a hay field. All the way back to get him out I said anything but wise, loving and careful words. I will never forget the pain in his face as the dad he loved berated him mercilessly and I've since apologized. I wish I could say I have never committed that sin again, but someone might tell you the truth so I will not even try to sell that one. One thing I can say is that every time I open my mouth hurtfully, even in a "small" way, I still see my son's face. With God's help and that image I am attempting to put my selfish agenda aside in order to be more what God would have me be. No doubt there are folks who have suffered head trauma, brain disorders or other conditions that cause such outbursts, but for the most of us it is just plain SIN that we need to confess. Then we can pray like David, **"Create in me a pure heart, O God, and renew a steadfast spirit within me. Do not cast me from your presence or take your Holy Spirit from me. Restore to me the joy of your salvation and grant me a willing spirit, to sustain me."** (Ps 51:10-12)

## The HUMBLE are the winners

**Ps 86:1 Hear, O LORD, and answer me, for I am poor and needy.**

**Ps 34:6-7 This poor man called, and the LORD heard him; He saved him out of all his troubles. The angel of the LORD encamps around those who fear him, and He delivers them.**

**Ps 119:22 Remove from me scorn and contempt, for I keep your statutes.**

**Matt 5:3 "Blessed are the poor in spirit, for theirs is the kingdom of heaven."**

"I do it." So many times we've seen this attitude in the actions of a two-year old. Toddlers have a very strong streak of independence, but sadly this is a picture of many adults who all too often fail to give their problems and needs to God. Instead of dropping immediately to our knees, we try everything in the book until finally we come to the point of saying, "I've tried everything else, guess it's time to pray". Solomon said, **"Pride goes before destruction, a haughty spirit before a fall."** (Prov 16:18) How often we make the situations in our lives worse by our "I do it" attitude. God loves us so much and He says, **"For I know the plans I have for you," declares the LORD, "plans to prosper you and not to harm you, plans to give you hope and a future."** (Jer 29:11) He knows best how to accomplish His purposes for us, so it only makes sense that humility and obedience to Him would make life a lot easier and far more enjoyable. Oh that we would be able to say with David, **"Remove from me scorn and contempt, for I keep your statutes"** The poor in spirit (the humble, those who come to God first) have the kingdom of heaven already. Sounds like a win win plan to me.

## FINISHED!

**John 19:30 When He had received the drink, Jesus said, "It is finished." With that, He bowed His head and gave up His spirit.**

**Gen 3:15 "And I will put enmity between you and the woman, and between your offspring and hers; He will crush your head, and you will strike his heel."**

**John 4:34 "My food," said Jesus, "is to do the will of Him who sent me and to finish His work."**

**Heb 9:14 How much more, then, will the blood of Christ, who through the eternal Spirit offered himself unblemished to God, cleanse our consciences from acts that lead to death, so that we may serve the living God!**

As I think about that day nearly two thousand years ago, the day we call "Good Friday", where did we ever come up with that title for the darkest day in history when the SON of God was murdered by His own creation? The only good thing about that day was that He redeemed any and all who will believe. Pondering this there are a few things I wonder about. Did the Pharisees really think they could get rid of this threat to their power base; did Satan really think he could put the Son of God permanently out of the way? Jesus taught the truth of the Kingdom and He set people free from sin and it's dominion. Souls were being changed and the enemies of God could not tolerate such things. Little did they realize the truth of what they would accomplish that day. Little did they know that Jesus would "finish" the work He came to do and provide forever the freedom He had preached to all who would accept it. Satan learned that day the full meaning of God's declaration **"He will crush your head, and you will strike his heel."** Praise the Lord! Salvation was finished and three days later, oh three days later, He arose and lives forevermore! Hallelujah, hallelujah, hallelujah! Now the question is, will we eat the "food" (John 4:34) that Jesus ate and do His will?

## Winning by Losing

**John 19:30 When he had received the drink, Jesus said, "It is finished." With that, he bowed his head and gave up his spirit.**

**Is 53:10 Yet it was the LORD's will to crush him and cause him to suffer, and though the LORD makes his life a guilt offering, He will see his offspring and prolong his days, and the will of the LORD will prosper in his hand.**

**John 4:34 "My food," said Jesus, "is to do the will of him who sent me and to finish his work."**

**1 Cor 5:7 Get rid of the old yeast that you may be a new batch without yeast-as you really are. For Christ, our Passover lamb, has been sacrificed.**

Just a couple of months ago at the Super Bowl the NY Giants pulled a surprising upset and became the world football team. We all know that to take the prize you have to win but there is a realm where that does not hold up. On the day that Jesus hung on that cruel cross He could have easily called twelve legions of angels to set Him free. The thing is He knew that if He were going to win and if He were going to destroy death and sin, He had to lose this battle. Satan thought he had the upper hand and was killing this Son of God for good, but little did he realize that in three days Jesus would walk forth from that grave. Jesus won the war by losing that one battle and so it will be with us when we completely surrender to Jesus Christ. We will become winners in the greatest sense of the word, for it is in losing self and putting on Him that the war is won. Our Lord defeated Satan and provides that victory for us. **"For whoever wants to save his life will lose it, but whoever loses his life for me will find it"** (Matt 16:25)

## Is Jesus Christ YOUR LORD?

**Rom 10:12-13 For there is no difference between Jew and Gentile-the same Lord is Lord of all and richly blesses all who call on him, for, "Everyone who calls on the name of the Lord will be saved."**

**Rom 14:9 For this very reason, Christ died and returned to life so that he might be the Lord of both the dead and the living.**

**Rev 19:16 On his robe and on his thigh he has this name written:**
**KING OF KINGS AND LORD OF LORDS.**

If you ask Mr. Webster he will tell you that Lord is defined as "one having authority over another, or a person with great power in a field." In order for one to claim Jesus as Savior one must also recognize Him as Lord. I heard a television preacher say that it is one thing to kneel at the altar and say you want Jesus as your Savior and Lord, but it is after rising that the rubber meets the road. You have to do what you just prayed. It takes resolution and determination to live the life of Jesus as Lord. No more excuses like I'm too busy to spend (invest) time with God. No more saying I don't understand the Bible so there's no use to read it. No longer is the status quo sufficient. Jesus Christ is King of kings and Lord of lords therefore it is of great importance to kneel before Him as such, now. **"Therefore God exalted him to the highest place and gave him the name that is above every name, that at the name of Jesus every knee should bow, in heaven and on earth and under the earth, and every tongue confess that Jesus Christ is Lord, to the glory of God the Father."** (Phil 2:9-11) One day **all** will bow, but only those who have truly made Him Lord will spend eternity with Him, **"Not everyone who says to me, 'Lord, Lord,' will enter the kingdom of heaven, but only he who does the will of my Father who is in heaven."** (Matt 7:21) As for me, I would rather make Him my Lord NOW rather than be made to acknowledge Him later. How about you?

## Praise the Lord oh my soul!

**Ps 103:1 Praise the LORD, O my soul; all my inmost being, praise his holy name. 2 Praise the LORD, O my soul, and forget not all his benefits-**

**Ps 111:1 Praise the LORD. I will extol the LORD with all my heart in the council of the upright and in the assembly.**

**John 4:24 "God is spirit, and his worshipers must worship in spirit and in truth."**

**Phil 1:9 And this is my prayer: that your love may abound more and more in knowledge and depth of insight,**

We know that some men have told their wives "look, I told you once that I love you and I will let you know if anything changes." That line does not go far in correcting a troubled marriage nor does such an attitude toward God go far in bringing Him the honor and glory He is due. And, it surely doesn't help us get to know this precious Savior. Jesus willingly left the glory of His home in heaven, became a baby human being, walked the dirty cruel paths of this earth and in the last few hours endured unspeakable pain and rejection. Crucifixion was the most debasing form of death a person could bear and in fact the Scripture states that, **"Christ redeemed us from the curse of the law by becoming a curse for us, for it is written: "Cursed is everyone who is hung on a tree."** (Gal 3:13) What's more our Lord died **willingly,** knowing that heaven with His Father, the redemption of all who believe and numberless other joys lay ahead. **"Let us fix our eyes on Jesus, the author and perfecter of our faith, who for the joy set before him endured the cross, scorning its shame, and sat down at the right hand of the throne of God."** (Heb 12:2) How can we even profess to know Him and not do whatever we must to bring Him praise? Answer, WE CANNOT.

## Coming Again

**Acts 1:11 "Men of Galilee," they said, "why do you stand here looking into the sky? This same Jesus, who has been taken from you into heaven, will come back in the same way you have seen him go into heaven."**

**Matt 24:30 "At that time the sign of the Son of Man will appear in the sky, and all the nations of the earth will mourn. They will see the Son of Man coming on the clouds of the sky, with power and great glory."**

**Mark 13:26 "At that time men will see the Son of Man coming in clouds with great power and glory."**

**John 14:3 "And if I go and prepare a place for you, I will come back and take you to be with me that you also may be where I am. 4 You know the way to the place where I am going."**

It's 4:30 in the afternoon and daddy will soon be home. A four-year-old with the pet dog stands steadily gazing out the window in eager anticipation of his arrival. He doesn't care how or exactly when the magical event will occur, he just knows HE WILL see his dad. The truth is, he may not get there until 5:30, but that's OK; it only matters that he is coming and it's worth the wait. Jesus told His disciples on the day He went home to the Father, **"It is not for you to know the times or dates the Father has set by his own authority."** (Acts 1:7) Of the ten virgins in Matthew chapter 25 five were wise enough to bring extra oil for their lamps and thus were ready at the midnight hour when the bridegroom came. Oh that we would be like them and that child, not caring how or exactly WHEN He will come but only that HE IS COMING! What does it matter if it is today, tomorrow or not for a thousand years? The key is to BE READY WITH JOYFULL ANTICIPATION!

## Seek HIM

**Matt 5:37 "Simply let your 'Yes' be 'Yes,' and your 'No,' 'No'; anything beyond this comes from the evil one."**

**Col 4:6 Let your conversation be always full of grace, seasoned with salt, so that you may know how to answer everyone.**

**James 5:12 Above all, my brothers, do not swear-not by heaven or by earth or by anything else. Let your "Yes" be yes, and your "No," no, or you will be condemned.**

I once knew of a couple that had a little problem. He overheard her telling someone on the phone that he had said something that he could not remember ever saying. When she finished her conversation he asked her, "When did I say such and such?", to which she responded, "you didn't. I do this because if "I" tell people something they distrust it, but if they think "you" said it they believe me". To her it was easier to lie than to establish her own reputation of believability. I wonder how many of us do the same when it comes to God. We tell Him things we never carry through because either we're unable to or we really never intended to in the first place. We say we'll help or at least pray for a person and when we don't do what we've promised we wonder why they suspect our word. Sometimes we figure if God gets us out of a scrape, we'll reconsider and make good on the promises we've made to HIM. We may be able to put up a false front to our friends and family so they will think well of us, but God sees all things, we can't fool Him. Jesus had the solution. **"Let your 'Yes' be 'Yes,' and your 'No,' 'No"**. If we're always honest, we won't have to remember what we have told this one or that one. We will begin to become believable, spouses will grow closer and more unified, friends will be able to rely on us and everyone will know that what we say is true.

## We have fellowship

**1 John 1:7 But if we walk in the light, as He is in the light, we have fellowship with one another, and the blood of Jesus, his Son, purifies us from all sin.**

**Amos 3:3 Do two walk together unless they have agreed to do so?**

**1 John 1:3 We proclaim to you what we have seen and heard, so that you also may have fellowship with us. And our fellowship is with the Father and with his Son, Jesus Christ. 4 We write this to make our joy complete.**

**Matt 6:12 "Forgive us our debts, as we also have forgiven our debtors."**

"Walk in the light as He is in the light." Jesus walked in the light of His Father every day of His life here on earth and the way He was able to do that was by investing time in knowing Him. The result of that investment was multi faceted. He knew the fellowship of His Father and they walked in agreement because they agreed to do so. He also was able to forgive those who came against Him. How many of us would be better off if we knew our Lord better, agreed to walk with Him and were not in some bondage of unforgiveness? The answer to that can only come on an individual basis, but the truth is that too many who call themselves Christians are weak in the area of fellowship with the Lord. Ask yourself a few questions. Is my Bible as important as my cell phone? Do I carry it, check it often etc.? Am I investing time with the Lord daily? Am I in agreement with the Bible and know what it says about the subject I am struggling with? Am I able to forgive those who do not even deserve it? If the answers to any of these questions are "no", perhaps you need to make a change in your lifestyle. No, make that, you DO need to make a change.

## HE will finish the work

**Phil 1:6 being confident of this, that he who began a good work in you will carry it on to completion until the day of Christ Jesus.**

**Eph 2:4-5 But because of his great love for us, God, who is rich in mercy, made us alive with Christ even when we were dead in transgressions it is by grace you have been saved.**

**Phil 2:13 for it is God who works in you to will and to act according to his good purpose.**

**Rom 8:28 And we know that in all things God works for the good of those who love him, who have been called according to his purpose.**

We who are a little older remember cars that if they made it to 100,000 miles had at best been overhauled at least once. Today at that mileage a car is just nicely broken in, yet when one fails to run perfectly, oh how we groan, expecting Ford, GM, or Chrysler to create an auto that never quits. As Christians we have a Savior that never goes on vacation, never fails, and never forgets about His commitment to us. He loves us too much to allow us to become inert. His call on our life is to spread the gospel and be fruitful. **"Dear friends, let us love one another, for love comes from God. Everyone who loves has been born of God and knows God. Whoever does not love does not know God, because God is love."** (1 John 4:7-8) As Christians we need to be diligent to show God's love to our world. We have no excuse for not doing so because Jesus started a work in us the day we confessed our sin, repented of it and accepted Him as Lord and He will work through us if we will allow Him to. Let us be clay in the Potter's hands that others may know Him and that we may know His blessing.

## He will draw near to you

**James 4:8 Come near to God and He will come near to you. Wash your hands, you sinners, and purify your hearts, you double-minded.**

**Ps 73:28 But as for me, it is good to be near God. I have made the Sovereign LORD my refuge; I will tell of all your deeds.**

**Is 55:6 Seek the LORD while He may be found; call on him while He is near.**

**Heb 10:22 let us draw near to God with a sincere heart in full assurance of faith, having our hearts sprinkled to cleanse us from a guilty conscience and having our bodies washed with pure water.**

There are times when we feel alone and anxious and we're not quite sure where to turn or what to do in a given situation. We struggle with a particular problem in our lives and there seems to be no victory or joy, just a lot of guilt. "I just don't know how to lose weight, quit smoking, be kinder to others", and on and on. Does this sound all too familiar? James and others offer the solution to these anxieties and many more in our day-to-day walk. When we "Draw near to God" we experience His presence and we're much more likely to take the straight path. If we only see Him as some ethereal being that's out there somewhere it becomes too easy to do things that are displeasing to Him, but if we DRAW NEAR it will become harder for us to sin and cause Him pain. Paul asked, "**Do you not know that your body is a temple of the Holy Spirit, who is in you, whom you have received from God? You are not your own; you were bought at a price. Therefore honor God with your body.**" (1 Cor 6:19-20) When we are near to God we honor Him and act like the temples of the Holy Spirit that we are. In turn we know His help and guidance and enjoy His loving presence. So why stay away?

## Show your faith by your actions

**James 2:14-17** What good is it, my brothers, if a man claims to have faith but has no deeds? Can such faith save him? Suppose a brother or sister is without clothes and daily food. If one of you says to him, "Go, I wish you well; keep warm and well fed," but does nothing about his physical needs, what good is it? In the same way, faith by itself, if it is not accompanied by action, is dead.

**Prov 3:27-28** Do not withhold good from those who deserve it, when it is in your power to act. Do not say to your neighbor, "Come back later; I'll give it tomorrow" when you now have it with you.

**Matt 25:42** "For I was hungry and you gave me nothing to eat, I was thirsty and you gave me nothing to drink,"

"Do we own our stuff, or does our stuff own us"? It's possible for us to lay claim to Jesus Christ as our Savior, yet fail to show His love to those around us. It is the DOING of our faith that makes us really shine as "CHRISTians". "James wrote **"You have faith; I have deeds." Show me your faith without deeds, and I will show you my faith by what I do."** (James 2:18) He knew the truth and lived it and in essence is saying that it is never enough to merely **say** the words. We must be willing to do as Jesus would do and go on to put into practice what we say. In our times that might mean hugging someone afflicted with AIDS, taking in a pregnant single girl, adopting a child through World Vision (or another charity), or it may mean giving a glass of cold water on a warm day to that neighbor that bugs us so much. If we own our stuff we will be willing to share whatever God lays on our hearts to give, but if our stuff owns us we will turn a deaf ear. Simply put, if we are rightly related to our things we will realize that ALL we have, our stuff AND our family, is only on loan to us.

## Trouble Free?

**Acts 5:41 The apostles left the Sanhedrin, rejoicing because they had been counted worthy of suffering disgrace for the Name.**

**Matt 5:10-12 "Blessed are those who are persecuted because of righteousness,**

**for theirs is the kingdom of heaven. "Blessed are you when people insult you, persecute you and falsely say all kinds of evil against you because of me. Rejoice and be glad, because great is your reward in heaven, for in the same way they persecuted the prophets who were before you."**

**Rom 5:3 Not only so, but we also rejoice in our sufferings, because we know that suffering produces perseverance;**

**James 1:2 Consider it pure joy, my brothers, whenever you face trials of many kinds,**

We live in a day when we hear preaching that presents the gospel as a cure all for every ill in our lives. Just become a Christian and you will have no problems, you'll always feel good and you won't have any or at least many financial or other worries. But the Word of God is quite specific that we WILL have trials and tribulations. Jesus lived a life of woe, He was mocked and jeered at; they tried to stone Him and they did crucify Him. He told us that, **"If the world hates you, keep in mind that it hated me first. If you belonged to the world, it would love you as its own. As it is, you do not belong to the world, but I have chosen you out of the world. That is why the world hates you."** (John 15:18-19) Life won't always be easy and it will get harder after we come to know Jesus as our Savior, the closer we live to Him. Those who proclaim "life will be just great when you become a Christian" are watering down the truth. Yes, life will be great, but not because it is trouble free. It will be great in spite of problems and this greatness will come from the joy of knowing the God of the universe as Savior and friend.

## Taking Ownership

**Luke 18:14 "I tell you that this man, rather than the other, went home justified before God. For everyone who exalts himself will be humbled, and he who humbles himself will be exalted."**

**Job 9:20 Even if I were innocent, my mouth would condemn me; if I were blameless, it would pronounce me guilty.**

**Rom 5:1 Therefore, since we have been justified through faith, we have peace with God through our Lord Jesus Christ,**

**Matt 5:3 "Blessed are the poor in spirit, for theirs is the kingdom of heaven."**

There are times when people think it's necessary to point out to us and to God just how good they are. The Pharisee in Luke 18 did that. He even thanked God that he was not like that sinner of a tax collector. Jesus was very quick to point out the difference between these two men when he said, "I tell you this man went home justified.", referring to the tax collector. Job's statement, "even if I were innocent," indicates that we all are guilty of some sort of sin. The Pharisee in the story had guilt, (pride anyway), and evidently found it easier to point out the problems in the other guy's life than to deal with the sin in his own. Since we are all justified by faith and it takes a poor (humble) spirit to bring us to the point where we can take ownership of our sins, acknowledge and confess them, wouldn't we feel the presence and love of God more often if we were to put God's principles into practice? The answer is a very short, YES, we would.

## Will He find faith?

**Luke 18:8** "I tell you, he will see that they get justice, and quickly. However, when the Son of Man comes, will he find faith on the earth?"

**Deut 32:20** "I will hide my face from them," he said, "and see what their end will be; for they are a perverse generation, children who are unfaithful.

**Prov 20:6** Many a man claims to have unfailing love, but a faithful man who can find?

**Luke 17:26-27** "Just as it was in the days of Noah, so also will it be in the days of the Son of Man. People were eating, drinking, marrying and being given in marriage up to the day Noah entered the ark. Then the flood came and destroyed them all.

The return of our precious Lord is close and I ask two questions. Will it come as a complete surprise to us and what will He find? The second posed by Jesus in today's passage challenges us, the church. One commentator says this about the subject — *"Would they be found persevering in prayer, and "believing" that God would yet avenge them; or would they cease to pray "always, and faint?" This is not to be understood, therefore, as affirming that when Christ comes to judgment there will be few Christians on the earth, and that the world will be overrun with wickedness. That "may be" true, but it is not the truth taught here"* (from Barnes' Notes) Jesus was well aware that Israel had a reputation for waxing hot then cold when it came to the things of God and it seems that He is implying the same about His church. We need to be like the five wise virgins, **"At that time the kingdom of heaven will be like ten virgins who took their lamps and went out to meet the bridegroom. Five of them were foolish and five were wise. The foolish ones took their lamps but did not take any oil with them. The wise, however, took oil in jars along with their lamps."** — (Matt 25:1-4) It is imperative that we keep watching and in prayer and true to the teachings of our Lord Jesus, IF indeed He truly is our Lord. Jesus cannot be just "fire insurance". If He is our Savior, He must be our LORD.

## To whom much is given

**Luke 12:48b "From everyone who has been given much, much will be demanded; and from the one who has been entrusted with much, much more will be asked."**

**Luke 16:10 "Whoever can be trusted with very little can also be trusted with much, and whoever is dishonest with very little will also be dishonest with much. 11 So if you have not been trustworthy in handling worldly wealth, who will trust you with true riches? 12 And if you have not been trustworthy with someone else's property, who will give you property of your own?"**

"To whom much is given….." Ok that let's me off, I have so very little. But wait a minute, maybe it doesn't. You're blessed to live in the USA where you are free to worship, travel, invest, save, spend, come and go as you wish and many other privileges. Most of us have food to eat, in fact sometimes too much. We have a roof over our heads, multiple autos, savings accounts, vacations etc. and that's just the material side to say nothing of the freedom to worship our God, having the word of God in hand, Christian radio, and numberless other blessings. Add to that our natural talents and abilities like carpentry, music, art etc. and spiritual gifts of encouragement, discernment, administration and many more. The truth is that we, especially here in America, have been given generously from the hand of God and are guilty of not always making good use of what we have. Jesus said **"Whoever can be trusted with very little can also be trusted with much,"** Oh that we would be worthy of much, not only to be trusted with more, but oh to be worthy of greater intangible things like knowing our Lord better and seeing precious souls comes to Jesus Christ as Savior and Lord. All this and more are ours if those of us who claim to belong to Jesus would begin to appreciate and honor God with ALL we've been given.

## Seek First

**Hag 1:3-4 Then the word of the LORD came through the prophet Haggai: "Is it a time for you yourselves to be living in your paneled houses, while this house remains a ruin?"**

**Ps 132:3-5 "I will not enter my house or go to my bed I will allow no sleep to my eyes, no slumber to my eyelids, till I find a place for the LORD, a dwelling for the Mighty One of Jacob."**

**Matt 6:33 "But seek first his kingdom and his righteousness, and all these things will be given to you as well."**

**Phil 2:21 For everyone looks out for his own interests, not those of Jesus Christ.**

The Lord spoke through Haggai to accuse the Hebrews of thinking more of their personal comfort than of their spiritual condition. They were living in fine houses with wood paneling and all the niceties of the day. At the same time they were paying no heed to the state of the temple, God's house. It lay in shambles and they just ignored it, after all they were comfortable. It never occurred to them that the source of their everyday problems might be the attitude they held toward God. **"Now this is what the LORD Almighty says: "Give careful thought to your ways. You have planted much, but have harvested little. You eat, but never have enough. You drink, but never have your fill. You put on clothes, but are not warm. You earn wages, only to put them in a purse with holes in it."** (Hag 1:5-6) Much earlier King David had felt the need for honoring God when he said that he would not sleep until he found a place for God. Jesus said we are to seek HIM first and later yet the Apostle Paul saw the age old problem with selfishness in the church. He wrote to the Philippians that they were more concerned with their own interests than they were those of the Lord. Note he does not say needs. In our day many THINGS vie for our attention, **"...but only one thing is needed. Mary has chosen what is better, and it will**

**not be taken away from her."** (Luke 10:42) That ONE THING is our Lord and Savior.

## Gifts yet today?

**Luke 1:20 And now you will be silent and not able to speak until the day this happens, because you did not believe my words, which will come true at their proper time."**

**Mark 9:19 "O unbelieving generation," Jesus replied, "how long shall I stay with you? How long shall I put up with you? Bring the boy to me."**

**Mark 16:14 Later Jesus appeared to the Eleven as they were eating; he rebuked them for their lack of faith and their stubborn refusal to believe those who had seen him after he had risen.**

"In my opinion, God does not use the gift of ____ today." I've heard this said so many times. Usually, though not always, it is in reference to one of the gifts of the Spirit and usually by one who wants to limit God. I'm not sure why we attempt to put God in a box and try to tell Him what He can or cannot do, but I am sure that He never changes. **"Jesus Christ is the same yesterday and today and forever".** (Heb 13:8) One more thing for certain, there are consequences to doubting Him and His abilities. Zechariah was unable to speak from the time of his doubt until the birth if John. The disciples who doubted that Jesus had risen were scolded severely by Him. On the other hand, at Pentecost 3000 souls were saved because Jesus was honored and the Holy Spirit showed up. Peter, the wimp, the coward, who even cursed when asked if he was one of Christ's followers, now spoke boldly saying, **"These men are not drunk, as you suppose. It's only nine in the morning! No, this is what was spoken by the prophet Joel: "In the last days, God says, I will pour out my Spirit on all people."** (Acts 2:15-17) When he preached his first sermon and 3000 believed, it was not necessarily because of him, but because Jesus was lifted up and not doubted. Let us allow God to be who He is, yesterday, today and forever, and be given the privilege of seeing Him work in OUR day.

## In my opinion

**Luke 7:33-36 "For John the Baptist came neither eating bread nor drinking wine, and you say, 'He has a demon.' The Son of Man came eating and drinking, and you say, 'Here is a glutton and a drunkard, a friend of tax collectors and "sinners." 'But wisdom is proved right by all her children."**

**Mark 1:6 John wore clothing made of camel's hair, with a leather belt around his waist, and he ate locusts and wild honey.**

**Luke 5:29 Then Levi held a great banquet for Jesus at his house, and a large crowd of tax collectors and others were eating with them.**

A funny thing happened on the way to the kingdom. Somewhere along the road, man decided that his ways of evaluating things are better than God's way. John had a demon because he didn't eat the right diet and Jesus was a glutton and a drunkard because he did eat. It seems that man thinks he has all the answers. The trouble is that we filter our decisions through our own experiences and preferences. The Pharisees didn't see any way that "Messiah" could come from Nazareth, that He could not be of the elite crowd nor that He could be hanging around with the likes of the men He chose for His apostles. After all, they were mostly uneducated fishermen. We tend to look at "the package" even as Samuel did, **But the LORD said to Samuel, "Do not consider his appearance or his height, for I have rejected him. The LORD does not look at the things man looks at. Man looks at the outward appearance, but the LORD looks at the heart."** (1 Sam 16:7) Eliab was tall, dark and handsome so Samuel was sure he had to be the one to replace Saul, BUT God looks on the heart. Maybe it's about time that we learn that lesson and start seeing things the way God does when choosing pastors, electing deacons and elders and on and on according to their talents, abilities and most importantly their Spiritual gifts. When it comes to positions in ministry, better to have an open slot than to fill it with a person not gifted by God in that area.

## Time alone with Him

**Matt 14:23 After he had dismissed them, he went up on a mountainside by himself to pray. When evening came, he was there alone,**

**Mark 6:46 After leaving them, he went up on a mountainside to pray.**

When you think of Jesus Christ, the incarnate Son of God, what kind of picture do you envision? Maybe some see a superhero type who's able to leap tall buildings with a single bound or stop a locomotive with one hand. We know that Jesus could have done anything, since the Father was His source of strength through the Holy Spirit. On the other hand, He was well aware of the limitations of His human body and counted it of utmost importance to invest time with His Father. In so doing He set an example for us. We so often stumble, trip and fall in our daily walk and there is a very strong possibility that we would fail less often if we INVEST more time with our Lord. Suppose someone told you that you could get a 500% return in forty-eight hours on a certain investment. Most of us would jump at that chance. Listen to the prophet Haggai, **"Then the word of the LORD came through the prophet Haggai: "Is it a time for you yourselves to be living in your paneled houses, while this house remains a ruin?" Now this is what the LORD Almighty says: "Give careful thought to your ways. You have planted much, but have harvested little. You eat, but never have enough. You drink, but never have your fill. You put on clothes, but are not warm. You earn wages, only to put them in a purse with holes in it."** (Hag 1:3-6) WOW! It seems very safe to say that you and I would be far more successful in our daily walk if we invested more time in the Lord. We could lose that weight, love that unlovable person, save that money, tithe more, be loved more, be less critical of others and the list goes on and on. If Jesus Christ, the Son of God, needed time alone to pray, what does that say about us and what are we going to do about it???

## "I will repay"

**Rom 12:17-21 Do not repay anyone evil for evil. Be careful to do what is right in the eyes of everybody. If it is possible, as far as it depends on you, live at peace with everyone. Do not take revenge, my friends, but leave room for God's wrath, for it is written: "It is mine to avenge; I will repay," says the Lord. On the contrary: "If your enemy is hungry, feed him; if he is thirsty, give him something to drink. In doing this, you will heap burning coals on his head." Do not be overcome by evil, but overcome evil with good.**

**Matt 5:5 "Blessed are the meek, for they will inherit the earth."**

**Col 3:14 And over all these virtues put on love, which binds them all together in perfect unity.**

"Put on love" is the command from the Apostle Paul. When we are attacked in one way or another our tendency is to find a way to bring pain upon the attacker. Yes, they need to pay for what they have done but Jesus said it is the meek who inherit the earth. Again, Paul tells us not to repay evil with evil. When we take it upon ourselves to do the avenging we take things out of God's hands. It is only when we can be "meek" and "put on love" that GOD is free to correct the situation. His ways and thoughts are not the same as ours. **"For my thoughts are not your thoughts, neither are your ways my ways," declares the LORD. "As the heavens are higher than the earth, so are my ways higher than your ways and my thoughts than your thoughts".** (Is 55:8-9) God has the best eternal interest at heart, both for us and for our enemy. "I am sure that I am correct and that I know how to deal with this person", BUT my being sure plus $1.50 will only get me a Cappuccino. God does know best and HIS WAYS are designed to bring our enemies into a relationship with His Son, while OURS usually focus on vengeance. And, after all, I am most glad that it is GOD who has dealt with MY sin and not those whom I have sinned against.

## "In spirit and in truth"

**Rev 3:20 "Here I am! I stand at the door and knock. If anyone hears my voice and opens the door, I will come in and eat with him, and he with me."**

**John 4:23 "Yet a time is coming and has now come when the true worshipers will worship the Father in spirit and truth, for they are the kind of worshipers the Father seeks. 24 God is spirit, and his worshipers must worship in spirit and in truth."**

**Is 26:3 You will keep in perfect peace him whose mind is steadfast, because he trusts in you.**

Maybe you've had the following conversation, "Hey honey, there's somebody at the door" then one of you goes to see who it is. When someone comes knocking it's because they want to be in your presence and Jesus told John to let us know that HE KNOCKS AT OUR HEART'S DOOR. He desires to be a part of our lives and knocks gently never bulldozing in for He is a true gentleman. He only asks us for our worship in spirit and in truth, no dress code, no required meeting place, no formal agenda, just **"God is spirit, and his worshipers must worship in spirit and in truth."** WE are the ones who have set requirements in place. WE are the ones who expect certain language, appearance and the like. God through Isaiah gives His take on our rules and regulations **"These people come near to me with their mouth and honor me with their lips, but their hearts are far from me. Their worship of me is made up only of rules taught by men."** (Is 29:13) Did you hear that? True worship for the Lord Jesus Christ comes from the depths of the heart. Worship that conforms only to man-made rules is empty and a rebuff to God for He says, **"their hearts are far from me"**.

# OH NO, what do I serve!

**Luke 10:41** "Martha, Martha," the Lord answered, "you are worried and upset about many things, 42 but only one thing is needed. Mary has chosen what is better, and it will not be taken away from her."

**Mark 4:19** "but the worries of this life, the deceitfulness of wealth and the desires for other things come in and choke the word, making it unfruitful."

**Ps 27:4** One thing I ask of the LORD, this is what I seek: that I may dwell in the house of the LORD all the days of my life, to gaze upon the beauty of the LORD and to seek him in His temple.

**Gal 5:6** For in Christ Jesus neither circumcision nor uncircumcision has any value. The only thing that counts is faith expressing itself through love.

 Company is coming. Those three words strike terror into many a lady. "What will I cook? I have so much to do. The floor needs to be swept, pick up junk, put away stuff" and on and on. Yes, there are things to do when company is on the way but when those chores rob us of the enjoyment of the visit maybe we need to ask, just where should our priorities lie? Martha was all aflutter with preparing a special meal. I mean it's not every day that Jesus stops by the house. Okay Martha, He does deserve a good food, but if you put your all into a nice seven course meal and miss out on what He is teaching are you really gaining anything? Is He going to be impressed? Remember He's the one who fed five thousand with very little fish and bread and even had leftovers. Everyone had a fulfilling meal and did not miss one word of what He had to offer. Yes, there are times when a fancy meal may be in order, but that meal or any other should never deprive us of time with family and friends or loved ones and especially our Lord.

## Let Your Light Shine

**Luke 11:33-36 "No one lights a lamp and puts it in a place where it will be hidden, or under a bowl. Instead he puts it on its stand, so that those who come in may see the light. Your eye is the lamp of your body. When your eyes are good, your whole body also is full of light. But when they are bad, your body also is full of darkness. See to it, then, that the light within you is not darkness. Therefore, if your whole body is full of light, and no part of it dark, it will be completely lighted, as when the light of a lamp shines on you."**

**Matt 5:16 "In the same way, let your light shine before men, that they may see your good deeds and praise your Father in heaven."**

The way some Christians act you might get the impression that being a child of God is all about benefits and little if anything about responsibility. This idea in plain English is a lie from the pit of hell. When we accept Jesus' salvation we become indebted to Him and we are rescued from sin to honor and live for Him, **"What a wretched man I am! Who will rescue me from this body of death? Thanks be to God-through Jesus Christ our Lord! So then, I myself in my mind am a slave to God's law, but in the sinful nature a slave to the law of sin."** (Rom 7:24-25) Paul says he is a slave to God and we need to have the same mindset. This salvation is not for my personal enjoyment but it is for the glory of God and as such I must live accordingly. No longer do I want the preacher to tell me what a good person I am, but rather I want him to challenge me to grow in my relationship with Jesus. As a true Christian I am no longer satisfied with a life of ease, but rather my utmost desire is that HE be honored in all I do and say, NO MATTER WHAT. Above all I want to be a lamp on a lamp stand with the sole purpose of attracting others to this precious Savior.

*Just A Thought*

## "I LOVE YOU", OH really?

**Eph 5:22-29 Wives, submit to your husbands as to the Lord. For the husband is the head of the wife as Christ is the head of the church, his body, of which he is the Savior. Now as the church submits to Christ, so also wives should submit to their husbands in everything. Husbands, love your wives, just as Christ loved the church and gave himself up for her to make her holy, cleansing her by the washing with water through the word, and to present her to himself as a radiant church, without stain or wrinkle or any other blemish, but holy and blameless. In this same way, husbands ought to love their wives as their own bodies. He who loves his wife loves himself. .... This is a profound mystery but I am talking about Christ and the church. However, each one of you also must love his wife as he loves himself, and the wife must respect her husband.**

These three little words seem so easy to say some times, but are oh so hard to say at others. Many spouses do not hear "I love you" nearly often enough. Valentine's Day, admittedly the most romantic day of the year, and it's one of those days when the words flow so easily. We need to look, though, beyond the pitter-patter heart situation and consider what "I love you" really means. Men everywhere love to tell their mates that Paul says they are to submit to them and he makes it quite clear in the Ephesians passage above, **"Now as the church submits to Christ, so also wives should submit to their husbands in everything."** The catch is that the church can submit to Christ only because He earned the right to demand it by His redemptive work on the cross. Likewise the husband must earn the right to be the head of the household by giving himself for his wife and his family. Second only to the Lord, they must be the focus of all that he does. That doesn't mean merely in the financial arena, for many a financial success has failed the family. The truly happy, loved-filled marriage, now or in the future, is one where a man truly loves his wife and she truly respects her husband.

## Beautiful Feet

**Is 52:7 How beautiful on the mountains are the feet of those who bring good news,**

**who proclaim peace, who bring good tidings, who proclaim salvation, who say to Zion, "Your God reigns!"**

**Rom 10:15 And how can they preach unless they are sent? As it is written, "How beautiful are the feet of those who bring good news!"**

**Mark 16:15-16 He said to them, "Go into all the world and preach the good news to all creation. Whoever believes and is baptized will be saved, but whoever does not believe will be condemned."**

Suppose for a minute that you've fallen from a pier into the water. You're momentarily stunned, unable to get your bearings and it's hard to tell up from down. Just as you're about to lose your breath someone lifts you out of the water into the safety of a small boat. My guess is that you'd think that person is pretty special. This is only an illustration, but it puts forth the truth that every day souls slip out of this world into a Christless eternity. People say somebody ought to do something. The Bible says that **you** can have beautiful feet by sharing the good news of the gospel, AND in so doing be obedient to the directive of our Lord Jesus. **"Go (as you live your life) into all the world and preach the gospel."** This is not optional. We are saved to serve the living GOD and must be doing just that. If you think you would be grateful to the one who pulled you into the boat, can you imagine the impact you would make on someone you share the Good News with? Now they would know the joyful assurance of the presence of Jesus Christ in their life and they would assuredly see your feet as beautiful. My wish is to have beautiful feet and my prayer is that you desire the same.

## On The Cross

**Phil 2:5-8 Your attitude should be the same as that of Christ Jesus: Who, being in very nature God, did not consider equality with God something to be grasped, but made himself nothing, taking the very nature of a servant, being made in human likeness. And being found in appearance as a man, He humbled Himself and became obedient to death even death on a cross!**

**Matt 16:24-25 Then Jesus said to his disciples, "If anyone would come after me, he must deny himself and take up his cross and follow me. For whoever wants to save his life will lose it, but whoever loses his life for me will find it.**

I have my rights! How often have you heard or said just that? We all have a problem with "self" altogether too much of the time. Think for a couple of minutes about this. Jesus, the very Son of God, second member of the trinity, creator of all that is, (**Through him all things were made; without him nothing was made that has been made.** (John 1:3)), resident of heaven, King of kings, Lord of lords and much more, laid all that aside to become one of us. He humbled Himself as the Apostle Paul wrote even to death on a cross. The act of crucifixion was the cruelest form of punishment of the day, yet Jesus in submission was willing to give up His rights in order that He could pay for our sin. Paul calls to our attention, as does Jesus Himself, that we are to do the same. None of us merit in any way any type of special honor. If we lay claim to the love of Jesus we must (that's MUST) forget about special treatment of any sort and allow HIM to be our master in EVERYTHING. Pastor, deacon, elder, church dinner planner or janitor are all on the same level. In fact those in leadership are to be the GREATEST example of servanthood. Remember that just hours before Judas would betray our Lord and He would face that cross He knelt down and washed the feet of all the disciples including Judas, the betrayer. Now there is a true role model. When was the last time YOU were that humble before an enemy? Isn't it about time to be?

*Just A Thought*

# Only ONE?

**Luke 17:17-19 Jesus asked, "Were not all ten cleansed? Where are the other nine? Was no one found to return and give praise to God except this foreigner?" Then he said to him, "Rise and go; your faith has made you well."**

**Ps 106:13 But they soon forgot what he had done and did not wait for his counsel.**

**2 Chron 32:25 But Hezekiah's heart was proud and he did not respond to the kindness shown him; therefore the LORD's wrath was on him and on Judah and Jerusalem.**

More than likely we all have sent a gift to someone then waited for what seemed like forever to receive a thank you. Thoughts like "I wonder if they even got it", or "boy they must have really appreciated it" go through our minds. Maybe even, "How could they be so thoughtless? Don't they know the effort and love I put into that gift?" If Jesus' story of the ten lepers who were healed is any indicator, about ninety percent of us are guilty of not being thankful to God for His blessings in our lives. In the Luke passage only one was grateful enough to take the time to come back and worship the Lord. David in the Psalm above said, **"they soon forgot."** Hezekiah was proud and refused to respond to the kindness of the Lord, thus incurring the His wrath. The Apostle Paul writes, **"For although they knew God, they neither glorified him as God nor gave thanks to him, but their thinking became futile and their foolish hearts were darkened. Although they claimed to be wise, they became fools and exchanged the glory of the immortal God for images made to look like mortal man and birds and animals and reptiles."** (Rom 1:21-23) From these scriptures we learn that we all can be prone to hearts of foolishness and lack of gratefulness, forgetting the goodness of the Lord. In all probability wouldn't our being thankful and remembering God's blessings yield more peace and joy in our lives? YES it would.

## It Is God Who Judges

**Ps 43:1-5 Vindicate me, O God, and plead my cause against an ungodly nation; rescue me from deceitful and wicked men. You are God my stronghold. Why have you rejected me? Why must I go about mourning, oppressed by the enemy? Send forth your light and your truth, let them guide me; let them bring me to your holy mountain, to the place where you dwell. Then will I go to the altar of God, to God, my joy and my delight. I will praise you with the harp, O God, my God. Why are you downcast, O my soul? Why so disturbed within me? Put your hope in God, for I will yet praise him, my Savior and my God.**

**Ps 35:1 Contend, O LORD, with those who contend with me; fight against those who fight against me.**

**Ex 15:2 The LORD is my strength and my song; He has become my salvation. He is my God, and I will praise him, my father's God, and I will exalt him.**

How often we make the mistake of trying to manage our own problems? "I can do this" is our common response to everything from the attacks of Satan to everyday difficulties. The truth is, I CAN NOT handle these things myself. David was well aware of that fact and that is why he cried out more than once **"Vindicate me, O God"**. One reason for our need of GOD'S vindication is that He knows all the reasons behind what is going on and why I am feeling so put upon. I only see the surface of the situation, which is more than likely not the whole story. God also knows the very best way to accomplish His purposes. Even though I think I do, I don't really know how best to address the issue. As I yield to Him and allow Him to become my strength and shield, I will experience victory and vindication that far surpasses my understanding. It matters not the source of our problem, the answer is always the same "HE IS ABLE", we are not.

## Different Rules

**Eph 6:12 For our struggle is not against flesh and blood, but against the rulers, against the authorities, against the powers of this dark world and against the spiritual forces of evil in the heavenly realms.**

**Heb 12:1-3 Therefore, since we are surrounded by such a great cloud of witnesses, let us throw off everything that hinders and the sin that so easily entangles, and let us run with perseverance the race marked out for us. Let us fix our eyes on Jesus, the author and perfecter of our faith, who for the joy set before him endured the cross, scorning its shame, and sat down at the right hand of the throne of God. Consider him who endured such opposition from sinful men, so that you will not grow weary and lose heart.**

In the wars America has endured there have been many heroes, men and women who have accomplished the seemingly impossible and they deserve our thanks and notice. One big difference, though, between these wars and our warfare as Christians is that they fought a visible enemy where we fight invisible powers that if seen would frighten us mere humans. For this reason, the rules of engagement are different. The Apostle Paul tells us to submit to Christ, **"Therefore, I urge you, brothers, in view of God's mercy, to offer your bodies as living sacrifices, holy and pleasing to God this is your spiritual act of worship. Do not conform any longer to the pattern of this world, but be transformed by the renewing of your mind. Then you will be able to test and approve what God's will is His good, pleasing and perfect will.** (Rom 12:1-2)The world would tell us to fight our own battles, but though it may sound simplistic, "letting go and letting God" is the only way we can know victory. Submission to Christ, allowing and using His power is the rule to be obeyed. He defeated the enemy already at the cross and we are true heroes when we accept His victory.

## Press On

**Phil 3:14 I press on toward the goal to win the prize for which God has called me heavenward in Christ Jesus.**

**2 Cor 4:17 For our light and momentary troubles are achieving for us an eternal glory that far outweighs them all. 18 So we fix our eyes not on what is seen, but on what is unseen. For what is seen is temporary, but what is unseen is eternal.**

**1 Thess 2:12 encouraging, comforting and urging you to live lives worthy of God, who calls you into his kingdom and glory.**

Imagine if you will the reaction of the fans and the media if a runner in a mile event suddenly sits down on the side of the track for a rest. Maybe it's a football game and there has just been an interception; the carrier has a clear opportunity to make it safely into the end zone but he stops to look up into the bleachers and say hello to a friend. The Bible likens life to a race; we sometimes call it a rat race. The Christian life, though, is a race climaxing with the amazing reward of living with God in His heaven, yet too many of us are like the athletes above, taking side trips, not keeping our eyes on the goal. A true football fan might even suggest that the player above be kicked off the team. WE have to always run the Christian race with the goal in our sights. That goal must be to honor our Savior and to look forward to seeing Him with the joyful anticipation of hearing Him say "Well done". (Luke 19:17) All of this so that we like the Apostle Paul may be able to say, **"I have fought the good fight, I have finished the race, I have kept the faith. Now there is in store for me the crown of righteousness, which the Lord, the righteous Judge, will award to me on that day-and not only to me, but also to all who have longed for his appearing."** (2 Tim 4:7-8)

## "All in All"

**Col 3:11** Here there is no Greek or Jew, circumcised or uncircumcised, barbarian, Scythian, slave or free, but Christ is all, and is in all.

**Gal 3:29** If you belong to Christ, then you are Abraham's seed, and heirs according to the promise.

**Gal 6:14** May I never boast except in the cross of our Lord Jesus Christ, through which the world has been crucified to me, and I to the world.

**Gal 2:20** I have been crucified with Christ and I no longer live, but Christ lives in me. The life I live in the body, I live by faith in the Son of God, who loved me and gave himself for me.

A. B. Simpson penned the words to the hymn, "Himself", in which he describes various reasons people come to Christ. Carefully read these words. *"Once it was the blessing, now it is the Lord; Once it was the feeling, now it is His Word; Once His gift I wanted, now the Giver own; Once I sought for healing, now Himself alone. Once 'twas painful trying, now 'tis perfect trust; Once a half salvation, now the uttermost! Once 'twas ceaseless holding, now He holds me fast; Once 'twas constant drifting, now my anchor's cast. All in all forever, Jesus will I sing, Everything in Jesus, and Jesus everything."* In Christ there is no race, creed, color, nor denomination. In Christ HE is everything. If I am in Him I will not be locked into the definitions the world places on mankind, for as Jesus becomes my "all in all", I will begin to think like Him. WE tend to look at life based on day-to-day needs and wants, but HE looks on the heart. Oh that we would see everything through HIS eyes.

## Worship and Wholeness

**Heb 10:25 Let us not give up meeting together, as some are in the habit of doing, but let us encourage one another-and all the more as you see the Day approaching.**

**Matt 18:19-20 "Again, I tell you that if two of you on earth agree about anything you ask for, it will be done for you by my Father in heaven. For where two or three come together in my name, there am I with them."**

**Acts 2:42 They devoted themselves to the apostles' teaching and to the fellowship, to the breaking of bread and to prayer.**

**1 Cor 5:4 When you are assembled in the name of our Lord Jesus and I am with you in spirit, and the power of our Lord Jesus is present,**

Some people would dare to proclaim, "I don't need anybody. I can take care of my own life." This is simply not true for we all need others with whom to share our lives. In the famous passage from "For Whom The Bell Tolls" by John Donne, there's a powerful statement "...No man is an island, entire of itself; every man is a piece of the continent, a part of the main." Paul puts it another way, "**The body is a unit, though it is made up of many parts; and though all its parts are many, they form one body. So it is with Christ. For we were all baptized by one Spirit into one body-whether Jews or Greeks, slave or free-and we were all given the one Spirit to drink.**" (1 Cor 12:12-13) The truth that arises out of all this is that when we fail to come together for worship we are cheating three entities. OURSELVES, for we deprive ourselves of the support and the privilege of being a part of the rest of the body. OTHERS, for we deprive others of the honor of supporting us and being part of a complete body. And most importantly, we dishonor JESUS CHRIST for He is the One who gave everything for the body that it might be whole. After all, HE is the bridegroom and HE is the reason we come together anyway.

## Look ahead, never back

**Luke 9:62 Jesus replied, "No one who puts his hand to the plow and looks back is fit for service in the kingdom of God."**

**Ps 78:8 They would not be like their forefathers a stubborn and rebellious generation, whose hearts were not loyal to God, whose spirits were not faithful to him.**

**Heb 10:37 For in just a very little while, "He who is coming will come and will not delay.**

**38 But my righteous one will live by faith. And if he shrinks back, I will not be pleased with him."**

From experience I can attest that once you start across a field with a plow it is absolutely necessary to keep looking ahead. If not, the furrow will most likely be crooked and may even uproot something that's supposed to be there. How often have you taken your eyes off the road for only a second and found yourself on the berm or headed to the other lane? In the same way, when we give our lives to Jesus Christ we need to keep focused on Him. If we allow family, friends, old habits and the like to distract us we will not be productive for the Lord and we may even rob ourselves of the joy of His provision and presence in our lives. Think about this, you hire a carpenter to do some remodeling in your home. He comes for a couple of days and then calls every day for a few weeks to say he has more pressing things to attend to. Your living room is in shambles and he's concerned with everything but his obligation to you. Likewise God sent His one and only Son to suffer, die and rise again for the redemption of man. If a person comes to Him and proclaims, "I want this salvation", then remains involved, maybe even more so, with the former sinful life than with this great God, why should God bless them?

# Purpose in your Heart

**Dan 1:8 But Daniel resolved not to defile himself with the royal food and wine, and he asked the chief official for permission not to defile himself this way.**

**Ruth 1:17-18 Where you die I will die, and there I will be buried. May the LORD deal with me, be it ever so severely, if anything but death separates you and me." 18 When Naomi realized that Ruth was determined to go with her, she stopped urging her.**

**Acts 11:23 When he arrived and saw the evidence of the grace of God, he was glad and encouraged them all to remain true to the Lord with all their hearts.**

Daniel was totally unaware of how he would impact people over centuries right on to our day, but the fact is when he set his heart to be obedient to God he laid down an undeniable challenge to all of us. Will YOU and I be loyal to this God who sacrificed His very life on our behalf? Jesus gave His all to pay a bill we could never pay and we can do no less than return that love by living TOTALLY for Him. We so often moan and groan about our problems and struggle needlessly because we don't, or don't want to, realize that in our attempt to control life ourselves we are rejecting God's help. The Israelites were told in Haggai, **Therefore, because of you the heavens have withheld their dew and the earth its crops. I called for a drought on the fields and the mountains, on the grain, the new wine, the oil and whatever the ground produces, on men and cattle, and on the labor of your hands."** (Hag 1:10-11) But some say, "I don't know what God wants of me" and that sounds like a valid question on the surface, but how much effort have WE put forth into knowing Him and His ways? Do you spend (make that INVEST) time seeking to know more? God's Word is filled with all the wisdom, directions and examples we need and all we have to do is study it. Imagine one day looking Jesus in the eye and having to tell Him that you just didn't have the time to give Him; you had too many other things going on. If- WE PURPOSE (resolve, make up our minds) that we are going to make HIM our priority in EVERYTHING, we will have His peace and all that HE HAS PURPOSED FOR US.

## Do not be deceived

**1 John 1:8 If we claim to be without sin, we deceive ourselves and the truth is not in us.**

**Eccl 7:20 There is not a righteous man on earth who does what is right and never sins.**

**James 3:2 We all stumble in many ways. If anyone is never at fault in what he says, he is a perfect man, able to keep his whole body in check.**

**1 John 1:10 If we claim we have not sinned, we make him out to be a liar and his word has no place in our lives.**

There's a tendency in the church to be smug and self-righteous. We're proud of the fact that we're not guilty of murder, adultery, covetousness or any of the several "serious" things we call sin. Furthermore, as Christians we have subtle ways of covering OUR sin. For example, we gossip under the guise if a "prayer request" and then you know we can't pray without all the "facts", or at least the facts as WE see them. It never enters our minds that only God knows the real circumstances and all too often our judgment of others is under the false face of "concern" for their situation. "Why doesn't he just get a job or go to a better doctor, etc.; if they just had MY 'word of wisdom' they'd be able to defeat the struggle in their life." Yet we overeat and say, "I just can't help myself" and probably we'd reject another's "word of wisdom" for ourselves. More serious than that, don't ask us to move out of our comfort zone. We fail to love lost souls, even though we profess to, and think people need to clean up, put on the correct clothing and a good appearance, and then come to church." After all, it's just plain not honoring to God if one is not dressed properly etc. Besides that, there are those who just don't smell good." In those and many other ways we who profess Christ sin and in fact need to own those sins and apply, **"If we confess our sins, He is faithful and just and will forgive us our sins and purify us from all unrighteousness." (1 John 1:9)**

## What Guilt?

**1 Thess 5:23 May God himself, the God of peace, sanctify you through and through. May your whole spirit, soul and body be kept blameless at the coming of our Lord Jesus Christ.**

**Phil 1:6 being confident of this, that he who began a good work in you will carry it on to completion until the day of Christ Jesus.**

**1 Cor 1:8-9 He will keep you strong to the end, so that you will be blameless on the day of our Lord Jesus Christ. God, who has called you into fellowship with his Son Jesus Christ our Lord, is faithful.**

**Jude 24 To him who is able to keep you from falling and to present you before his glorious presence without fault and with great joy**

The songwriters (Noland & Fergurson) penned the words, "**He is able, more than able to do much more than I could ever dream, He is able, more than able, to make me what He wants me to be.**" Oh how true and He is able more than able to keep me pure and blameless before the Father. What does it mean though to be blameless? According to the dictionary there are several synonyms, which make it appear that to be blameless would mean there is no guilt, no fault, no culpability, and no onus or load to be borne. How can that be when I have sinned, I have broken God's rules and I have hurt others? Yes, there is guilt, fault, culpability and a load to bear, BUT Jesus took all of that with Him on that cruel cross. Many times we see the cross portrayed as a thing of beauty entwined with lilies but in reality it was anything but beautiful. It was an ugly, cruel means of a torturous death. The only beauty was and is in the fact that He took my blame, my sin and set me free. So when Satan points His ugly finger at me and says, "It is all your fault" I can point to the Cross and say "Yes, but HE paid it all".

## HUMBLE??

**Luke 14:11 "For everyone who exalts himself will be humbled, and he who humbles himself will be exalted."**

**Ps 18:27 You save the humble but bring low those whose eyes are haughty.**

**Prov 18:12 Before his downfall a man's heart is proud, but humility comes before honor.**

**Luke 18:14b "For everyone who exalts himself will be humbled, and he who humbles himself will be exalted."**

In our world today we glorify superstars who are paid unbelievable millions for their talent and crowd pleasing ability. Even Christians fall into this trap of standing in awe of athletes, actors, musicians etc. with their superegos and find it hard to put into practice the command of our Lord to be humble. But, we all need to understand that human nature and human ego are totally in opposition to God. James explains it this way, **"Listen, my dear brothers: Has not God chosen those who are poor in the eyes of the world to be rich in faith and to inherit the kingdom he promised those who love him? But you have insulted the poor. Is it not the rich who are exploiting you? Are they not the ones who are dragging you into court? Are they not the ones who are slandering the noble name of him to whom you belong?** (James 2:5-7) Unfortunately the egotistical rich sometimes take advantage of those with less. A few years ago the Supreme Court decided that private lands could be seized for the private investment of the wealthy. This decision is what James was talking about. Oh, praise the Lord that there are those whom God has blessed with wealth who are very humble and dedicated to Christ, but such is not the human tendency. God has chosen the poor and humble to inherit His Kingdom. Above all we are to obey our God and take the humble road, a road we will never know we are traveling, but God and others will.

## The Gates of Hell Shall Not Prevail

**Matt 16:16-18 Simon Peter answered, "You are the Christ, the Son of the living God." Jesus replied, "Blessed are you, Simon son of Jonah, for this was not revealed to you by man, but by my Father in heaven. And I tell you that you are Peter, and on this rock I will build my church, and the gates of Hades will not overcome it."**

**1 John 4:4 You, dear children, are from God and have overcome them, because the one who is in you is greater than the one who is in the world.**

With one quick glimpse at the evening news you can tell that Satan is going full speed ahead in His attempts to harm and destroy all that God created and loves. And as if that isn't bad enough, the Church seems to be too weak and splintered to take a solid stand for what is right and righteous. Some fight to approve those living in sin to be qualified as ministers of the Gospel. (YES, Jesus loves the sinner, but no unredeemed sinner can be an emissary of Him.) Political correctness, which usually leads to the denial of Jesus Christ, is the rule. **"Whoever acknowledges me before men, I will also acknowledge him before my Father in heaven. But whoever disowns me before men, I will disown him before my Father in heaven."** (Matt 10:32-33) He is Lord, He is "the way, the truth and the life", and strict adherence to that truth and to His example of how to live in a sin sick world is all that can be seriously considered. Hell can unleash its total fury on the Church, but it can never destroy it. Jesus Christ won that battle, the war and everything else when He walked out of the tomb. So why does the Church act so weak? The truth is that fear of the world and the enemy causes many to succumb. Remember what Timothy said, **"For God did not give us a spirit of timidity, but a spirit of power, of love and of self-discipline."** (2 Tim 1:7)

## There is no fear in true fear!

**Ps 34:9-10 Fear the LORD, you his saints, for those who fear him lack nothing. The lions may grow weak and hungry, but those who seek the LORD lack no good thing.**

**Ps 89:7-8 In the council of the holy ones God is greatly feared; He is more awesome than all who surround him. O LORD God Almighty, who is like you? You are mighty, O LORD, and your faithfulness surrounds you.**

**Rev 15:3-4 and sang the song of Moses the servant of God and the song of the Lamb: "Great and marvelous are your deeds, Lord God Almighty. Just and true are your ways, King of the ages. Who will not fear you, O Lord, and bring glory to your name? For you alone are holy. All nations will come and worship before you, for your righteous acts have been revealed."**

"Great and mighty is the Lord our God; great and mighty is He." To Fear the Lord is an awesome thing and the source of all peace, grace and assurance. Fearing God means to have a reverent awe or a profound reverence, especially toward God. **"There is no fear in love. But perfect love drives out fear, because fear has to do with punishment. The one who fears is not made perfect in love."** (1 John 4:18) Loving the Lord in perfection removes fear of Him from our lives. If we truly love Him we are assured of His eternal love, mercy and grace. It is the one who does not love and revere this King of kings that needs to fear. When His perfect love casts out fear we are one with God the Father, joint heirs with Christ His Son and as such know His consistent presence and joy. I recently heard a lady say in reference to her children, "I don't understand how they can hear the truth and stay in their sinful ways". Good question, yet statistics tell us that a high percentage of "Christians" remain unchanged, maybe never truly saved to begin with. I plead with you that if you do not have that assurance of Him and His presence, seek it now and live in the joy He offers.

## Is it faith if the love is not there?

**James 2:14-17** What good is it, my brothers, if a man claims to have faith but has no deeds? Can such faith save him? Suppose a brother or sister is without clothes and daily food. If one of you says to him, "Go, I wish you well; keep warm and well fed," but does nothing about his physical needs, what good is it? In the same way, faith by itself, if it is not accompanied by action, is dead.

**1 Cor 13:3** If I give all I possess to the poor and surrender my body to the flames, but have not love, I gain nothing.

**James 2:26** As the body without the spirit is dead, so faith without deeds is dead.

**Philemon 1:6** I pray that you may be active in sharing your faith, so that you will have a full understanding of every good thing we have in Christ.

It is one thing to CLAIM to be a Christian and quite another to BE one. Many people think that just because they live in the USA (a Christian nation??) they are Christians. Others believe that church attendance and various other good things will save them. The Bible makes it very clear that if we claim to be a Christian there are certain things that will be evident in our lives such as a life change, being kind and loving and a desire to share the Gospel with the lost, to name just a couple. In short we will no longer be satisfied with just going to church and acting the part. Now we will want more of Jesus and care not the cost. Friends may go away and some people may call us fanatics, but a closer walk with our friend, Jesus Christ, is all that matters. A true Christian puts his/her all into this relationship and wants only to know Him better and be what He wants them to be.

## I am NOT my own

**1 Cor 6:19-20 Do you not know that your body is a temple of the Holy Spirit, who is in you, whom you have received from God? You are not your own; you were bought at a price. Therefore honor God with your body.**

**2 Cor 6:16 What agreement is there between the temple of God and idols? For we are the temple of the living God. As God has said: "I will live with them and walk among them, and I will be their God, and they will be my people."**

**Titus 2:14 who gave himself for us to redeem us from all wickedness and to purify for himself a people that are his very own, eager to do what is good.**

If I go and buy a tool for my shop, that tool becomes mine and I can use it however or whenever I want. Whatever its purpose, I can put it to use. Sometimes I utilize a tool for something other than what it was designed for, with good or not so good results. Some of us have even been known to talk to our tools making statements like "I own you and you will do what I want you to". While that remark is a little inane it does portray a truth we need to know. We spend a few dollars and expect the best performance possible and even more. Jesus paid a very high price for our redemption and He asks for and deserves our total commitment and service to Him. How can we give HIM less than our ALL when He gave His very life? Jesus said, **"By their fruit you will recognize them. Do people pick grapes from thornbushes, or figs from thistles?"** (Matt 7:16) This would seem to be saying that if we are not living to please Christ nor bearing His good fruit in our lives, **"Each one should use whatever gift he has received to serve others, faithfully administering God's grace in its various forms."** 1 Peter 4:10), we might not even belong to Him ourselves. Woodrow Wilson once said, *"The princes among us are those who forget themselves and serve mankind.* (Now that's Christianity!) How about you and me?

## Free to what?

**1 Cor 8:9 Be careful, however, that the exercise of your freedom does not become a stumbling block to the weak.**

**Matt 18:6 "But if anyone causes one of these little ones who believe in me to sin, it would be better for him to have a large millstone hung around his neck and to be drowned in the depths of the sea."**

**Rom 14:20-21 Do not destroy the work of God for the sake of food. All food is clean, but it is wrong for a man to eat anything that causes someone else to stumble. It is better not to eat meat or drink wine or to do anything else that will cause your brother to fall.**

**1 Cor 10:24 Nobody should seek his own good, but the good of others.**

In past thoughts we have talked about being free, remember, **"So if the Son sets you free, you will be free indeed."** (John 8:36) We must be very careful, though, that we do not use that freedom for the wrong ends. Our freedom is real and for our benefit in Christ to His glory, but it is never to be used for selfish purposes. Truly being free from bondage to sin is to be in bondage to the King of kings. He never has anything but our best interest at heart and He wants for us what will bring Him glory and what will bring us true and lasting joy. Part of that joy comes from witnessing to and seeking the well being of others. True freedom means I want my brother and sister to be able to enjoy what I do. That cannot happen if I am not careful to show them the real love of Christ. If I know my brother struggles with something, I will not flaunt my freedom in his face and thus cause him to fall. Freedom must be self-propagating and that can only be if I do not misuse mine.

## Who put the "GOOD" in Good Friday?

**John 19:28-30 Later, knowing that all was now completed, and so that the Scripture would be fulfilled, Jesus said, "I am thirsty." A jar of wine vinegar was there, so they soaked a sponge in it, put the sponge on a stalk of the hyssop plant, and lifted it to Jesus' lips. When he had received the drink, Jesus said, "It is finished." With that, he bowed his head and gave up his spirit.**

**Is 53:10 Yet it was the LORD's will to crush him and cause him to suffer, and though the LORD makes his life a guilt offering, he will see his offspring and prolong his days, and the will of the LORD will prosper in his hand.**

There used to be an ad that went like this "Who put the OOOH in Oreo?" Of course they were talking about Oreo cookies, good eating! The question today is," Who put the good in Good Friday?" and the answer is, Jesus of course. But this Friday almost 2000 years ago was anything but good. Jesus was falsely accused and executed for crimes He did not commit and as that day drew to a close He simply stated the truth that made that Friday good by saying, "It is finished." When walking the paths of this life as a man, Jesus had made it clear that He had one purpose in life, **"My food," said Jesus, "is to do the will of him who sent me and to finish his work."** (John 4:34) ("My food", or what fulfills me, is to do the will of the Father who sent me here by becoming the atonement for sin.) As death drew near and His goal in sight, He knew that He had indeed finished the work at hand. In so doing He made that Friday truly a "Good Friday" for now we as redeemed sinners are related to the Father through His Son. Many years later Paul writes that we are to get rid of the old yeast, our selfish religious garbage, and put on the truth of Jesus. **Get rid of the old yeast that you may be a new batch without yeast-as you really are. For Christ, our Passover lamb, has been sacrificed.** (1 Cor 5:7) He was our Passover Lamb and He made Good Friday good, now go and live like He lived.

## Where are the other nine?

**Luke 17:17-19 Jesus asked, "Were not all ten cleansed? Where are the other nine? Was no one found to return and give praise to God except this foreigner?" Then he said to him, "Rise and go; your faith has made you well."**

**Ps 106:13 But they soon forgot what he had done and did not wait for his counsel.**

**Rom 1:21 For although they knew God, they neither glorified him as God nor gave thanks to him, but their thinking became futile and their foolish hearts were darkened.**

**John 5:23 "that all may honor the Son just as they honor the Father. He who does not honor the Son does not honor the Father, who sent him."**

As Jesus was walking down the road that day ten lepers approached Him and boldly asked to be healed. He took compassion on them and they were made whole. As they left to go and present themselves to the priest, I am sure that all ten looked at their bodies and knew they were now well; but only one, and he a Samaritan, returned to thank the Lord. Percentages do not always have great meaning, however this case would indicate that ninety percent of those who experience God's restoration are so absorbed in themselves they do not even have time to thank the One who restored them. What a shame it is if we are willing to accept His help and salvation, but are only interested in our own gains. It seems that for nine of the ten lepers it was more important to get on with their lives than to give glory to their Healer. How very much happens in our own day to day lives for which we never say "Thank You"! More than we know, I bet.

## Oh that You would bless me

**1 Chron 4:10 Jabez cried out to the God of Israel, "Oh, that you would bless me and enlarge my territory! Let your hand be with me, and keep me from harm so that I will be free from pain." And God granted his request.**

**Gen 32:26 Then the man said, "Let me go, for it is daybreak." But Jacob replied, "I will not let you go unless you bless me."**

**Eph 1:3 Praise be to the God and Father of our Lord Jesus Christ, who has blessed us in the heavenly realms with every spiritual blessing in Christ.**

**Matt 6:13 "And lead us not into temptation, but deliver us from the evil one."**

All of us surely want God's blessing on our lives, but according to James chapter 1 the reason we don't see that blessing more often is that we ask with all the wrong motives. In Jabez' prayer he seems to be seeking freedom from two kinds of PAIN, which is the meaning of his name given him by his mother. The first is that he be kept from harm; when others sin against us we are hurt. And secondly, he desired to be free from pain that results when he hurts others, both their pain and his, because when we sin against God or another person they are hurt and so are we. Both kinds of pain in his request are real and to be free from only one would still leave the other. He also wanted God to enlarge his borders and as His servant he desired to bring honor to Him. Like Jacob he was desperate for such a blessing. It is my conviction that both men knew the importance of **"Let your hand be with me"** and without God's hand on us we will surely know pain. Oh what blessing awaits the one who seeks GOD'S blessing and is focused on HIS honor and glory. When our desire for enlarged borders is for the purpose of drawing others to Christ, we will know the greatest blessing of God.

# Imagine ……

**Rev 1:17-18** When I saw him, I fell at his feet as though dead. Then he placed his right hand on me and said: "Do not be afraid. I am the First and the Last. I am the Living One; I was dead, and behold I am alive for ever and ever! And I hold the keys of death and Hades."

**Dan 10:15-17** While he was saying this to me, I bowed with my face toward the ground and was speechless. Then one who looked like a man touched my lips, and I opened my mouth and began to speak. I said to the one standing before me, "I am overcome with anguish because of the vision, my lord, and I am helpless. How can I, your servant, talk with you, my lord? My strength is gone and I can hardly breathe."

**Dan 8:18** While he was speaking to me, I was in a deep sleep, with my face to the ground. Then he touched me and raised me to my feet.

"Well, I'll tell you one thing, when I get to heaven I'm going to ask the Lord about…" Many of us have made that statement. There are things in life we don't understand, myself included, about which we'd like to know the whys and wherefores when we see Him face to face. The popular song goes like this – "Surrounded by Your Glory, what will my heart feel? Will I dance for you, Jesus? Or in awe of You, be still? Will I stand in Your presence, or to my knees will I fall? Will I sing 'Hallelujah!'? Will I be able to speak at all? I can only imagine! Yeah! I can only imagine!" One thing is for sure; it will be an awesome experience to be before the One who so loved me. He will owe me no explanation for how my life went and whether I fall to my knees or on my face, it will be less than I owe Him when I think of the ultimate price He paid.

## There is no way I can...

**Phil 4:13 I can do everything through him who gives me strength.**

**John 15:4-5 "Remain in me, and I will remain in you. No branch can bear fruit by itself; it must remain in the vine. Neither can you bear fruit unless you remain in me. "I am the vine; you are the branches. If a man remains in me and I in him, he will bear much fruit; apart from me you can do nothing."**

**Is 41:10 So do not fear, for I am with you; do not be dismayed, for I am your God. I will strengthen you and help you; I will uphold you with my righteous right hand.**

**2 Cor 12:9 But he said to me, "My grace is sufficient for you, for my power is made perfect in weakness." Therefore I will boast all the more gladly about my weaknesses, so that Christ's power may rest on me.**

I do not know how I would function without my computer. Many hours are spent here studying, writing and of course playing. (Free Cell or Scrabble) There, my secret is out. But, I have to admit that when I try to do some things I draw a blank and then it's time to call a pro to get me back on track. I mostly just stumble along and I'm sure it would be quicker and less trying if I would get some training. Many of us stumble through our Christian life, barely eking by, never quite sure how to take the next step. The Apostle Paul said, "I can do all things" and what he meant was that he was enabled by the Holy Spirit to live his life pleasing to his God. We have the same assurance that we can also live pleasing to God, BUT, there are requirements. We must "abide" in Jesus. To do this we must intimately know Him. We must also be so yielded to Him that we become obedient to all He asks of us. THEN we can rely totally on His "grace that is sufficient". Do you desire enough to do what it takes to "**do everything through Him who gives me strength**"?

## No Cakewalk

**1 Cor 9:24-27** Do you not know that in a race all the runners run, but only one gets the prize? Run in such a way as to get the prize. Everyone who competes in the games goes into strict training. They do it to get a crown that will not last; but we do it to get a crown that will last forever. Therefore I do not run like a man running aimlessly; I do not fight like a man beating the air. No, I beat my body and make it my slave so that after I have preached to others, I myself will not be disqualified for the prize.

**Luke 13:24** "Make every effort to enter through the narrow door, because many, I tell you, will try to enter and will not be able to"

**Eph 6:12** For our struggle is not against flesh and blood, but against the rulers, against the authorities, against the powers of this dark world and against the spiritual forces of evil in the heavenly realms.

**2 Cor 5:9** So we make it our goal to please him, whether we are at home in the body or away from it.

Many a hunter has entered the woods in pursuit of that trophy whitetail. Some even climb a mountain they've never seen before in search of "the one", but it is usually the hunter who has done their homework that bags the elusive big rack. Sometimes a marriage falls apart and one or both spouses are unaware that it's because they have never invested much of anything into that marriage, (unfortunately many put more into the wedding than they do the marriage.) It is the athlete who hones his skills of the game by arduously repeating them that becomes the next super star. Like all of the above, the same holds true in our walk with the Lord Jesus. As with the hunter, the truly successful married couple or the star athlete, it is the Christian who puts forth EFFORT into their spiritual life that will become the mature, joy-filled, peaceful and even happy person.

It is not a cakewalk, but it is worth the effort and after all, in light of His sacrifice for us, HE deserves no less.

## For Our Sins

**Is 53:4-5 Surely He took up our infirmities and carried our sorrows, yet we considered Him stricken by God, smitten by him, and afflicted. But He was pierced for our transgressions, He was crushed for our iniquities; the punishment that brought us peace was upon Him, and by His wounds we are healed.**

**Gal 3:13 Christ redeemed us from the curse of the law by becoming a curse for us, for it is written: "Cursed is everyone who is hung on a tree."**

**Heb 9:28 so Christ was sacrificed once to take away the sins of many people; and he will appear a second time, not to bear sin, but to bring salvation to those who are waiting for him.**

**1 Peter 2:24 He himself bore our sins in his body on the tree, so that we might die to sins and live for righteousness; by his wounds you have been healed.**

When Jesus endured that horrible sham of a trial. When He carried that cross down the Via Delarosa and up to Golgotha. When He let the Roman soldiers drive those nails through His hands and feet. When the onlookers mocked and jeered. When they taunted, "If you are the Christ, come down from that cross." It was His determination to do the will of the Father. He was committed to paying the price of my sin and yours. His great love for us overcame any mocker's taunts, even though he possessed the means to leave that whole scene. Remember His words, **"Do you think I cannot call on my Father, and he will at once put at my disposal more than twelve legions of angels?"** (Matthew 26:53) BUT, His love and concern for my eternal destiny and yours kept Him on that cruel cross. Someone asked "how can I say thank you for all He has done?" I can say thanks by giving Him my very being to live for and serve Him. It is that simple. When He was on that cross I WAS on His mind. Lord, may my mind be totally on YOU.

## True Greatness

**John 12:26 Whoever serves me must follow me; and where I am, my servant also will be. My Father will honor the one who serves me.**

**Luke 6:46 "Why do you call me, 'Lord, Lord,' and do not do what I say?"**

**Rom 14:17-18 For the kingdom of God is not a matter of eating and drinking, but of righteousness, peace and joy in the Holy Spirit, because anyone who serves Christ in this way is pleasing to God and approved by men.**

**1 John 5:3 This is love for God: to obey his commands. And his commands are not burdensome,**

Human beings seem to be enamored with greatness. In present history men like Bill Gates, Donald Trump, superstar athletes and movie stars, etc. all command great attention and admiration. Even Christians seem to fall into this vile trap. It is a pure delusion of Satan. A.W. Tozer has the following to say about this dangerous evil. *"If the church were a body wholly unaffected by the world we could toss the above problem over to the secular philosophers; but the truth is that the church also suffers from this evil notion! Christians have fallen into the habit of accepting the noisiest and most notorious among them as the best and the greatest. They too have learned to equate popularity with excellence. In open defiance of the Sermon on the Mount, they have given their approval not to the meek but to the self-assertive; not to the mourner but to the self-assured; not to the pure in heart who see God but to the publicity hunter who seeks headlines!"* True greatness comes from service to God not from public acclaim. In God's eyes it is the person who unselfishly yields to Him their very being that is the great one. The one who would wash the feet of an enemy, even as Jesus washed Judas' feet, is greater than any public figure that is constantly drawing attention to themselves. Oh that we would BELIEVE and LIVE OUT what the word teaches.

## "More Than Me?"

**Luke 14:26 "If anyone comes to me and does not hate his father and mother, his wife and children, his brothers and sisters-yes, even his own life-he cannot be my disciple."**

**Matt 10:37 "Anyone who loves his father or mother more than me is not worthy of me; anyone who loves his son or daughter more than me is not worthy of me;"**

**Phil 3:8 What is more, I consider everything a loss compared to the surpassing greatness of knowing Christ Jesus my Lord, for whose sake I have lost all things. I consider them rubbish, that I may gain Christ**

Many things compete for our attention and affections. Allurements come in all shapes and sizes. For a child it may be that special toy (usually the one someone else has), or for an adult it may well be that promotion, degree, raise, spouse, etc. The draw of the goal becomes all consuming and other things are neglected as our focus becomes more and more intense. Sad to say, our ambitions may come before God. Sometimes even family members or friends will encourage us to become obsessed with what interests us most. Moses addressed this issue in, **If your very own brother, or your son or daughter, or the wife you love, or your closest friend secretly entices you, saying, "Let us go and worship other gods" (gods that neither you nor your fathers have known, gods of the peoples around you, whether near or far, from one end of the land to the other), do not yield to him or listen to him. Show him no pity. Do not spare him or shield him.** (Deut 13:6-8) That is awfully good advice. If anything or anyone tries in any way to draw us away from our Lord we need to end it right then and there. Jesus has to be the entire focus of our lives. Remember He is the one who said, **"But seek first his kingdom and his righteousness, and all these things will be given to you as well."** (Matt 6:33)

## THIRSTY?

**Ps 42:2 My soul thirsts for God, for the living God. When can I go and meet with God?**

**Ps 63:1 O God, you are my God, earnestly I seek you; my soul thirsts for you, my body longs for you, in a dry and weary land where there is no water.**

**John 7:37-28 On the last and greatest day of the Feast, Jesus stood and said in a loud voice, "If anyone is thirsty, let him come to me and drink. Whoever believes in me, as the Scripture has said, streams of living water will flow from within him."**

When we're thirsty we seek something to drink. Out on the road we may have coffee, a soda or bottled water. Thirst causes our mouth to dry out somewhat; it creates an overall feeling of the need for liquid and on a hot summer day we need to drink even though we may not feel thirsty. If our body gets too short for moisture serious health problems can occur. Someone shared with me a few days ago about a loved one who was experiencing some of the symptoms of dehydration and this person wound up in the hospital with an IV to replace lost fluid. Our spiritual lives suffer in the same way when we do not "thirst" for the Word of God. Jesus promised — **Matt 5:6 "Blessed are those who hunger and thirst for righteousness, for they will be filled."** If we don't have a genuine thirst that's met in God our SOUL will dehydrate. That real thirst will not be satisfied with a brief reading of a few verses and a short wish list prayer. Earnest thirst seeks intimacy with our Lord. It seeks to know Him and allows Him TIME to speak to us and respond to our prayers. Prayer is supposed to be a conversation with God and thirst for Him will allow Him to bless us with a sense of His presence. Are you genuinely thirsty?

## "Where your treasure is"

**2 Cor 4:18 So we fix our eyes not on what is seen, but on what is unseen. For what is seen is temporary, but what is unseen is eternal.**

**Matt 6:21 "For where your treasure is, there your heart will be also."**

**Phil 3:14 I press on toward the goal to win the prize for which God has called me heavenward in Christ Jesus.**

No one likes to talk about the brevity of life. We praise the medical industry when they find a cure for some disease or a better surgical procedure and we take special vitamin concoctions and supplements all in an effort to live longer, but the truth of the matter is that life is short and death will come. In fact the Bible makes this fact clear, **"The length of our days is seventy years or eighty, if we have the strength; yet their span is but trouble and sorrow, for they quickly pass, and we fly away." (Ps 90:10)** In our day the average life expectancy is a little over eighty and even if we live to be more than one hundred it still is only a speck in time. Death is immanent but for the Christian this is not bad news because we will at that point be united with our precious Jesus. The only question we need to consider is this, "Did I use my time effectively for HIM?" Matthew recorded Jesus' statement **"For where your treasure is, there your heart will be also."** The truth of this statement is self-defining. If I am focused on Jesus and His kingdom I will be living a life that seeks to honor HIM. We need to ask ourselves if He is our all compelling purpose and desire.

## Forgive What?

**Col 3:13-14 Bear with each other and forgive whatever grievances you may have against one another. Forgive as the Lord forgave you. And over all these virtues put on love, which binds them all together in perfect unity.**

**Matt 5:44 "But I tell you: Love your enemies and pray for those who persecute you,"**

**Matt 6:14-15 "For if you forgive men when they sin against you, your heavenly Father will also forgive you. But if you do not forgive men their sins, your Father will not forgive your sins."**

**Mark 11:25 "And when you stand praying, if you hold anything against anyone, forgive him, so that your Father in heaven may forgive you your sins."**

There are times when we are tempted to harbor some sort of resentment. After all, someone has really hurt us and they have not even shown any hint of remorse or feeling sorry; what's more, there are limits, we think. Read the above verses over once more. Do you see anything that says forgive after they apologize? The truth is they may never get around to that. Jesus set the ideal example in this issue. From that cruel cross He did not look down and ask if those who had just driven the nails through His hands and feet were sorry. Rather He looked to heaven and said **Luke 23:34 Jesus said, "Father, forgive them, for they do not know what they are doing."** What Would Jesus Do? Jesus would forgive even those who mocked Him and nailed Him to that tree. Note that He says, "They do not know what they are doing." There are times when I've hurt someone and I'm totally unaware of what I've done. So it is with most of us. We seldom would intentionally injure another, nor would they us. Even setting that all aside, if I forgive, I set my spirit free from the tyranny and health destruction of harboring unforgiveness. It is said that as many as eighty-five percent of people in mental health facilities need only to forgive (even themselves) and their mental problems would go away. No wonder Jesus had so much to say on this subject.

## Is He MY Shepherd?

**Ps 23:1 The LORD is my shepherd, I shall not be in want.**

**Ps 84:11 For the LORD God is a sun and shield; the LORD bestows favor and honor; no good thing does he withhold from those whose walk is blameless.**

**Matt 6:33 "But seek first his kingdom and his righteousness, and all these things will be given to you as well."**

**Phil 4:19 And my God will meet all your needs according to his glorious riches in Christ Jesus.**

Whenever we are facing a danger, the twenty-third Psalm often comes to mind. Even those who do not have a relationship with Jesus want to claim the promises it contains. The truth, though, is that only those who have received God's salvation through faith in Jesus Christ can lay claim to the promises here. After sinning David confessed, **"For I know my transgressions, and my sin is always before me. Against you, you only, have I sinned and done what is evil in your sight,"** (Ps 51:3-4) Confession (owning up to and feeling sorry for what we have done) is the first step that must be followed by repentance which means turning from our sin. Look at how David stated it." **Create in me a pure heart, O God, and renew a steadfast spirit within me. Do not cast me from your presence or take your Holy Spirit from me. Restore to me the joy of your salvation and grant me a willing spirit, to sustain me."** (Ps 51:10-12) We then must seek God and His direction in our day-to-day life. Read what God wants from us – **"You do not delight in sacrifice, or I would bring it; you do not take pleasure in burnt offerings. The sacrifices of God are a broken spirit; a broken and contrite heart, O God, you will not despise."** (Ps 51:16-17) Confess, repent and present yourself to God, then place full confidence in the *twenty-third Psalm*.

## ME WORRY??

**Matt 6:25-26 "Therefore I tell you, do not worry about your life, what you will eat or drink; or about your body, what you will wear. Is not life more important than food, and the body more important than clothes? Look at the birds of the air; they do not sow or reap or store away in barns, and yet your heavenly Father feeds them. Are you not much more valuable than they? 27 Who of you by worrying can add a single hour to his life?"**

**Ps 55:22 Cast your cares on the LORD and he will sustain you; He will never let the righteous fall.**

**Matt 6:31 "So do not worry, saying, 'What shall we eat?' or 'What shall we drink?' or 'What shall we wear?"**

**Heb 13:5 Keep your lives free from the love of money and be content with what you have, because God has said, "Never will I leave you; never will I forsake you."**

I recently read that when a fork is being used for an eating utensil it can last almost indefinitely; however, if used to drive nails etc it will soon be of no use at all. The author then went on to relate this in regard to a person obsessed with the cares of life. Some characteristics that can soon become evident are fatigue, anger, self-criticism, sleeplessness, shortness of breath and even headaches and gastro-intestinal problems. People were not made to worry, but they were created to rely upon the Creator who has promised to **"meet all your needs according to his glorious riches in Christ Jesus"**. (Phil 4:19) To be in a state of worry and fretting is to slap God in the face (by doubting Him) and is hazardous to our health. Total trust in the One who gave Himself for our salvation will bring peace, health and assurance. Which would you rather have?

## The Seat of Honor

**Luke 14:7-11 When he noticed how the guests picked the places of honor at the table, he told them this parable: "When someone invites you to a wedding feast, do not take the place of honor, for a person more distinguished than you may have been invited. If so, the host who invited both of you will come and say to you, 'Give this man your seat.' Then, humiliated, you will have to take the least important place. But when you are invited, take the lowest place, so that when your host comes, he will say to you, 'Friend, move up to a better place.' Then you will be honored in the presence of all your fellow guests. For everyone who exalts himself will be humbled, and he who humbles himself will be exalted."**

**Prov 15:33 The fear of the LORD teaches a man wisdom, and humility comes before honor.**

**Mark 9:35 Sitting down, Jesus called the Twelve and said, "If anyone wants to be first, he must be the very last, and the servant of all."**

Pride is a very deceitful taskmaster. In this parable Jesus warns us about taking the seat of honor and having to endure being moved to a lower position. Even Christians fall into the trap of wanting (needing) to be honored and sometimes try to take the high seat. They feel the need to be recognized or praised in the world. This reminds me of the missionary who felt low because no big crowd met him and his family when they came home after many years of service in a foreign land. It was then his wife reminded him that they were NOT HOME YET. Jesus said, **"Be careful not to do your 'acts of righteousness' before men, to be seen by them. If you do, you will have no reward from your Father in heaven."** (Matt 6:1) Recognition by the world may be alluring, but it also leads to disillusionment and abasement. Which do you think is more rewarding, the accolades of the world or the "well done" of the One who paid for our redemption?

## Christmas, What a Beautiful Gift

**Luke 1:67-69** His father Zechariah was filled with the Holy Spirit and prophesied: "Praise be to the Lord, the God of Israel, because he has come and has redeemed his people. He has raised up a horn of salvation for us in the house of his servant David

**Ps 111:9** He provided redemption for his people; He ordained his covenant forever holy and awesome is his name.

**Eph 1:7-9** In him we have redemption through his blood, the forgiveness of sins, in accordance with the riches of God's grace that he lavished on us with all wisdom and understanding. And he made known to us the mystery of his will according to his good pleasure, which he purposed in Christ

**John 3:16** "For God so loved the world that he gave his one and only Son, that whoever believes in him shall not perish but have eternal life."

Most of us have heard the newer carol titled, "A Strange Way to Save the World". Strange it was and is, to our finite way of thinking, for the Son of God to become a man, to lower Himself to our estate, only to die that we might be saved. However strange it was, it is the perfect and only way of salvation, I am sure we can agree on that. But the next step is, what do we do with that salvation? Some people just praise the Lord they are going to heaven and are quite satisfied that the pastor is preaching such wonderful salvation messages. However, what should happen next is that we grow beyond that initial point and be challenged to develop a deep walk with God through His Holy Spirit. Some will laugh at us for doing so, but God is the One we had better please, not our world. If He would endure such suffering to save us, the very least we can do is give Him our all. One suggestion is to take a reality check on why you attend a particular church or why you attend church at all. Look at every phase of your life in that same way, not just WHAT you do, but WHY you do it, then invest time in prayer and act on whatever the Holy Spirit reveals.

## Condemnation is a Choice

**John 3:17** "For God did not send his Son into the world to condemn the world, but to save the world through him."

**John 5:45-47** "But do not think I will accuse you before the Father. Your accuser is Moses, on whom your hopes are set. If you believed Moses, you would believe me, for he wrote about me. But since you do not believe what he wrote, how are you going to believe what I say?"

**John 8:15-16** "You judge by human standards; I pass judgment on no one. But if I do judge, my decisions are right, because I am not alone. I stand with the Father, who sent me."

**John 12:47** "As for the person who hears my words but does not keep them, I do not judge him. For I did not come to judge the world, but to save it."

Christmas, no matter how much the world may try to alter it, is the celebration of the arrival of man's redemption into this world. Jesus, born as a baby in human form, came for the sole purpose of redeeming fallen creation. That redemption is a free gift that cannot be earned or merited in any way. When one rejects redemption, they are choosing condemnation. The question often arises "how can a loving God send a soul to hell?" The truth of the matter is that He does not; God is honoring the choice of that soul. The one who says "I want nothing to do with God" seals his/her own place in eternity. Just as a beautiful gift is not a gift or of any benefit to the recipient until it is received, God's gift of living here in His light every day and spending eternity in heaven is not ours until we accept it. Remember, the choice is ours and that choice binds God to honor what we choose. It is my prayer today that you, dear reader, have chosen the gift of salvation, not condemnation.

## The Bright and Morning Star

**Matt 2:2 and asked, "Where is the one who has been born king of the Jews? We saw his star in the east and have come to worship him."**

**Luke 1:78-79 because of the tender mercy of our God, by which the rising sun will come to us from heaven to shine on those living in darkness and in the shadow of death, to guide our feet into the path of peace."**

**Rev 22:16 "I, Jesus, have sent my angel to give you this testimony for the churches. I am the Root and the Offspring of David, and the bright Morning Star."**

**Rev 22:5 There will be no more night. They will not need the light of a lamp or the light of the sun, for the Lord God will give them light. And they will reign for ever and ever.**

Oh how awesome is the Christmas season. There are lights, trees, food, family and friends, joy and all kinds of excitement, stores decorated with bright colors and Santa is everywhere. All these are symbols that remind us of the greatest gift ever given, Jesus coming to earth as man to redeem us from the pit of hell. One of these symbols is the star so many place on top of our Christmas trees. Ah, the star, a reminder of our Lord's advent, God's guidance to the men of old and so much more. But it offers one more thing, the sweet promise that HE WILL COME AGAIN. There is a day coming when we will not need a flashlight, a lamp, or even the sun, for He is the "light". I pray today that when we see the star we will be reminded and be like the wise men – **"When they saw the star, they were overjoyed. On coming to the house, they saw the child with his mother Mary, and they bowed down and worshiped him.** (Matt 2:10-11) Oh "Bright and Morning Star" be honored in us today.

# Watch and PRAY!!!

**Luke 11:4 "And lead us not into temptation."**

**Matt 26:41 "Watch and pray so that you will not fall into temptation. The spirit is willing, but the body is weak."**

**1 Cor 10:13 No temptation has seized you except what is common to man. And God is faithful; he will not let you be tempted beyond what you can bear. But when you are tempted, he will also provide a way out so that you can stand up under it.**

**Rev 2:10 "Do not be afraid of what you are about to suffer. I tell you, the devil will put some of you in prison to test you, and you will suffer persecution for ten days. Be faithful, even to the point of death, and I will give you the crown of life."**

Can God lead us into temptation? Can or does God want us to be tempted? The answer is that God cannot be tempted and He does not tempt man. (James 1:13) But, if we remember Job's story, God sort of put Job on the spot **"Then the LORD said to Satan, 'Have you considered my servant Job? There is no one on earth like him; he is blameless and upright, a man who fears God and shuns evil.'"** (Job 1:8) I believe God was proud of his servant, Job and also had faith in him that he would remain true no matter what. If God allows temptation to come into our lives it has a dual purpose. First, it is to be for His honor and glory, and second to grow us in Him. One thing is for sure; the closer we are to God the easier will be the escape from it. If we can bring ourselves to ask Him to deliver us from the temptations the enemy brings along and from the things God allows, we have taken one giant step toward Him. It is never a walk in the park, but when we are full of Him the trek becomes more like walking on the level than mountain climbing.

# Forgive Us

**Matt 6:12 "Forgive us our debts, as we also have forgiven our debtors."**

**1 John 1:7-10 But if we walk in the light, as he is in the light, we have fellowship with one another, and the blood of Jesus, his Son, purifies us from all sin. If we claim to be without sin, we deceive ourselves and the truth is not in us. If we confess our sins, he is faithful and just and will forgive us our sins and purify us from all unrighteousness. If we claim we have not sinned, we make him out to be a liar and his word has no place in our lives.**

**Matt 6:14-15 "For if you forgive men when they sin against you, your heavenly Father will also forgive you. But if you do not forgive men their sins, your Father will not forgive your sins."**

For some reason it's not hard at all to seek God's forgiveness when we mess up (SIN) "Well the Lord knows I didn't mean to do that and anyway I have confessed it". All that may be true but there is another stipulation. If we expect HIM to forgive US, WE have to forgive OTHERS for what they've done or what we think they have done against us. I don't find any verse that allows for any exceptions. Actually Jesus told a parable about the need to forgive. A guy was forgiven by his master what we are told would be millions today, yet the man refused to forgive a twenty-dollar debt owed to him; so the master then rescinded his forgiveness of the man and turned him over to be tortured. Check it out in Matt. 18:22-35. Jesus concludes the parable with, **"This is how my heavenly Father will treat each of you unless you forgive your brother from your heart."** (Matt 18:35) We have no choice and it matters not the offense; we must forgive if we want to be forgiven. Jesus came, died and rose again to extend forgiveness to us. Can we in any way do less? NO, because we can only be forgiven as we do the same.

## Daily Bread????

**Matt 6:11 "Give us today our daily bread."**

**Job 23:12 I have not departed from the commands of his lips; I have treasured the words of his mouth more than my daily bread.**

**Matt 4:4 Jesus answered, "It is written: 'Man does not live on bread alone, but on every word that comes from the mouth of God.'"**

**Matt 6:34 "Therefore do not worry about tomorrow, for tomorrow will worry about itself. Each day has enough trouble of its own."**

There are people in this world who think they are broke if there is less than five-thousand dollars in their checking account and then there are others who don't consider themselves broke until the overdraft notices start arriving. This fact shows that we look at our daily bread differently. In Acts the early church had all in common and when there was a need someone sold property and presented the money to the apostles. Our state of wealth depends on our state of mind. When Jesus stopped at the well in Samaria the disciples had gone for food. When they returned Jesus was no longer hungry **"But he said to them, "I have food to eat that you know nothing about."** (John 4:32). If we give ourselves to God He will see to our every need. **"The lions may grow weak and hungry, but those who seek the LORD lack no good thing."** (Ps 34:10) The point is that we often think we need far more than we actually do. The daily bread we really need is Jesus and to live out His Word, to be more regular with tithes and offerings, to donate to feed a child in another country, to volunteer at a local charity, or maybe simply send a card or make a call, or in some way encourage another person. In short, what we MUST do is be about the Father's business.

## THY will be done

**Matt 6:10 "your will be done on earth as it is in heaven."**

**Matt 12:50 "For whoever does the will of my Father in heaven is my brother and sister and mother."**

**Matt 26:42 He went away a second time and prayed, "My Father, if it is not possible for this cup to be taken away unless I drink it, may your will be done."**

**Acts 13:22 After removing Saul, he made David their king. He testified concerning him: 'I have found David son of Jesse a man after my own heart; he will do everything I want him to do.'**

How easy it is to mutter the words "thy will be done", but what are the implications and requirements that go along with that statement? For our precious Lord it meant death, and not only that, but probably the most gruesome form of death known to man. It meant His willingness to suffer for our redemption. In David's case it meant the desire to do whatever God wanted him to do. For us it should be the willingness to put our totality on the line for Him. Jesus said, **"For whoever does the will of my Father in heaven is my brother and sister and mother."** The will of the Father is **"Therefore go and make disciples of all nations, baptizing them in the name of the Father and of the Son and of the Holy Spirit, and teaching them to obey everything I have commanded you. And surely I am with you always, to the very end of the age."** (Matt 28:19-20) It's not all that complicated really if you want to be in His will, just live like you really believe in and love this Jesus Christ. Will it be easy? Not always. Will it mean perfection? No, but it will mean a close relationship with our Brother and Savior. It will mean we will confess and be forgiven of our sins. And it will mean living in the care, love and guidance of our loving Father. Sounds like a win-win situation to me.

## His Kingdom

**Matt 6:10 "your kingdom come."**

**Matt 4:17 From that time on Jesus began to preach, "Repent, for the kingdom of heaven is near."**

**Col 1:13 For he has rescued us from the dominion of darkness and brought us into the kingdom of the Son he loves,**

**Matt 7:21 "Not everyone who says to me, 'Lord, Lord,' will enter the kingdom of heaven, but only he who does the will of my Father who is in heaven."**

When an elected official takes office it's often said, "I hope he works to enact the promises made on the campaign trail". We want the politician to make good on his promises because we believe they are for the benefit of our society. God's kingdom is for the ultimate benefit of ALL society and when He is given the reins of our hearts He works toward that eternal goal. When we become part of His kingdom it is imperative that we begin to live like a citizen of it. For His kingdom to come He must have loyal subjects who will be obedient at any and all costs. The Apostle Paul asks us, **"Do you not know that your body is a temple of the Holy Spirit, who is in you, whom you have received from God? You are not your own; you were bought at a price. Therefore honor God with your body"**. (1 Cor 6:19-20) He also reminds us, **"the kingdom of God is not a matter of eating and drinking, but of righteousness, peace and joy in the Holy Spirit, because anyone who serves Christ in this way is pleasing to God and approved by men."** (Rom 14:17-18) We are really not our own and if we truly belong to Him and desire His kingdom we will want to forsake the desires of this world and take on total allegiance to our Savior. If we do not want to live for Him now why would we ever want to live with Him for eternity?

# Our Father

**Matt 6:9 "This, then, is how you should pray: "'Our Father in heaven, hallowed be your name,"**

**Is 64:8 Yet, O LORD, you are our Father. We are the clay, you are the potter; we are all the work of your hand.**

**Matt 5:16 "In the same way, let your light shine before men, that they may see your good deeds and praise your Father in heaven."**

**Matt 5:48-6:1 "Be perfect, therefore, as your heavenly Father is perfect. "Be careful not to do your 'acts of righteousness' before men, to be seen by them. If you do, you will have no reward from your Father in heaven."**

If one of us were to claim to be related to the President there may be certain questions to be answered. We may have to explain the basis on which we make that claim and under certain circumstances documents verifying the facts may have to be produced. There might even be some who would question our claim unless they heard the President himself attest to the relationship. In like manner when we claim to be a Christian certain proofs must be offered. Isaiah portrays the child of God as clay in the Father's hand, moldable and compliant to His will. He made us and He has every right to direct each step we take. Jesus told us, **"let your light shine before men"**. If you are His, you will not be hiding that fact nor will you be ashamed to have others know that you are His child. When the Savior said, **"Be perfect, therefore, as your heavenly Father is perfect"** He meant that we are to be sorry for and repentant of our sin. He also intends for us to live our lives to please Him. He is well aware of our humanity and our need of His Holy Spirit to be our strength and guide in order to do this. Is He YOUR Father?

## "Be it unto me"

**Luke 1:38** "I am the Lord's servant," Mary answered. "May it be to me as you have said." Then the angel left her.

**Ps 116:16** O LORD, truly I am your servant; I am your servant, the son of your maidservant; you have freed me from my chains.

**Rom 4:18-21** Against all hope, Abraham in hope believed and so became the father of many nations, just as it had been said to him, "So shall your offspring be." Without weakening in his faith, he faced the fact that his body was as good as dead-since he was about a hundred years old-and that Sarah's womb was also dead. Yet he did not waver through unbelief regarding the promise of God, but was strengthened in his faith and gave glory to God, being fully persuaded that God had power to do what he had promised.

**Ps 119:38** Fulfill your promise to your servant, so that you may be feared.

Mary had no way of fully understanding what Gabriel was saying to her, but she did know enough to say, **"May it be to me as you have said."** She grasped that what was being told her was truth and that whether she fully understood or not she needed to be obedient. There are many times when we do not know exactly what our obedience might look like, but it is never possible to go wrong by obeying even when we cannot see for a while the outcome. Abraham waited many, many years before the birth of Isaac, and yet **"Without weakening in his faith"**. Will it be easy? Maybe not, but it will always be right. There is never a time when it is not correct to say "be it unto me". For as David said, He is our Salvation" and if we can trust Him with our eternal state we surely can leave our current circumstances and future entirely in His hand.

## My thoughts and my actions

**Ps 19:14 May the words of my mouth and the meditation of my heart be pleasing in your sight, O LORD, my Rock and my Redeemer.**

**Ps 51:15 O Lord, open my lips, and my mouth will declare your praise.**

**Heb 11:4 By faith Abel offered God a better sacrifice than Cain did. By faith he was commended as a righteous man, when God spoke well of his offerings. And by faith he still speaks, even though he is dead.**

**Heb 13:15 Through Jesus, therefore, let us continually offer to God a sacrifice of praise-the fruit of lips that confess his name.**

Think for a moment about the possibility of your spouse claiming to love you, yet their actions and constant eyeing of others cause you to question the depth of that love. Or a "friend" who doubts your word and never spends time with you, but always seems to have time for coffee with someone else. Isn't that what Christians who seldom pray, study God's Word, attend church, witness or show love to a hurting person are doing to God? The early Christians stayed on track because **"They devoted themselves to the apostles' teaching and to the fellowship, to the breaking of bread and to prayer."** (Acts 2:42) David prayed that the words of his mouth and the meditations of his heart would be acceptable. If that is our prayer as well, we may need to change some of our habits. Anything occupying our time that does not draw us toward God has to go. We must start loving the unlovely, caring for the lost, crying over the fate of those who know not Jesus Christ and listen to and read only what will encourage our walk with Him. Paul said, **"Finally, brothers, whatever is true, whatever is noble, whatever is right, whatever is pure, whatever is lovely, whatever is admirable-if anything is excellent or praiseworthy-think about**

**such things."** (Phil 4:8) If our words and thoughts are to be pure we have to heed THE WORD.

## Not of this world

**John 18:36 Jesus said, "My kingdom is not of this world. If it were, my servants would fight to prevent my arrest by the Jews. But now my kingdom is from another place."**

**Is 9:6 For to us a child is born, to us a son is given, and the government will be on his shoulders. And he will be called Wonderful Counselor, Mighty God, Everlasting Father, Prince of Peace.**

**Luke 17:20-21 Once, having been asked by the Pharisees when the kingdom of God would come, Jesus replied, "The kingdom of God does not come with your careful observation, nor will people say, 'Here it is,' or 'There it is,' because the kingdom of God is within you."**

**Dan 2:44 "In the time of those kings, the God of heaven will set up a kingdom that will never be destroyed, nor will it be left to another people. It will crush all those kingdoms and bring them to an end, but it will itself endure forever.**

What ever gave any of us the idea that being a Christian was a means to a life of ease here on earth? Jesus said, "My Kingdom is not of this world" and that is what He meant. Being a Christian means that the world may reject and even persecute us, BUT it also means that in the coming Kingdom of God we will enjoy the very presence of THE very God of all. **"I have told you these things, so that in me you may have peace. In this world you will have trouble. But take heart! I have overcome the world."** (John 16:33) **"If the world hates you, keep in mind that it hated me first"** (John 15:18) Jesus Christ is not a cure-all for life's woes. But He is the source of eternal life and joy. He calls upon those who claim His name to live as He lived in love and service to those who so desperately need Him. Question, which would you rather have, a multi-million dollar bank account or the assurance that you and those you love will be together in the KINGDOM of Jesus Christ? Oh Lord Jesus, open our eyes.

## Would we be struck dumb?

**Luke 1:18-20 Zechariah asked the angel, "How can I be sure of this? I am an old man and my wife is well along in years." The angel answered, "I am Gabriel. I stand in the presence of God, and I have been sent to speak to you and to tell you this good news. And now you will be silent and not able to speak until the day this happens, because you did not believe my words, which will come true at their proper time."**

**Num 20:12 But the LORD said to Moses and Aaron, "Because you did not trust in me enough to honor me as holy in the sight of the Israelites, you will not bring this community into the land I give them."**

**Mark 9:19 "O unbelieving generation," Jesus replied, "how long shall I stay with you? How long shall I put up with you?"**

**Rev 3:19 Those whom I love I rebuke and discipline. So be earnest, and repent.**

When a husband says to his wife "I love you" he has to put action behind those words. He needs to provide for her, protect, honor and in other ways demonstrate that love. He can utter the line thousands of times, but things like a few simple loving hugs will SHOW it with far more power than all those times of saying it. The Christian (?) can say "I love God", but if he/she does not show it in many ways it is but a **"a resounding gong or a clanging cymbal."** (1 Cor 13:1) This passage goes on to tell us that love is the most powerful way to show our Christianity. **"Love the Lord your God with all your heart and with all your soul and with all your mind and with all your strength."** (Mark 12:30) Believing that God is God is one thing, but believing that He has our best interest at heart is another. Zechariah failed to believe and was struck dumb; Moses failed and was forbidden entry to the Promised Land. How many of us are lacking in joy and happiness because we do not fully love God, nor believe what He says, nor make Him first in our lives?

# Wake up, Church

**Rev 3:1-4 "To the angel of the church in Sardis write: These are the words of him who holds the seven spirits of God and the seven stars. I know your deeds; you have a reputation of being alive, but you are dead. Wake up! Strengthen what remains and is about to die, for I have not found your deeds complete in the sight of my God. Remember, therefore, what you have received and heard; obey it, and repent. But if you do not wake up, I will come like a thief, and you will not know at what time I will come to you. Yet you have a few people in Sardis who have not soiled their clothes. They will walk with me, dressed in white, for they are worthy.**

**Is 61:10 I delight greatly in the LORD; my soul rejoices in my God. For He has clothed me with garments of salvation and arrayed me in a robe of righteousness, as a bridegroom adorns his head like a priest, and as a bride adorns herself with her jewels.**

Why do folks go to church? Some go because it is the thing to do, some for the fellowship, some feel guilty if they don't and some go to worship God. For the later, God is so important in their life that a Sunday without church is like a day without sunshine. Then there are those who have gone for so long that they just automatically follow the same routine even mindlessly. If we attend church it should be to give something to our precious Savior, our praises and worship, our love, our very lives. We need to be like the few at Sardis who **"have not soiled their clothes"**. They walked with God every step and going to church was a glorious day of worship to the Lord. If we have an close relationship with Christ we will be sure we are at His side every minute of every day and we will avoid the trap of living for ourselves six days a week then grudgingly give Him one or two hours on the seventh. So what place does HE have in your life today?

## The letter kills; the Spirit gives life

**Gal 4:9 But now that you know God-or rather are known by God-how is it that you are turning back to those weak and miserable principles? Do you wish to be enslaved by them all over again?**

**Gal 1:6 I am astonished that you are so quickly deserting the one who called you by the grace of Christ and are turning to a different gospel**

**Gal 3:24 So the law was put in charge to lead us to Christ that we might be justified by faith. 25 Now that faith has come, we are no longer under the supervision of the law.**

**Heb 7:18 The former regulation is set aside because it was weak and useless**

As Moses was leading the people to the Promised Land, God gave him the law to provide for them a sense of direction. They had been under Egyptian law and had no idea how to govern themselves. He gave this law as a guide for how they were to live their lives before Him, which also provided the needed wisdom to live with each other. But down through the ages they added so many customs to it that blinded them to the fullness of the law itself. It was in fact their customs that created the contention between them and Jesus. The Galatians had come to Christ through faith and were growing in that freedom and love; however, along the way they were introduced to some of the "weak and miserable" principles of the law, weak because they offered no hope of deliverance and miserable because they were so demanding and impossible to keep. In the post resurrection era all the former ways have only one purpose and that is to bring us to the Lord Jesus Christ. At that point it is HIM ALONE with His forgiveness and restoration plus NOTHING ELSE. Trying to keep the law will only bring discouragement and prevent us from knowing His fullness. Do not be fooled, only trust Him.

## There is ALWAYS hope!!!!

**2 Cor 4:8-12 We are hard pressed on every side, but not crushed; perplexed, but not in despair; persecuted, but not abandoned; struck down, but not destroyed. We always carry around in our body the death of Jesus, so that the life of Jesus may also be revealed in our body. For we who are alive are always being given over to death for Jesus' sake, so that his life may be revealed in our mortal body. So then, death is at work in us, but life is at work in you.**

**2 Cor 1:8-10 We do not want you to be uninformed, brothers, about the hardships we suffered in the province of Asia. We were under great pressure, far beyond our ability to endure, so that we despaired even of life. Indeed, in our hearts we felt the sentence of death. But this happened that we might not rely on ourselves but on God, who raises the dead. He has delivered us from such a deadly peril, and he will deliver us. On him we have set our hope that he will continue to deliver us,**

Oh me, oh my, the world is falling apart. Among other things there are so many wrong decisions made by the government. While this may seem to be true if you consistently watch the evening news (I recommend listening to Christian radio instead of watching the major networks), it is so far from truth. **"the faith and love that spring from the hope that is stored up for you in heaven and that you have already heard about in the word of truth, the gospel".**

(Col 1:5) There is never a reason to despair because we know the Source of hope. With God hoping is having, rather than wishing. We who have made Jesus our LORD and Savior know His peace and security and can hope in Him. Yesterday the radio carried a news story of the folks in New Jersey who called their representatives, putting an end to a bill that would have given some special rights to same sex couples. There are many reasons things are bad and getting worse, but if Christians will pray, believe, hold fast to Jesus as LORD and act like they really care by lawfully and peaceably expressing themselves instead of just complaining, we would see a different nation. What kind of American Christian are you???

## Don't lose heart!

**2 Cor 4:16-18 Though outwardly we are wasting away, yet inwardly we are being renewed day by day. For our light and momentary troubles are achieving for us an eternal glory that far outweighs them all. So we fix our eyes not on what is seen, but on what is unseen. For what is seen is temporary, but what is unseen is eternal.**

**Rom 5:3-5 Not only so, but we also rejoice in our sufferings, because we know that suffering produces perseverance; perseverance, character; and character, hope. And hope does not disappoint us, because God has poured out his love into our hearts by the Holy Spirit, whom he has given us**

**1 Cor 11:31-32 But if we judged ourselves, we would not come under judgment. When we are judged by the Lord, we are being disciplined so that we will not be condemned with the world.**

All together too often we tend to fall into a self-pity party and as a result we can lose sight of the reality of Jesus Christ and what He is to us. Paul reminds us that outwardly our physical bodies are wasting away. If you don't believe that just think of what you could and did do twenty years ago. But these are light and momentary problems, after all, **"the length of our days is seventy years or eighty, if we have the strength;"** (Ps 90:10) and we must find a way to focus on the eternal and not this temporary life. The way to do that is to give the Lord full control. Only then can we know the truths of His Word and learn that our trials and tribulations are the training ground to produce in us character. Also, you and I are to judge our own actions and motives. Is our focus on ourselves or on Him? If the former we will receive His discipline and if the latter we need not fear His judgment because just as with our children there is no discipline needed when we live in obedience to Him.

## ME LOST ??

**Is 9:6-7 For to us a child is born, to us a son is given, and the government will be on his shoulders. And he will be called Wonderful Counselor, Mighty God, Everlasting Father, Prince of Peace. Of the increase of his government and peace there will be no end. He will reign on David's throne and over his kingdom, establishing and upholding it with justice and righteousness from that time on and forever. The zeal of the LORD Almighty will accomplish this.**

**Gal 4:4-7 But when the time had fully come, God sent his Son, born of a woman, born under law, to redeem those under law, that we might receive the full rights of sons. Because you are sons, God sent the Spirit of his Son into our hearts, the Spirit who calls out, "Abba, Father." So you are no longer a slave, but a son; and since you are a son, God has made you also an heir.**

Sadly many people in our world are totally unaware that they are lost and thanks to Satan's lies they invest much time and effort trying to prove they aren't. The father of all lies is blinding them to truth and they fall prey to the greatest lie of all eternity. Working tirelessly they try to prove evolution and other falsehoods and many times are fighting that still small voice knocking on the door of their hearts. The Bible is truth and tells us that ever since Eve took a bite of that fruit we have been separated from God. **"Therefore, just as sin entered the world through one man, and death through sin, and in this way death came to all men, because all sinned".** (Rom 5:12) Sin, the cause of that separation, is the reason we are lost (unable to commune with God and unable to enter His home), but praise be to God He provided the cure for that problem.

**"Not only is this so, but we also rejoice in God through our Lord Jesus Christ, through whom we have now received reconciliation."** (Rom 5:11) If you dear reader do not know this Jesus and His peace, joy, love, mercy and salvation please come to Him today. He is waiting with arms open wide for YOU!

## Do what HE would do

**Matt 1:5 Salmon the father of Boaz, whose mother was Rahab,**

**Matt 1:5 Boaz the father of Obed, whose mother was Ruth,**

**Matt 1:6 David was the father of Solomon, whose mother had been Uriah's wife,**

**John 8:11 "Then neither do I condemn you," Jesus declared. "Go now and leave your life of sin."**

**John 4:29 "Come, see a man who told me everything I ever did.**

How easy it is to TALK ABOUT doing what Jesus would do, but DOING it is quite another story. Rahab the harlot, Ruth a Moabitess and Bathsheba the adulteress were given the distinction of being listed in the lineage of Jesus Christ. These women were the scum of the earth in Jewish circles of their day, but the Holy Spirit made sure they were mentioned. The woman taken in adultery was by law punishable by death, but Jesus gently picked her up from that shameful position and told her, **"Go now and leave your life of sin."** The woman at the well had been married five, count them, five times and was now unmarried, just living with a man, but Jesus lovingly let her know that He is the long expected Messiah. All of these women had tainted histories, but in love and compassion God honored all of them because they had faith in Him and despised their former sin. I wonder how many men and women today have checkered pasts and now love Jesus but are forbidden to serve Him by a church that CLAIMS Jesus but acts nothing like Him? It is time we did more than just TALK about what He would do and START DOING IT, because the bigger question is how many souls are heading toward hell because of a hard-nosed, judgmental, legalistic body of so called believers?

## We have sinned

**Dan 9:4-6 "O Lord, the great and awesome God, who keeps his covenant of love with all who love him and obey his commands, 5 we have sinned and done wrong. We have been wicked and have rebelled; we have turned away from your commands and laws. 6 We have not listened to your servants the prophets, who spoke in your name to our kings, our princes and our fathers, and to all the people of the land.**

**2 Chron 7:14 if my people, who are called by my name, will humble themselves and pray and seek my face and turn from their wicked ways, then will I hear from heaven and will forgive their sin and will heal their land.**

**1 John 1:8-10 If we claim to be without sin, we deceive ourselves and the truth is not in us. If we confess our sins, he is faithful and just and will forgive us our sins and purify us from all unrighteousness. If we claim we have not sinned, we make him out to be a liar and his word has no place in our lives.**

"Lord God, maker of heaven and earth, who will come to You. We confess today that as a nation, as a church and as individuals we have sinned. We have put many other labels on our transgressions and not called sin sin. We have thrown You out of our schools, legalized the murder of unborn babies and have followed the ways of evil rather than good. Those who call themselves yours often try to keep You in a box, forbidding You access to their daily lives, in essence saying, "there are two sides of life". Oh Lord, forgive us and teach us to give You **all** that You are due. Lord may we like the Psalmist pray, **"May the words of my mouth and the meditation of my heart be pleasing in your sight, O LORD, my Rock and my Redeemer."** (Ps 19:14) "Teach us, mold us and make us like Yourself, oh Jesus, our Salvation. In Your precious name." Amen

## "You have forsaken your first love"

**Rev 2:4 "Yet I hold this against you: You have forsaken your first love."**

**Jer 2:2-3 "Go and proclaim in the hearing of Jerusalem: "'I remember the devotion of your youth, how as a bride you loved me and followed me through the desert, through a land not sown. Israel was holy to the LORD, the firstfruits of his harvest;**

**Matt 24:12-14 Because of the increase of wickedness, the love of most will grow cold, but he who stands firm to the end will be saved. And this gospel of the kingdom will be preached in the whole world as a testimony to all nations, and then the end will come.**

**Phil 1:9 And this is my prayer: that your love may abound more**

Last evening I heard a person ask a televangelist why they were always so vague about how God would bless people if they were to give money to their particular ministry. The answer given was very good and for me it strengthened a couple of my thoughts on the subject. First, if I give money to a church, a parachurch, minister or a Christian organization I am in fact giving it to the Lord. When I give a gift to a loved one I should not have any expectation of controlling how they use that gift, so why would it be any different in giving to my Lord. Secondly, if I give money to the Lord only to get a certain blessing from Him I have given for the wrong reason. When I leave my first love I begin to seek only that which will appease ME. When I give money to the Lord and expect to be blessed in some specific way or I want to have control over that gift, I just may have drawn away from that first love. Furthermore, every ministry is to be open and above reproach legally etc. with the use of monies it receives and that should be the only legitimate control of such money which is used for the furtherance of the Gospel. One test of allegiance to Jesus Christ is giving him tithes and offerings expecting absolutely nothing in return. It is THEN that He can and will bless us beyond measure.

## That "WOW" Factor

**Est 2:18** And the king gave a great banquet, Esther's banquet, for all his nobles and officials. He proclaimed a holiday throughout the provinces and distributed gifts with royal liberality.

**Song 3:11** Come out, you daughters of Zion, and look at King Solomon wearing the crown, the crown with which his mother crowned him on the day of his wedding, the day his heart rejoiced.

**Song 1:2-4** Let him kiss me with the kisses of his mouth- for your love is more delightful than wine. Pleasing is the fragrance of your perfumes; your name is like perfume poured out. No wonder the maidens love you! Take me away with you-let us hurry! Let the king bring me into his chambers.

It's the big day. The groom is standing at the altar peering up that aisle then voila, there she is. His heart nearly stops. She is so beautiful and soon she will be all his. She's having similar thoughts and needs an arm to keep her balanced as she walks slowly toward this man she loves so deeply. Today their hearts are filled with that "WOW" thought, but life seems to get in the way all too soon and the "WOW" becomes wow or less. I have found that if I take a moment and just look at my Ruthie (I purposely quit calling her my wife much of the time because that is not her identity) and remember how much she meant to me on that "WOW" day it helps keep the "WOW" in our marriage. I told that to a young couple I was counseling and a few days later he related to me how proud he had become of his wife just by reminding himself of the "WOW" fact. Oh how true that on that special day we feel such strong emotions, but if these aren't nursed and fed we may well become no more than another statistic. Having a strong loving life takes serious devotion to the one who once made you and still can make you say "WOW". So may I suggest that you try just looking at your mate and see what you once saw and I will venture that you will like the outcome.

## Do what is right

**1 John 2:28-29** And now, dear children, continue in him, so that when he appears we may be confident and unashamed before him at his coming. If you know that he is righteous, you know that everyone who does what is right has been born of him.

**Matt 7:16-20** "By their fruit you will recognize them. Do people pick grapes from thornbushes, or figs from thistles? Likewise every good tree bears good fruit, but a bad tree bears bad fruit. A good tree cannot bear bad fruit, and a bad tree cannot bear good fruit. Every tree that does not bear good fruit is cut down and thrown into the fire. 20 Thus, by their fruit you will recognize them."

**Titus 2:12-14** It teaches us to say "No" to ungodliness and worldly passions, and to live self-controlled, upright and godly lives in this present age, while we wait for the blessed hope-the glorious appearing of our great God and Savior, Jesus Christ, who gave himself for us to redeem us from all wickedness and to purify for himself a people that are his very own, eager to do what is good.

**1 John 3:7** Dear children, do not let anyone lead you astray. He who does what is right is righteous, just as he is righteous

"Christian" is a word that conjures up many thoughts in peoples' minds. Some think that because America is called a Christian Nation, they are automatically Christians. Others think that because they attend church regularly, do good deeds, give to charity etc. they can lay claim to that name. The truth is that only those who accept Jesus Christ as Savior and live a life pleasing to Him are in fact CHRISTians. Those who say no to sin and it's allure and live like Jesus would live are the only ones who are His. Jesus said, "by their fruit you will recognize them". Paul said, **"But the fruit of the Spirit is love, joy, peace, patience, kindness, goodness, faithfulness, gentleness and self-control. Against such things there is no**

**law. Those who belong to Christ Jesus have crucified the sinful nature with its passions and desires."** (Gal 5:22-24) This is the true measure of the fruit Jesus was talking about and if we are exemplifying this kind of life style we are Christians. So how is it with you?

## "Live at peace..."

**Luke 23:34 "Father, forgive them, for they do not know what they are doing."**

**Matt 5:44 But I tell you: "Love your enemies and pray for those who persecute you,"**

**Rom 12:14-18 Bless those who persecute you; bless and do not curse. Rejoice with those who rejoice; mourn with those who mourn. Live in harmony with one another. Do not be proud, but be willing to associate with people of low position. Do not be conceited. Do not repay anyone evil for evil. Be careful to do what is right in the eyes of everybody. If it is possible, as far as it depends on you, live at peace with everyone.**

**1 Peter 2:20 But how is it to your credit if you receive a beating for doing wrong and endure it? But if you suffer for doing good and you endure it, this is commendable before God.**

Someone said to me the other day, "I can only be pushed so far". As long as we live with that mindset we can expect and will have trouble and heartache at every corner. Co-workers, friends, and sometimes even family will do things (accidentally or purposefully) that push us toward that imaginary line. Oh how many friendships, careers, and even marriages have been destroyed by selfish actions AND reactions. The state and the federal governments set laws and guidelines that serve to protect our welfare. Speed limits are one example and when such restrictions are violated the results can be disastrous. Last summer it appears that six teens lost their lives because the driver attempted to drive and text at the same time. God gives us many guidelines and rules in the Bible, but contrary to public opinion they are not set to dampen our fun, but rather to enhance and make our lives fuller and safer. I have a question; is it possible that your last "discussion" with your spouse really centered around one of you attempting to have your own way over the other? Question two, are both of you now aware that this selfish action caused both of you pain? Question three, could it be that God's way would have been better? You and I have ego problems and being human we do not want to admit that fact, but life would be so much better if we would.

## Give thanks, just give thanks

**Ps 100:4 Enter his gates with thanksgiving and his courts with praise; give thanks to him and praise his name.**

**1 Thess 5:18 give thanks in all circumstances, for this is God's will for you in Christ Jesus.**

**Job 1:20-21 Then he fell to the ground in worship and said: "Naked I came from my mother's womb, and naked I will depart. The LORD gave and the LORD has taken away; may the name of the LORD be praised."**

**Phil 4:6 Do not be anxious about anything, but in everything, by prayer and petition, with thanksgiving, present your requests to God.**

It would be futile to search the Bible for the phrase "give thanks when all is going well", because what it teaches is the very opposite. Give thanks period. That's it. Just give thanks. The prophet Isaiah in speaking for God said, **"For my thoughts are not your thoughts, neither are your ways my ways," declares the LORD. "As the heavens are higher than the earth, so are my ways higher than your ways and my thoughts than your thoughts."** (Is 55:8-9) Because God is God He knows the whole story. Having the ability to see the end from the beginning enables Him to allow the things that will bring us to where we need to be. For some of us that means being hit upside the head with a baseball bat, while others only require a gentle nudge. I know, because He has had to break several bats in His attempts to get MY attention. One sign of becoming mature in the Lord is to be thankful in "ALL" things. Matters not if life is a bowl of cherries or a bowl of cherry pits for as long as God is in the driver's seat we can be thankful. He is taking us on a journey that will one day lead us into His very presence. The day that happens, **"then I shall know fully, even as I am fully known."** (1 Cor 13:12b) "What a day, glorious day, that will be" and as the songwriter penned, "It will be worth it all, when we see Jesus".

## Thankful in Everything?

**1 Thess 5:18 give thanks in all circumstances, for this is God's will for you in Christ Jesus.**

**Job 1:21 "Naked I came from my mother's womb, and naked I will depart. The LORD gave and the LORD has taken away; may the name of the LORD be praised."**

**Eph 5:20 always giving thanks to God the Father for everything, in the name of our Lord Jesus Christ.**

**Col 3:17 And whatever you do, whether in word or deed, do it all in the name of the Lord Jesus, giving thanks to God the Father through him.**

This past couple of weeks has been a very hard time for me. Several trips and calls to the doctor, blood work, antibiotics and consults. To date we're not sure what's wrong and still have a CT scan of my sinuses to go. They think it's probably at least in part a chronic sinus problem. At any rate it has been a chance for me to try out this "praise in everything" thing. Have I felt good, have I experienced relief by praising or has it been a picnic? No, but it has been a lot easier to deal with. Honestly I have felt like David, **"My God, my God, why have you forsaken me? Why are you so far from saving me, so far from the words of my groaning? O my God, I cry out by day, but you do not answer, by night, and am not silent."** (Ps 22:1-2) I also learned like David, **"Yet you brought me out of the womb; you made me trust in you.** (Ps 22:9) You see, when I came to totally trust Him I remembered that He **is** and **has** all the answers. Peter told the Lord, **"Lord, to whom shall we go? You have the words of eternal life. We believe and know that you are the Holy One of God."** (John 6:68-69) How about you? Do you need to, **"Cast all your anxiety on him because he cares for you"?** (1 Peter 5:7) What's stopping you?

## Beware – evil will breed evil..

**Prov 17:13** If a man pays back evil for good, evil will never leave his house.

**1 Sam 24:17-18** "You are more righteous than I," he said. "You have treated me well, but I have treated you badly. 18 You have just now told me of the good you did to me; the LORD delivered me into your hands, but you did not kill me

**1 Sam 31:2-3** The Philistines pressed hard after Saul and his sons, and they killed his sons Jonathan, Abinadab and Malki-Shua. The fighting grew fierce around Saul, and when the archers overtook him, they wounded him critically.

**2 Sam 21:1** During the reign of David, there was a famine for three successive years; so David sought the face of the LORD. The LORD said, "It is on account of Saul and his blood-stained house; it is because he put the Gibeonites to death."

How many of us can't figure out why so many bad things are happening, both to us and to our country. For some time the USA has, as a nation, murdered babies, sought to legitimize certain sins (homosexuality i.e.), punished Christians for sharing their faith and a host of other atrocities, then we wonder why horrendous fires, floods, droughts and the like fall on us. It is time for us as a nation to corporately repent and turn around. Admittedly (for political reasons) that is very unlikely to take place nationally, but it can happen if each and every Christian who claims to know and love Jesus Christ will get down on their knees, repent of personal sin and the sin of our nation and then seek our Lord to change our country. Guess what, HE WILL! Wouldn't it be great to hear "Merry Christmas" without expecting it to be a negative headline on the evening news? Saul sinned greatly and the entire nation suffered even after his death. The Untied States of America has so gravely sinned and it needs us as Christians to take the lead in repentance. Will you join me in doing just that?

## "I am become all things…"

**1 Cor 9:22-23 To the weak I became weak, to win the weak. I have become all things to all men so that by all possible means I might save some. I do all this for the sake of the gospel, that I may share in its blessings.**

**1 Cor 9:19 Though I am free and belong to no man, I make myself a slave to everyone, to win as many as possible.**

**2 Cor 6:3 We put no stumbling block in anyone's path, so that our ministry will not be discredited.**

**Heb 10:24 And let us consider how we may spur one another on toward love and good deeds.**

Somehow the church has lost the emphasis that it must have. We seem to focus on beautiful houses of worship, the proper decorum of worship and many other things that have nothing at all to do with the Gospel. In the early church, **They devoted themselves to the apostles' teaching and to the fellowship, to the breaking of bread and to prayer. Everyone was filled with awe, and many wonders and miraculous signs were done by the apostles.** (Acts 2:42-43) They focused on Jesus. Many of us find a special blessing in a certain style of worship. That, in and of its self, may be all right, but when adherence to these things prevents us from being SALT and LIGHT to the lost around us we've become selfish and counter-productive to serving our God and to the Church as a whole. The total focus of worship must be Jesus and when it is, we will know Him in a very special way. We must put aside our personal preferences if they come even close to blocking our effectiveness for Christ. People in droves are walking away from churches that have no relevance in their lives. It's time we were like the Apostle Paul and changed our thinking, bringing church into the 21$^{st}$ century, never compromising our basis beliefs but putting aside dress, time and style of worship and other non-essential constraints, that we may win this generation to Him.

# Grow Up

**Heb 5:12-13 In fact, though by this time you ought to be teachers, you need someone to teach you the elementary truths of God's word all over again. You need milk, not solid food! Anyone who lives on milk, being still an infant, is not acquainted with the teaching about righteousness.**

**Is 28:13 So then, the word of the LORD to them will become: Do and do, do and do, rule on rule, rule on rule; a little here, a little there so that they will go and fall backward, be injured and snared and captured.**

**Heb 6:1 Therefore let us leave the elementary teachings about Christ and go on to maturity, not laying again the foundation of repentance from acts that lead to death, and of faith in God,**

**1 Cor 13:11 When I was a child, I talked like a child, I thought like a child, I reasoned like a child. When I became a man, I put childish ways behind me**

Some babies progress from milk to cereal to real food much quicker than others. Perhaps you've seen that happen. But unfortunately it takes place in the church in reverse. There are many who do not progress past the milk of Scripture, or do so at a very slow rate. They're like the ones Isaiah was talking about who, "**Do and do, do and do, rule on rule, rule on rule;**" They're so happy that the pastor preaches so much on salvation and stay content to not be challenged to move on. The writer of Hebrews noted "**Anyone who lives on milk, being still an infant, is not acquainted with the teaching about righteousness.**" Our physical body does not do well on milk alone and neither does the spiritual body. While milk is nature's most perfect food, a steady diet of it will cause great physical harm just as never growing up in the Lord will cause great spiritual harm. Do not ever become satisfied to feed only on salvation, but rather seek to move on to a deeper life in the Lord, getting to know Him more intimately every day.

## HE will take care of you

**1 Peter 5:7** Cast all your anxiety on him because he cares for you.

**1 Sam 30:6** David was greatly distressed because the men were talking of stoning him; each one was bitter in spirit because of his sons and daughters. But David found strength in the LORD his God.

**Ps 37:5** Commit your way to the LORD; trust in him and he will do this:

**Matt 6:25** "Therefore I tell you, do not worry about your life, what you will eat or drink; or about your body, what you will wear. Is not life more important than food, and the body more important than clothes?"

"OOOHHHH I just don't know what I am going to do. The first of the month is still two weeks away and the account is empty. The kids need shoes, the dog should see the vet, the car is acting up, I have this ache in my leg and a multitude of other problems". Sound familiar? Some people have given themselves hypertension and even heart attacks with worry." I have to figure a way out of this". YES, there are times when we need to make adjustments in our lifestyle, confess sin, or change attitudes, BUT a lot of the time by worrying about these kinds of problems we are fretting about things over which we have absolutely no control. Life has its trials but we fail to put the proper trust in the One who so loves us. Somehow we believe He can get us into heaven, but He is not able to help us in our day-to-day living. Here is the good news. HE CAN and HE WANTS TO. We just have to do this, "Cast all your cares on HIM." If we suffer and struggle, **we** are the problem. All we have to do is allow Him to be LORD of ALL and He will handle ALL.

*Just A Thought*

## If you obey

**John 15:9-10 "As the Father has loved me, so have I loved you. Now remain in my love. If you obey my commands, you will remain in my love, just as I have obeyed my Father's commands and remain in his love"**

**Eph 3:17-18 so that Christ may dwell in your hearts through faith. And I pray that you, being rooted and established in love, may have power, together with all the saints, to grasp how wide and long and high and deep is the love of Christ,**

**1 John 2:28 And now, dear children, continue in him, so that when he appears we may be confident and unashamed before him at his coming.**

**Luke 6:47-48 "I will show you what he is like who comes to me and hears my words and puts them into practice. He is like a man building a house, who dug down deep and laid the foundation on rock."**

Some years ago we found a kitten in our haymow that had been abandoned by his mother. It took weeks of patient hand feeding and trust building before a friend of ours was able to catch him. Almost immediately after being caught and lovingly held that kitten became so content and responsive. Jesus told us to remain in Him and He also told us to love our neighbor. The two are tightly linked. Our neighbors are in need of the salvation Christ offers and like that kitten they have to come to see that we really have their best interest at heart. Our kitten ultimately was given a very loving home where he enjoyed a very happy life. Maybe if we could cease from pelting stones at those who need Christ, and instead shed some of His love on people, they would be more likely to see who He really is. Imagine the joy of offering to Jesus a soul in need of Him just by loving that soul like He does. Or, how about Christians who have failed and are in need of a loving arm to draw them securely back into Jesus' arms and back to the love and support of the church. THIS is true obedience.

## "The Lord doesn't seem to hear my prayers"

**Prov 15:29** The LORD is far from the wicked but he hears the prayer of the righteous.

**Ps 34:16** the face of the LORD is against those who do evil, to cut off the memory of them from the earth.

**Ps 138:6** Though the LORD is on high, he looks upon the lowly, but the proud he knows from afar.

**Matt 25:46** "Then they will go away to eternal punishment, but the righteous to eternal life."

So many of us would identify with the above title and can fill in the blank with our own list of "whys", but if we take another look at today's verses it's quite easy to see at least one reason our prayers seem to go unanswered. The Lord hears the righteous. Maybe it would help to define the word "righteous". Mr. Webster says that righteous is *"acting or being in accordance with what is just, honorable, and free from guilt or wrong: UPRIGHT with synonyms like virtuous, noble, moral, ethical."* While it is true that as Christians we are positionally righteous, that righteousness Christ has bestowed upon us has to work itself out in our daily lives. James says, **"But someone will say, "You have faith; I have deeds." Show me your faith without deeds, and I will show you my faith by what I do."** (James 2:18) I read yesterday of Bruce Olson who was shot with an arrow, stabbed with a spear, came down with amoebic dysentery then hepatitis and held captive twice, yet returned a third time and eventually was able to share Jesus with the Motilone Indians in Venezuela having gained their trust. His faith was evident and his call undeniable, so driven by the love of Christ he persevered. We probably will never have to endure what he did, but if our faith is not evident every day just why should the Lord answer our prayers. And this is only one of the reasons the Bible gives for unanswered prayers. Why not look up others for yourself.

## By their fruit and by their love...

**Matt 7:17-20** "Likewise every good tree bears good fruit, but a bad tree bears bad fruit. A good tree cannot bear bad fruit, and a bad tree cannot bear good fruit. Every tree that does not bear good fruit is cut down and thrown into the fire. Thus, by their fruit you will recognize them."

**Matt 12:48-50** He replied to him, "Who is my mother, and who are my brothers?" Pointing to his disciples, he said, "Here are my mother and my brothers. For whoever does the will of my Father in heaven is my brother and sister and mother."

**Matt 22:39-40** "And the second is like it: 'Love your neighbor as yourself.' All the Law and the Prophets hang on these two commandments."

**James 2:8-9** If you really keep the royal law found in Scripture, "Love your neighbor as yourself," you are doing right. But if you show favoritism, you sin and are convicted by the law as lawbreakers.

If you go to the garden looking for a cucumber you don't go to a tomato plant. If you're looking for grapes you don't head to the apple orchard. But speaking of apple trees, there you'd expect to see apples. When you look at a Christian you expect to see an example of Jesus Christ. Jesus said we would be known by our love and by our fruit. Those who are His will be loving, kind, caring and will bear another's burden. You can know if you are part of the family of God by looking at your own love and fruit. Do we live lives worthy of being called Christians? I read this morning of a lady who always went to a branch post office because the people there treated her with kindness, now that's fruit. We are called to, **"For whoever does the will of my Father in heaven is my brother and sister and mother."** (Matthew 12:48) **"Love your neighbor as yourself."** (Matt 22:40) Where do you stand when it comes to bearing fruit? Jesus loved and spent time with the leper, the woman at the well and the maniac of Gadara, and He loves you and me. How can we do less than love our neighbor?

## You are free indeed!

**John 8:34-36** Jesus replied, "I tell you the truth, everyone who sins is a slave to sin. Now a slave has no permanent place in the family, but a son belongs to it forever. So if the Son sets you free, you will be free indeed."

**Ps 19:13** Keep your servant also from willful sins; may they not rule over me. Then will I be blameless, innocent of great transgression.

**Luke 4:18** "The Spirit of the Lord is on me, because he has anointed me to preach good news to the poor. He has sent me to proclaim freedom for the prisoners and recovery of sight for the blind, to release the oppressed,"

**Gal 5:1** It is for freedom that Christ has set us free. Stand firm, then, and do not let yourselves be burdened again by a yoke of slavery.

The law of the land requires that once a person is convicted of a breach of that law there must be a punishment. Depending on the severity of the offense such punishment may be light or up to life in prison or even death. It appears that there are within the church those who believe the same should apply there. Jesus said "I am come to set you free". Sin puts us in bondage and will destroy us if we do not deal with it. BUT **"If we confess our sins, he is faithful and just and will forgive us our sins and purify us from all unrighteousness."** (1 John 1:9) With that forgiveness and cleansing comes freedom from the bondage and any additional penalty. Know the freedom He offers. Two things to remember; 1) Take your sin seriously. Confess, repent and accept His forgiveness. 2) Take your forgiveness seriously. Never let anyone tell you that you are still guilty. There are consequences we will live with, but the guilt is gone. And lastly, remember your sin for one purpose only, to serve as a reminder to avoid it from here on or help someone else to avoid it. You are FREE if you have confessed and received His forgiveness, so live in that freedom.

## How to handle people!

**Prov 15:1-2 A gentle answer turns away wrath, but a harsh word stirs up anger. The tongue of the wise commends knowledge, but the mouth of the fool gushes folly.**

**Prov 25:15 Through patience a ruler can be persuaded, and a gentle tongue can break a bone.**

**Prov 10:12 Hatred stirs up dissension, but love covers over all wrongs.**

**Prov 28:25 A greedy man stirs up dissension, but he who trusts in the LORD will prosper.**

HGTV has a show (reality type??) called "The Next Design Star". One of the contestants made a comment that reminded me of today's scripture. She said, "If I want something, I will step on anyone to get it." Unfortunately even folks in the church have the same attitude. If someone hurts them they immediately seek vengeance or at the very least issue a tongue-lashing. Far too many Christians agree with the lady I quoted, thinking they have to step on others to get ahead, when in fact the truth is the exact opposite. It is the employer that treats his employees as human beings who will develop a strong and faithful work force and do well in business. It is the sales rep that puts the well being of the client at the forefront who will experience great success and sleep well at night. It is the church leader that truly loves those he's leading who will see God's blessing on the ministry. The writer of the letter to the Hebrews put it this way, **"Make every effort to live in peace with all men and to be holy; without holiness no one will see the Lord."** (Heb 12:14) Solomon and many other wise men and women have known the truth of that statement, and Solomon also said, **"Get wisdom, get understanding; do not forget my words or swerve from them."** (Prov 4:5) Jesus said, "As the Father has loved me, so have I loved you. Now remain in my love. If you obey my commands, you will remain in my love, just as I have

**obeyed my Father's commands and remain in his love."** (John 15:9-10) As we obey God we will know His blessing and His love. Sounds like a win win situation to me. What do you think?

## Oh the pain we cause

**Matt 6:12** "Forgive us our debts, as we also have forgiven our debtors."

**Matt 6:14—15** "For if you forgive men when they sin against you, your heavenly Father will also forgive you. But if you do not forgive men their sins, your Father will not forgive your sins."

**Mark 11:25** "And when you stand praying, if you hold anything against anyone, forgive him, so that your Father in heaven may forgive you your sins."

**Luke 6:37** "Do not judge, and you will not be judged. Do not condemn, and you will not be condemned. Forgive, and you will be forgiven."

Nearly twenty-six years ago I injured my back in an accident. I received treatment but was told that I needed to let the situation progress to a certain point before surgery would be of much help. From then until November of two thousand two I just dealt with it, but by that time the pain had reached an urgent level of needed treatment. Surgery was performed, releasing the damaged nerve from further irritation, but the problem then was that the nerve responded with an attitude. It said, "I know that you have fixed me, but I have been angry too long and I choose to remain irritated". That nerve reminds me of how we are when we refuse to forgive. Over time unforgiveness festers and boils causing pain to self, family, co-workers, and everyone else in our lives. It destroys marriages, families, churches and more. Unfortunately the one you need to forgive most often is yourself. If we confess and experience Jesus' forgiveness, how dare we not forgive ourselves. Our Lord Jesus requires us to forgive with good reason. Just as the nerve in my lower back causes me constant pain, aggravation and weariness, unforgiveness causes both physical and spiritual pain and sorrow and breaks our communion with the Lord. Oh Lord, help us forgive as you forgive.

# SAVED

**Acts 16:31 They replied, "Believe in the Lord Jesus, and you will be saved**

**John 1:12 Yet to all who received him, to those who believed in his name, he gave the right to become children of God**

**John 3:15-17 "that everyone who believes in him may have eternal life. "For God so loved the world that he gave his one and only Son, that whoever believes in him shall not perish but have eternal life. For God did not send his Son into the world to condemn the world, but to save the world through him."**

**John 6:45 "It is written in the Prophets: 'They will all be taught by God.' Everyone who listens to the Father and learns from him comes to me."**

*"Redeemed how I love to proclaim it! Redeemed by the blood of the Lamb; Redeemed through His infinite mercy, His child and forever I am."* Oh how Fanny Crosby could paint a picture with words. Blind in her eyes but totally sighted in her heart, she knew the truth of the Word. The refrain of "Redeemed" says, *"Redeemed, redeemed, Redeemed by the blood of the Lamb; Redeemed, redeemed, His child and forever I am."* I am HIS child, adopted into the family of God through salvation. When a couple adopts a son or daughter they expect them to acclimate into their life style. How is it then that people can accept Jesus as Savior and not make changes in their lives? If I belong to Him I should want to assume that role. Actors study hard to become the character they play and I've heard of folks who even get so into their part they sometimes have trouble sorting out who they really are. As "redeemed" children of the living God we have a new position, a new life and a new destiny so why not wholeheartedly get into that life. If we do, this will be true **"They will all be taught by God.' Everyone who listens to the Father and learns from him comes to me."** and we will always want to

bring honor to our God and Father. This is the sincerest desire of my heart. Is it yours?

# RED FLAGS

**1 John 4:1 Dear friends, do not believe every spirit, but test the spirits to see whether they are from God, because many false prophets have gone out into the world**

**Acts 17:11 Now the Bereans were of more noble character than the Thessalonians, for they received the message with great eagerness and examined the Scriptures every day to see if what Paul said was true.**

**1 Thess 5:21-22 Test everything. Hold on to the good. Avoid every kind of evil.**

**Rom 16:19 Everyone has heard about your obedience, so I am full of joy over you; but I want you to be wise about what is good, and innocent about what is evil.**

Everywhere we look now days someone is seeing red flags. I certainly am not so naïve that I would deny all red flags, but I fear many of them are false ones that the enemy has dangled out there to dissuade us from truth. Both Paul and John dealt with the same problem in their day. False prophets were going about teaching half-truths and outright lies. Sound familiar? The key to it all is this; does what's being said or taught line up with Scripture. There's no doubt that effort is required on our part that we know the "Word" in order to be discerning. Jesus' prayer is one example, **"My prayer is not for them alone. I pray also for those who will believe in me through their message, that all of them may be one, Father, just as you are in me and I am in you. May they also be in us so that the world may believe that you have sent me. I have given them the glory that you gave me, that they may be one as we are one: I in them and you in me. May they be brought to complete unity to let the world know that you sent me and have loved them even as you have loved me."** (John 17:20-23) A pastor friend told me that on the subject of unity he sees red flags. Well if unity was Jesus' prayer for us (and it was) the flags he sees are coming from the wrong source. The bottom line is this; know the truth and live by it. If we can do that we will be found very pleasing to our Lord.

## Pure Religion

**Rom 12:2 Do not conform any longer to the pattern of this world, but be transformed by the renewing of your mind. Then you will be able to test and approve what God's will is-his good, pleasing and perfect will.**

**John 17:14 I have given them your word and the world has hated them, for they are not of the world any more than I am of the world**

**1 Cor 3:19 For the wisdom of this world is foolishness in God's sight. As it is written: "He catches the wise in their craftiness"**

**James 1:27 Religion that God our Father accepts as pure and faultless is this: to look after orphans and widows in their distress and to keep oneself from being polluted by the world.**

There is an old story about the heart, the conscience and a knife. The knife is shaped like a triangle with three sharp blades. When driven through the heart it turns a little every time we do wrong. The pain is great, but as one sins more and more eventually the knife becomes dulled to the point that its turn causes no discomfort at all. The Word tells us over and over to be different from the world. Some claim that they are different because they keep their list of do's and don'ts. But Christ was different in that He loved everyone He came into contact with. He loved the woman at the well, the woman taken in adultery, the leper, and the woman who touched the very hem of His robe. He loved Judas so much He even washed his feet just hours before his betrayal and He loved Peter even when he denied Him. He expects us to be like Himself. We are to be different from the world in that we are to imitate Him. James says that religion acceptable to God is pure and faithful and it is to extend love. Oh God, help us to be religious in a way acceptable to You.

# REPUTATION

**Phil 2:7-8 but made Himself nothing, taking the very nature of a servant, being made in human likeness. And being found in appearance as a man, He humbled Himself and became obedient to death even death on a cross!**

**Matt 3:15 Jesus replied, "Let it be so now; it is proper for us to do this to fulfill all righteousness." Then John consented.**

**John 6:38 "For I have come down from heaven not to do my will but to do the will of him who sent me."**

**Eph 5:4 Nor should there be obscenity, foolish talk or coarse joking, which are out of place, but rather thanksgiving.**

There are many kinds of reputations we human beings do our best to protect. The politician builds up his image before the voters, the preacher polishes his/her appearance before the congregation and the actor will do most anything to keep the public attracted to his current movie or show. For some it is the amount of booze or drugs they are able to consume and still walk. For another who is a real jokester, the viler the gags the bigger the audience they attract. Then there is the leader who protects his power over people at all costs. To give up the current status is unthinkable; "elections are coming, feathers may get ruffled or I may become the brunt of jokes if I do what is right or forsake my life of sin". BUT, Jesus Christ, the Son of God, the one person who had a right to be honored and revered, put all aside to become a lowly carpenter and graduated to itinerant preacher only to die in the most degrading way known at the time. We Christians are often remiss to take a stand lest peers reject us. Brothers and sisters this cannot be. We, at the very least, owe Him so much that we must be His ambassadors no matter the cost.

## Safety inside the lines

**Prov 22:28 Do not move an ancient boundary stone set up by your forefathers.**

**Prov 23:10 Do not move an ancient boundary stone or encroach on the fields of the fatherless,**

**Hos 5:10 Judah's leaders are like those who move boundary stones. I will pour out my wrath on them like a flood of water.**

**Job 24:2 Men move boundary stones; they pasture flocks they have stolen. 3 They drive away the orphan's donkey and take the widow's ox in pledge.**

When I was a kid I remember playing baseball and getting tagged out because I happened to turn the wrong direction after coming to first base. It seems that if you turn toward second, even if you don't intend to try for it, you can be tagged. Rules and boundaries can be confusing at times and aggravating at others, but overall they are designed for our protection. God made boundaries to protect our society and us and when we stretch or cross those limits we set in motion what are often very serious and dangerous conditions. When a parent or a relative crosses the line and inappropriately touches a child, at the very least a life of confusion and emotional torture results. A teen lets her date go too far and finds herself in the position of having to tell mom and dad she is pregnant. A "harmless" (no such thing) flirtation brings on the destruction of a family. God gave lines to give us joy and freedom and when we break the rules we put ourselves into a place of captivity. Sin has great lure and presents itself as freedom, but as in the life of the meth user it hooks us and can bring us to the point of despair. Freedom is only found in obedience; that is why Proverbs says, "Do not move the ancient boundary stone". Oh that we would leave the stones in place and know His peace and joy.

## Ritualism

**Matt 28:18-20 Then Jesus came to them and said, "All authority in heaven and on earth has been given to me. Therefore go and make disciples of all nations, baptizing them in the name of the Father and of the Son and of the Holy Spirit, and teaching them to obey everything I have commanded you. And surely I am with you always, to the very end of the age."**

"Therefore go and make disciples." This was the charge Jesus gave to His church, those who claim His salvation. How could we have gotten so far off track? Could it be that we have taken on too many other agendas? Here are three "traditions" that should throw up red flags all over the place. First — A "pastoral ritualism" that assumes, among other things, that certain methods of worship are the best possible and ultimately the only ones. Second — A "social ritualism" in which the general consensus of opinion in a church dictates the list of "do's and don'ts" and one's degree of closeness to God is based on and evidenced by the keeping of that list. Third — A "personal ritualism" in which every man has his own opinion of the conditions under which he and others may be right with God. All of these omit the fact that it is for GOD ALONE to decide what is right and honoring to Him. When we demand our own way or tradition (our ritualism) we get caught up in dictating what God can and cannot do, stifling His work and neglecting our purpose in this world. Jesus said, "**...You nullify the word of God for the sake of your tradition. You hypocrites! Isaiah was right when he prophesied about you: "'These people honor me with their lips, but their hearts are far from me. They worship me in vain; their teachings are but rules taught by men."** (Matt 15:6-9)

# Tithe???

**Mal 3:8 "Will a man rob God? Yet you rob me. "But you ask, 'How do we rob you?'**
**"In tithes and offerings."**

**Prov 3:9 Honor the LORD with your wealth, with the firstfruits of all your crops;**

**Luke 20:24-25 "Show me a denarius. Whose portrait and inscription are on it?" "Caesar's," they replied. He said to them, "Then give to Caesar what is Caesar's, and to God what is God's."**

**Mark 10:21-22 Jesus looked at him and loved him. "One thing you lack," he said. "Go, sell everything you have and give to the poor, and you will have treasure in heaven. Then come, follow me." At this the man's face fell. He went away sad, because he had great wealth.**

Will a man rob God? Sad to say, but yes, men do rob God on a regular basis. We steal from Him in many ways. Jesus Christ gave His very life with one purpose in mind and that was to redeem His creation from the hands of the enemy. In the garden Eve bought Satan's lie and even today men/women continue to buy into the lies of the one who hates God. He cons us into thinking that we do not have time to read the Word or to pray and we cannot afford to tithe. In so doing we deny Him the ability to effectively work in our day-to-day life. The Bible is filled with promises for our welfare, but those promises have requirements. To be sure of a home in heaven we must accept Jesus' redemption. To enjoy the rest of His blessings we need to focus on adhering to His rules. When it comes to tithing God said **"Bring the whole tithe into the storehouse, that there may be food in my house. Test me in this," says the LORD Almighty, "and see if I will not throw open the floodgates of heaven and pour out so much blessing that you will not have room enough for it."** (Mal 3:10) In truth, we cannot afford not to be obedient to the commands of our God.

## Is this YOUR story?

**Rom 8:38-39 For I am convinced that neither death nor life, neither angels nor demons, neither the present nor the future, nor any powers, neither height nor depth, nor anything else in all creation, will be able to separate us from the love of God that is in Christ Jesus our Lord.**

*"Blessed assurance, Jesus is mine! Oh what a foretaste of glory divine! Heir of salvation, purchase of God, Born of His Spirit, washed in His blood."* When Fanny Crosby penned these words nearly a century ago she drew such a wonderful picture of salvation. Oh the security of being in Christ! He has promised to hold us in His own hands and never let go, even to the point of assuring us that no one can snatch us out of His hand. Crosby goes on to describe the joys of submission, the mercy He bestows, being "filled with His goodness and lost in His love." Wow, sounds like a deal to me! BUT listen to the chorus, *"This is my story, this is my song: Praising my savior all the day long. This is my story, this is my song: Praising my savior all the day long."* The life that is in Christ and the one who knows His joy will tell this story to a lost and dying world by the life they live, not only the words they speak. **"Whoever acknowledges me before men, I will also acknowledge him before my Father in heaven. But whoever disowns me before men, I will disown him before my Father in heaven."** (Matt 10:32-33) When was the last time you intentionally shared the Good News of salvation with a lost loved one, friend or someone God brought across your path? There is no higher calling than that and being able to sing "Blessed Assurance".

## Pray all the time!

**1 Thess 5:17 pray continually;**

**Luke 18:1 Then Jesus told his disciples a parable to show them that they should always pray and not give up**

**Luke 21:36 "Be always on the watch, and pray that you may be able to escape all that is about to happen, and that you may be able to stand before the Son of Man."**

**Eph 6:18 And pray in the Spirit on all occasions with all kinds of prayers and requests. With this in mind, be alert and always keep on praying for all the saints.**

Somehow prayer has seemed to drop to a 911 thing. When all else fails we decide to pray. Jesus said to, **"Be always on the watch, and pray"** I have heard of folks that have done intensive research into what ALWAYS means and have found that it means ALWAYS. Our lives need to be in constant communication with our Lord if we are to survive and make it to the next level. Video games have different levels for players of varying skills. The way a championship gamer gets to be a champ is to play, study and play, over and over. For some reason human beings find it easier to become winners in this world than to become champions for the One who gave His all for them. Prayer, talking to and with God, should be as easy and common as talking to a friend or spouse. He is willing and oh so desirous for that level of relationship. Even as you beam when a friend, a child or a mate wants to invest time in you, Jesus BEAMS and sets off a heavenly chorus of praise when you give Him your time. Do you want your life to have depth of meaning, constant peace, joy and the presence of God at every turn? Just pray, pray, pray and pray some more. Oh, and that does not require a specific physical position or anything but a heart attuned to God.

## Friend of God

**Acts 13:22 After removing Saul, he made David their king. He testified concerning him: 'I have found David son of Jesse a man after my own heart; he will do everything I want him to do.'**

**1 Kings 15:3 He committed all the sins his father had done before him; his heart was not fully devoted to the LORD his God, as the heart of David his forefather had been.**

**1 Kings 15:5 For David had done what was right in the eyes of the LORD and had not failed to keep any of the LORD's commands all the days of his life-except in the case of Uriah the Hittite.**

**James 2:23 And the scripture was fulfilled that says, "Abraham believed God, and it was credited to him as righteousness," and he was called God's friend.**

Oh what a blessing when a son or daughter is obedient and well behaved and a double blessing when they apologize sincerely if they do mess up. A parent feels especially close to that child; not that the others are not loved, but the compliant child is a breath of fresh air. God called David "a man after my own heart". Yes, David was one hundred percent human and as such he did sin, but the difference was that he took responsibility for that sin, confessed it and enjoyed the tender presence of the God he loved, the One to whom he was fully devoted. Listen to his confession to God – **"For I know my transgressions, and my sin is always before me. Against You, You only, have I sinned and done what is evil in your sight, so that You are proved right when You speak and justified when You judge. Surely I was sinful at birth, sinful from the time my mother conceived me.** (Ps 51:3-5) David was a man after God's heart, Abraham was a friend of God, and this was only true because they so believed in their Creator. Also, they were sincerely sorry for their sin (lying, adultery, murder) and poured out to Him their sorrow, the result being that they were what God's word says they were. May we also be friends of our God and people after God's own heart.

## Onward and upward

**Eph 5:14 for it is light that makes everything visible. This is why it is said: "Wake up, O sleeper, rise from the dead, and Christ will shine on you."**

**John 8:12 When Jesus spoke again to the people, he said, "I am the light of the world. Whoever follows me will never walk in darkness, but will have the light of life."**

**2 Cor 4:6 For God, who said, "Let light shine out of darkness," made his light shine in our hearts to give us the light of the knowledge of the glory of God in the face of Christ**

**Luke 15:17-18 "When he came to his senses, he said, 'How many of my father's hired men have food to spare, and here I am starving to death! I will set out and go back to my father"**

Join me, if you will, deep in a coalmine. The miner has been down there for hours wanting to get out and does not know how to reach the surface, the reason being that his light has gone out. Suddenly another miner appears with a new battery and replaces the old one. Ah, he can see, all is OK, but he makes no move toward the exit. You begin to wonder if this guy is really in his right mind. He has light so why doesn't he get a move on. Many Christians are like him. They have the light of Jesus but are complacent staying right where they are. It takes action as well as light to make our lives count for Jesus. The prodigal son "came to his senses", and then he acted, "I will set out and go". John the Baptist told his audience, **"Produce fruit in keeping with repentance."** (Matt 3:8) No more than the miner staying in the ground after having a light to show the way to safety, can a truly saved person be content to stay where they are. We have to get to know the Light, act upon His word and produce fruit for His honor and glory. We can find no better way to honor Him than by sharing Him.

## Keep your cup of love full, at home

**Prov 5:15 Drink water from your own cistern, running water from your own well.**

**Ps 128:3-4 Your wife will be like a fruitful vine within your house; your sons will be like olive shoots around your table. Thus is the man blessed who fears the LORD.**

**Heb 13:4 Marriage should be honored by all, and the marriage bed kept pure, for God will judge the adulterer and all the sexually immoral.**

**1 Peter 3:7 Husbands, in the same way be considerate as you live with your wives, and treat them with respect as the weaker partner and as heirs with you of the gracious gift of life, so that nothing will hinder your prayers.**

Solomon very vividly portrayed in his "Song of Songs" the value and preciousness of love between a married man and woman. In his dialogue with his "beloved" we can see the need for and enjoyment of that love. **"Let him kiss me with the kisses of his mouth for your love is more delightful than wine. Pleasing is the fragrance of your perfumes; your name is like perfume poured out. No wonder the maidens love you! Take me away with you-let us hurry! Let the king bring me into his chambers."** (Song 1:2-4) The world is full of men and women who either have no lover or desire many and seem to always be on the prowl for another notch on their belt. God made us with a great desire for sexual unity but expects us to meet that need within the bonds of marriage. Love and sex are a holy experience and as such are supposed to be respected and honored. The current trend in comedy (???) is to belittle and smear the value of that marital unity. There is nothing funny or humorous about sex. Two things come to mind, first – keep your cup of love full at home and you will know the real meaning of sexual union, and secondly – the next time you hear someone demeaning the value of love via supposed humor turn it off and refuse to listen, for **"Marriage should be honored by all"**. Let us start showing that honor.

## Is it love God or LOVE God?

**Matt 22:37-40 Jesus replied: "'Love the Lord your God with all your heart and with all your soul and with all your mind.' This is the first and greatest commandment. And the second is like it: 'Love your neighbor as yourself.' All the Law and the Prophets hang on these two commandments."**

**Mark 12:33 "To love him with all your heart, with all your understanding and with all your strength, and to love your neighbor as yourself is more important than all burnt offerings and sacrifices."**

**Rom 8:7-8 the sinful mind is hostile to God. It does not submit to God's law, nor can it do so. Those controlled by the sinful nature cannot please God.**

**1 John 5:2 This is how we know that we love the children of God: by loving God and carrying out his commands.**

There's an old saying that goes like this "if mama ain't happy, ain't nobody happy." While that's usually shared in a funny sense, it does portray the way many try to use God. As long as He answers all prayers the way we request and gets us out of all tight spots He is okay, but when things stay tough and life is hard God gets the blame and a cold shoulder. If you want proof, then just think about recent praises you've heard. Did they sound like this? "I praise the Lord for solving a problem in my life, for helping me with a test, for giving me a friend or maybe for taking an illness from me." Praise the Lord for those things, yes, but have you heard Him receive praise for the glory of His presence, for the joy of reading His Word or a book about the Christian walk, or for a current struggle with a disease? I recently heard a young lady praise the Lord that her gas was shut off. Now there is a true understanding of God's working in her life. Here is real love in that when God does not totally solve my every woe I still praise Him every moment of every day. Do we?

## Pass Grace On

**Matt 18:28-34 "But when that servant went out, he found one of his fellow servants who owed him a hundred denarii. He grabbed him and began to choke him. 'Pay back what you owe me!' he demanded. 9 "His fellow servant fell to his knees and begged him, 'Be patient with me, and I will pay you back.' "But he refused. Instead, he went off and had the man thrown into prison until he could pay the debt. When the other servants saw what had happened, they were greatly distressed and went and told their master everything that had happened."**

It is amazing how my sin is never even close to being as bad as yours. Trouble is having had that attitude I am beginning to see that my eyes have been just a bit clouded. God hates ALL sin, mine included, and in the parable above Jesus uses an allegory about money to make His point regarding debt and forgiveness, What we need to grasp here is that because of God's grace we have been forgiven our sin that put a smear on His purity; so we in turn must extend that grace and forgiveness to others, whether they hurt our feelings or whatever. When WE are sinned against it is an attack on our ego and self worth. When we sin against GOD we assault His value and ALL He is and ALL He does, including the sacrifice of His one and only Son for our benefit. So the question is how dare we not forgive those who offend us? Jesus said, **"Then the master called the servant in. 'You wicked servant,' he said, 'I canceled all that debt of yours because you begged me to. Shouldn't you have had mercy on your fellow servant just as I had on you?"** Shouldn't we? The obvious answer is YES. Then the story's conclusion, **"In anger his master turned him over to the jailers to be tortured, until he should pay back all he owed."** Does that mean we will not be allowed into heaven if we refuse to obey God's command to forgive? I don't know, but I am not about to take a chance. Are you?

## OH HOW HE SUFFERED !

**Luke 22:44 And being in anguish, he prayed more earnestly, and his sweat was like drops of blood falling to the ground.**

**Rev 19:13 He is dressed in a robe dipped in blood, and his name is the Word of God.**

**Is 50:6 I offered my back to those who beat me, my cheeks to those who pulled out my beard; I did not hide my face from mocking and spitting.**

**Matt 26:67 Then they spit in his face and struck him with their fists. Others slapped him 68 and said, "Prophesy to us, Christ. Who hit you?"**

**Mark 15:34 And at the ninth hour Jesus cried out in a loud voice, "Eloi, Eloi, lama sabachthani?" which means, "My God, my God, why have you forsaken me?"**

There are times when this Christian life brings us mocking and jeering from the world. Some of us faint in our attempts to live the Word. "I'll lose my friends if I get too serious about this Christianity thing." Isaiah told us, "**But He was pierced for our transgressions, He was crushed for our iniquities; the punishment that brought us peace was upon Him, and by His wounds we are healed.**" (Is 53:5) Jesus suffered ever so greatly. He sweat like drops of blood, endured floggings, His beard was plucked out then He gladly allowed those ugly nails to be driven through His hands and feet, all that He might bring reconciliation to His lost creation. I have watched the movie "The Passion of the Christ" several times. It is a reminder of how much He suffered for me, and personally I do not think that those responsible were able to present a full picture of His passion. Some today would present the Christian life as a life of ease, but why should we fare better than the One who paid our penalty. Many years ago in prayer I envisioned His sorrow and blood flowing down and I want to always remember that what little suffering I endure is

NOTHING compared to His. We should need no more encouragement than that to live a Christ-like life no matter what.

*Just A Thought*

## What is the character of God?

**Jonah 4:1-2 But Jonah was greatly displeased and became angry. He prayed to the LORD, "O LORD, is this not what I said when I was still at home? That is why I was so quick to flee to Tarshish. I knew that you are a gracious and compassionate God, slow to anger and abounding in love, a God who relents from sending calamity.**

**Ex 34:6 And he passed in front of Moses, proclaiming, "The LORD, the LORD, the compassionate and gracious God, slow to anger, abounding in love and faithfulness, 7 maintaining love to thousands, and forgiving wickedness, rebellion and sin. Yet he does not leave the guilty unpunished; he punishes the children and their children for the sin of the fathers to the third and fourth generation."**

**Ps 86:15 But you, O Lord, are a compassionate and gracious God, slow to anger, abounding in love and faithfulness.**

The Pharisees did it and so do many people today. They present the anger and vengeance of God as His only or main characteristics. Many people are hard and unforgiving so they want others to see God in the same way. Jonah knew God very well. He knew that He would forgive those evil Ninevites, but he hated them and wanted God to hate them as well. So great was his dislike for them that he risked not only his life and limb, to escape bringing the good news to Nineveh, but also the lives of everyone on his ship. That is the way it is when we place more value on our opinions than on God's true character. Jesus told the Pharisees, **"Woe to you, teachers of the law and Pharisees, you hypocrites! You travel over land and sea to win a single convert, and when he becomes one, you make him twice as much a son of hell as you are."** (Matt 23:15) God is loving, kind, forgiving and a thousand more adjectives to anyone who will come to Him. If only our world could see this kind of God they might be like those Ninevites and repent. What glory that would bring to Him.

## No one knows, but the Father

**Mark 13:32** "No one knows about that day or hour, not even the angels in heaven, nor the Son, but only the Father."

**Matt 24:37-39** "As it was in the days of Noah, so it will be at the coming of the Son of Man. For in the days before the flood, people were eating and drinking, marrying and giving in marriage, up to the day Noah entered the ark; and they knew nothing about what would happen until the flood came and took them all away. That is how it will be at the coming of the Son of Man."

**1 Thess 5:2** for you know very well that the day of the Lord will come like a thief in the night.

Complex mathematical codes and theories about the return of Christ are a dime a dozen. One story told of a group who were so sure that His return would occur on a date early in the last century they sold all they had and went up on a mountain to wait. If they were so sure, why did they SELL things? When He DOES come we will not need things or the money they represent. One theory using a 14,000-day base expected something great to happen on October 4, 2005. It is true that the return of our precious Lord may be soon, and it may not be, but we need to live EVERY DAY as if it would be that day. Jesus told of the virgins awaiting the bridegroom, **"At that time the kingdom of heaven will be like ten virgins who took their lamps and went out to meet the bridegroom. Five of them were foolish and five were wise. The foolish ones took their lamps but did not take any oil with them. The wise, however, took oil in jars along with their lamps."** (Matt 25:1-4) Let us be as the wise and be prepared every day, fully expecting the arrival of our full salvation, whether it is today or not for one hundred years. So the question of the day is this, "is your lamp trimmed and fueled?"

## He who watches over you

**Ps 121:1 I lift up my eyes to the hills where does my help come from?**
**2 My help comes from the LORD, the Maker of heaven and earth.**
**3 He will not let your foot slip he who watches over you will not slumber;**
**4 indeed, he who watches over Israel will neither slumber nor sleep.**
**5 The LORD watches over you the LORD is your shade at your right hand;**
**6 the sun will not harm you by day, nor the moon by night.**
**7 The LORD will keep you from all harm He will watch over your life;**
**8 the LORD will watch over your coming and going both now and forevermore.**

David once said, **"Even though I walk through the valley of the shadow of death, I will fear no evil, for you are with me; your rod and your staff, they comfort me."** (Ps 23:4) WOW! What confidence in the Lord. There is only one reason David could have such assurance. He made it a point to study, pray and invest time in his God. There's no other way he could be free of fear in death and know that God was always watching over him, tending to his needs and keeping his foot from slipping. David had learned the truth that Paul wrote so many years later, **"Therefore, I urge you, brothers, in view of God's mercy, to offer your bodies as living sacrifices, holy and pleasing to God-this is your spiritual act of worship. Do not conform any longer to the pattern of this world, but be transformed by the renewing of your mind. Then you will be able to test and approve what God's will is-his good, pleasing and perfect will."** (Rom 12:1-2) Just like David, we have to **intentionally** develop a relationship with **our** great God. Oh the joy and peace we forfeit if we do not. Everyone wants to make investments that will pay-off big time and here is the one that will do just that. Read the Psalm again and you will find that it's just what you have been looking for.

## Seek First

**Hag 1:3-4 Then the word of the LORD came through the prophet Haggai: "Is it a time for you yourselves to be living in your paneled houses, while this house remains a ruin?"**

**Ps 132:3-5 "I will not enter my house or go to my bed I will allow no sleep to my eyes, no slumber to my eyelids, till I find a place for the LORD, a dwelling for the Mighty One of Jacob."**

**Matt 6:33 "But seek first his kingdom and his righteousness, and all these things will be given to you as well."**

**Phil 2:21 For everyone looks out for his own interests, not those of Jesus Christ.**

The Lord spoke through Haggai to accuse the Hebrews of thinking more of their personal comfort than of their spiritual condition. They were living in fine houses with wood paneling and all the niceties of the day. At the same time they were paying no heed to the condition of the temple, God's house. It lay in shambles and they just ignored it, after all, they were comfortable. It never occurred to them that the source of their everyday problems might be the attitude they held toward God. "Now this is what the LORD Almighty says: **"Give careful thought to your ways. You have planted much, but have harvested little. You eat, but never have enough. You drink, but never have your fill. You put on clothes, but are not warm. You earn wages, only to put them in a purse with holes in it."** (Hag 1:5-6) David felt the need of honoring God when he said that he would not sleep until he found a place for God. (Ps 132:4-5 above) Jesus told us to seek Him first, yet Paul had a problem with selfishness in the church and wrote that everyone was more concerned with his or her own interests. (Phil 2:21) Note he does not say needs, but interests. In our day many things vie for our attention, **"...but only one thing is needed. Mary has chosen what is better, and it will not be taken away from her."** (Luke 10:42) That one thing is our Lord and Savior.

## Oh for a quiet life

**1 Thess 4:11 Make it your ambition to lead a quiet life, to mind your own business and to work with your hands, just as we told you,**

**2 Cor 5:9 So we make it our goal to please him, whether we are at home in the body or away from it.**

**1 Cor 7:20 Each one should remain in the situation which he was in when God called him.**

**1 Thess 4:1 Finally, brothers, we instructed you how to live in order to please God, as in fact you are living. Now we ask you and urge you in the Lord Jesus to do this more and more.**

"Oh my, there seems to be more to do than there are hours in a day. I just don't seem to be able to get it all done." One of the reasons we are so loaded with tasks and busyness is self (guilt, pride, the need for praise etc.) and we take on more than we should. The Apostle Paul says, **"Make it your ambition"** the KJV puts it this way, **"that ye study to be quiet".** Both translations make it clear that we have to work to live quietly. Busyness and stress come easily, like sin. They are alluring and attractive and as such appeal to our self. After all, what will people think if I don't agree to teach that class or do any number of other jobs? If we are to "study or make it our ambition to live quiet lives" we have to get alone with our Lord and receive direction from Him, then VOLUNTEER for the assignment HE gives. Two things will happen when we do so; first, all the important jobs will be filled and secondly, we will be free from stress in our lives because the load will be shared. Whether in the workplace, community, church or home many hands make light work. If every person is carrying his share of the load everyone will be burden free. Think about the advantages of a non-overloaded life.

## Ossified or Alive?

**Eph 4:18 They are darkened in their understanding and separated from the life of God because of the ignorance that is in them due to the hardening of their hearts.**

**James 4:4 You adulterous people, don't you know that friendship with the world is hatred toward God? Anyone who chooses to be a friend of the world becomes an enemy of God.**

**Rom 1:21 For although they knew God, they neither glorified him as God nor gave thanks to him, but their thinking became futile and their foolish hearts were darkened.**

**Rom 11:25 I do not want you to be ignorant of this mystery, brothers, so that you may not be conceited: Israel has experienced a hardening in part until the full number of the Gentiles has come in**

Our bodies need exercise in order to stay the least bit limber. If you have ever had serious surgery you know it is necessary to get up and about as soon as possible. The longer we remain in bed the harder it becomes to move. It hurts, but it will hurt even more if we don't. Atrophy will set in and muscles will become rigid and unbending. Unfortunately there are many in the church who have become like that. They have adopted legalistic views and stances that are anything but loving and Christlike. Paul explains it this way, **"For although they knew God, they neither glorified him as God nor gave thanks to him, but their thinking became futile and their foolish hearts were darkened."** (Rom 1:21) Knowing or claiming to know God is one thing, but **"knowing" God intimately** is another. The problem gets worse when we become like Jeremiah's description, **"Yet they did not listen or pay attention; they were stiff-necked and would not listen or respond to discipline."** (Jer 17:23) Our spiritual lives need to be stretched and molded as our God would have them or we will be of no use to Him. Choosing to follow men's fables and teachings before those of the Word leads to becoming darkened and filled with futile thinking.

## When I am weak I am very strong!

**2 Cor 12:10** That is why, for Christ's sake, I delight in weaknesses, in insults, in hardships, in persecutions, in difficulties. For when I am weak, then I am strong.

**2 Cor 12:9** But he said to me, "My grace is sufficient for you, for my power is made perfect in weakness." Therefore I will boast all the more gladly about my weaknesses, so that Christ's power may rest on me.

**Eph 6:10** Finally, be strong in the Lord and in his mighty power.

I wonder at times how long it took the Apostle Paul to learn the truth about how to be strong, after all, he said, **"though I myself have reasons for such confidence. If anyone else thinks he has reasons to put confidence in the flesh, I have more: circumcised on the eighth day, of the people of Israel, of the tribe of Benjamin, a Hebrew of Hebrews; in regard to the law, a Pharisee;"** (Phil 3:4-5) He was somebody in his day but he learned this powerful lesson. I grew up in an era where "real men" didn't cry, where they bucked-up and handled the situation. It took me a long time to learn that it takes a stronger person not to throw a punch than to throw one and it takes more fortitude to sob like a baby than to refuse a tear. Our society says we have to handle our lives ourselves, but a real man or woman knows that being truly strong is to fall in a heap at the foot of the cross and cry out to Jesus. Paul also learned, **"But whatever was to my profit I now consider loss for the sake of Christ. What is more, I consider everything a loss compared to the surpassing greatness of knowing Christ Jesus my Lord, for whose sake I have lost all things. I consider them rubbish, that I may gain Christ and be found in him, not having a righteousness of my own that comes from the law, but that which is through faith in Christ-the righteousness that comes from God and is by faith."** (Phil 3:7-9) So where do you and I find our strength?

## Like a drunken man

**Hab 3:16 I heard and my heart pounded, my lips quivered at the sound; decay crept into my bones, and my legs trembled. Yet I will wait patiently for the day of calamity to come on the nation invading us.**

**Jer 23:9 Concerning the prophets: My heart is broken within me; all my bones tremble. I am like a drunken man, like a man overcome by wine, because of the LORD and his holy words.**

**Dan 8:27 I, Daniel, was exhausted and lay ill for several days. Then I got up and went about the king's business. I was appalled by the vision; it was beyond understanding.**

**Rev 1:17 When I saw him, I fell at his feet as though dead. Then he placed his right hand on me and said: "Do not be afraid. I am the First and the Last"**

Many years ago while doing some electrical wiring I accidentally (I might add stupidly) got an extreme electrical shock. I even passed out momentarily. When I came to, my heart was racing and I was quite confused for a short time. This is as close as I can come in physical terms to describing what the prophets and John went through after face to faces with the Lord. The Lord and His holy words should produce in us that same amazement and sense of weakness and loss of control. Every weekend and even weekdays people totally lose control of all sense and sensibility while under the influence of alcohol. As a result kids are maimed and die, wives have broken bones, marred complexions and sometimes die, and families are left in horrific states; and this is just for starters. Paul said, **"Do not get drunk on wine, which leads to debauchery. Instead, be filled with the Spirit."** (Eph 5:18) Oh how much better to be filled with the Spirit. Kids have healthy family lives knowing the love of parents, wives know the joy of a husband that shows them respect and honor, husbands know the joy of what family is really supposed to be and families are filled with joy and peace. What a comparison. As for me, I far prefer the amazement of the Sovereign Lord to anything. How about you?

## Fight a good fight!

**1 Cor 9:24-27 Do you not know that in a race all the runners run, but only one gets the prize? Run in such a way as to get the prize. Everyone who competes in the games goes into strict training. They do it to get a crown that will not last; but we do it to get a crown that will last forever. Therefore I do not run like a man running aimlessly; I do not fight like a man beating the air. No, I beat my body and make it my slave...**

**2 Tim 2:5-7 Similarly, if anyone competes as an athlete, he does not receive the victor's crown unless he competes according to the rules. The hardworking farmer should be the first to receive a share of the crops. Reflect on what I am saying, for the Lord will give you insight into all this.**

Paul issued a serious warning, **"For our struggle is not against flesh and blood, but against the rulers, against the authorities, against the powers of this dark world and against the spiritual forces of evil in the heavenly realms."** (Eph 6:12) Perhaps if we were wrestling against flesh and blood we might win all on our own, at least for a while; BUT our enemies are not mere mortals. Sometimes it is people who cause us harm but the motivation comes from the evil within mankind. When Jesus was fasting alone in the desert (Matthew 4) Satan demonstrated that the enemy knows scripture only too well and is not above using it to trip us up. We need to know the Word and how to rely upon it and we need to know its author. Even in Bible times folks were well aware of the discipline it took to be an athlete. Olympic stars leave home and family to live at training camps where they eat and sleep their sport. They do it all for a moment of glory and will may be accused of cheating one way or another if they succeed. Some Christians (??) think they can accept Jesus as Savior then coast into heaven. Paul was not afraid to issue warning after warning against that mindset. The Christian life is a battle and if we are to win the "well done faithful servant", we must go into hard training. Do you take Jesus that seriously?

## The Eye, Source of Light or Not

**Matt 6:22 "The eye is the lamp of the body. If your eyes are good, your whole body will be full of light."**

**Luke 11:34-36 "Your eye is the lamp of your body. When your eyes are good, your whole body also is full of light. But when they are bad, your body also is full of darkness. See to it, then, that the light within you is not darkness. Therefore, if your whole body is full of light, and no part of it dark, it will be completely lighted, as when the light of a lamp shines on you."**

**2 Cor 11:3 But I am afraid that just as Eve was deceived by the serpent's cunning, your minds may somehow be led astray from your sincere and pure devotion to Christ.**

The eye is the source of light that enters the body and the soul. If the eye admits darkness and shadows, the whole will soon be following suit and living in that darkness. The desire to kick back and relax a little in front of the "boob tube" can be one example of darkness entering the eye. It seems that from the ads to the sit-coms the main thing presented is sex. Sex in and of its self is not wrong or evil. God created sex and blessed it. Look at, **"Marriage should be honored by all, and the marriage bed kept pure, for God will judge the adulterer and all the sexually immoral."** (Heb 13:4) Compare this verse to the last sit-com you watched. How about that joke the other day? **"Nor should there be obscenity, foolish talk or coarse joking, which are out of place, but rather thanksgiving,"** (Eph 5:4) If we aren't more careful about what comes into our minds through the eye and the ear we may well find ourselves filled with darkness. Look at what Jesus offered as the outcome of that, **"But if your eyes are bad, your whole body will be full of darkness. If then the light within you is darkness, how great is that darkness!"**

## Put NO stumbling block

**Rom 14:13 Therefore let us stop passing judgment on one another. Instead, make up your mind not to put any stumbling block or obstacle in your brother's way.**

**James 4:11 Brothers, do not slander one another. Anyone who speaks against his brother or judges him speaks against the law and judges it. When you judge the law, you are not keeping it, but sitting in judgment on it.**

**Matt 18:7 "Woe to the world because of the things that cause people to sin! Such things must come, but woe to the man through whom they come!"**

We often feel some degree of smugness if we do not commit what we consider to be sin. "I don't kill, covet, nor commit adultery, why I don't even smoke or drink. God must be impressed by my actions. It can't be sin or a stumbling block when I give the waitress a hard time and no tip just because my coffee cup got empty or my food was not exactly as ordered. And surely I'm not sinning if I don't feel pain when a drug user overdoses. (Even though that soul may have just landed in hell.) So what if I smear the reputation of another, after all they hurt me. And spreading rumors can't be entirely my fault. If that person hadn't been in their situation to begin with, there wouldn't be all that gossip to pass around. Oh and it cannot be sin if I fail to pray for lost family, friends, neighbors or even people I don't know." I'm reminded of the lady who spread a rumor about the pastor and quickly repented. When she apologized to him he asked her to drop a bag of feathers from the belfry then pick them all up. In a while she came back with all she could find and it was then she realized that just like the feathers she could not know where all her gossip had gone either. Can you blame a lost world for not wanting a Jesus who seems to endorse smugness, gossip, abusiveness, uncaring attitudes and selfishness? The Word says to not put out stumbling blocks. Kind of encourages us to take a hard look at all we do and say.

*Just A Thought*

## Seek not the approval of man

**John 5:44** "How can you believe if you accept praise from one another, yet make no effort to obtain the praise that comes from the only God?"

**John 3:19-20** "This is the verdict: Light has come into the world, but men loved darkness instead of light because their deeds were evil. Everyone who does evil hates the light, and will not come into the light for fear that his deeds will be exposed."

**John 12:42-43** "Yet at the same time many even among the leaders believed in him. But because of the Pharisees they would not confess their faith for fear they would be put out of the synagogue; for they loved praise from men more than praise from God."

**Matt 23:5** "Everything they do is done for men to see: They make their phylacteries wide and the tassels on their garments long; 6 they love the place of honor at banquets and the most important seats in the synagogues; 7 they love to be greeted in the marketplaces and to have men call them 'Rabbi.'

Man, it seems, is hung up on the approval of man. When we receive the attention of others there develops a sense of self-worth. We fall into the trap of admiring the one we believe has "arrived" for their money or possessions or position or any number of other things. The above verses fly in the face of that mindset. In reality it is the approval of God and His favor that is the only thing worth seeking. A.W. Tozer made this statement. *"Men and women who will make the honest once-for-all decision to exalt and honor God and His Christ over all, are precious to God above all treasures of earth or sea, for He knows that His honor is safe in such consecrated hands!"* It was He who created all things, it is in Him that all things exist and it is in Him that there is life, peace, joy and freedom. What it comes down to is that God must be first and foremost in us. If not, we may need to ask, "do I really believe at all?" Who do you seek to impress?

## He upset their apple cart

**Luke 20:5-6** They discussed it among themselves and said, "If we say, 'From heaven,' he will ask, 'Why didn't you believe him?' But if we say, 'From men,' all the people will stone us, because they are persuaded that John was a prophet."

**Mark 12:12** Then they looked for a way to arrest him because they knew he had spoken the parable against them. But they were afraid of the crowd; so they left him and went away.

**Acts 4:18-21** Then they called them in again and commanded them not to speak or teach at all in the name of Jesus. But Peter and John replied, "Judge for yourselves whether it is right in God's sight to obey you rather than God. For we cannot help speaking about what we have seen and heard." After further threats they let them go. They could not decide how to punish them, because all the people were praising God for what had happened.

Human beings love power and authority. It was true in Jesus' day and it is true today. Politicians say whatever they think will get them elected or reelected whether they believe it or not. The Pharisees were the religious rulers of their day. There was no way they could accept Jesus as the Messiah because he did not fit their image of what Messiah was to be. For one thing He came from Nazareth, "can anything good come from Nazareth?" and for another His words and actions were not politically correct. He upset their way of thinking and their authority was threatened. Even today there are those who have ideologies that differ from those of Jesus and so they will exalt themselves above Him. He warned about this state of mind – **"For everyone who exalts himself will be humbled, and he who humbles himself will be exalted."** (Luke 14:11) He also upsets our own applecart many times but that's because we think we know everything when in fact only He truly does." Jesus, you are life and you are the source of salvation and blessing. Let me never even try to usurp You in my life."

## A protective shell

**John 17:15-16** "My prayer is not that you take them out of the world but that you protect them from the evil one. They are not of the world, even as I am not of it."

**1 Chron 4:10** Jabez cried out to the God of Israel, "Oh, that you would bless me and enlarge my territory! Let your hand be with me, and keep me from harm so that I will be free from pain."

**Gal 1:4-5** who gave himself for our sins to rescue us from the present evil age, according to the will of our God and Father, to whom be glory for ever and ever. Amen.

**2 Tim 4:8** Now there is in store for me the crown of righteousness, which the Lord, the righteous Judge, will award to me on that day-and not only to me, but also to all who have longed for his appearing.

Jabez cried out to the Lord, **"Oh that You would bless me"**, (1 Chron 4:10) Jacob said, **"I will not let you go unless you bless me."** (Gen 32:26) Both men had learned that serving God was the only way to a successful life. Jabez asked the Lord to protect him from harm and to keep him from harming. He knew that causing pain to another would bring pain to himself. Jacob, whose very name meant "supplanter" and in our day we might say finagler or shyster, wrestled with God and wound up with a new name, Israel, meaning "soldier of God". Both men were greatly blessed and knew His presence in their lives. They had a protective shell over them because they had yielded to God and on the eve of His crucifixion Jesus prayed that same protective shell over us. We need to be like Jabez and Israel and allow the Lord His rightful place in us yielding our totality to Him that we may know the joy of His blessing in us.

## He's MY Lord

**Rom 10:9 That if you confess with your mouth, "Jesus is Lord," and believe in your heart that God raised him from the dead, you will be saved.**

**Matt 10:32 "Whoever acknowledges me before men, I will also acknowledge him before my Father in heaven."**

**1 John 4:2 This is how you can recognize the Spirit of God: Every spirit that acknowledges that Jesus Christ has come in the flesh is from God,**

There is a very nice chorus we all sing called "He is Lord". "He is Lord, He is Lord; He is risen from the dead and He is Lord. Every knee shall bow, every tongue confess that Jesus Christ is Lord." The day is coming when, **"'As surely as I live,' says the Lord, 'every knee will bow before me; every tongue will confess to God.'"** (Rom 14:11), and, **"They will make war against the Lamb, but the Lamb will overcome them because he is Lord of lords and King of kings-and with him will be his called, chosen and faithful followers."** (Rev 17:14) Look back up at Matthew 10:32 then consider singing, "He's MY Lord, He's MY Lord; He is risen from the dead and He's my Lord, and MY knee shall bow and MY tongue confess that Jesus Christ is Lord." Now bowing is an option, but then it will not be. Now we can honor Him freely but then those who now refuse will bow before Him and then perish. A friend once told me, "I don't know much about this church stuff, but I do know it is more than going to church on Sunday and living like hell the rest of the week." May I suggest that if Jesus is really "OUR" Lord we will not live that way? We will acknowledge Him every day in every way and **show** who He is, not just try to tell about Him. Oh and we need to see the other side of the coin, **"Whoever acknowledges me before men, I will also acknowledge him before my Father in heaven. But whoever disowns me before men, I will disown him before my Father in heaven."** (Matt 10:32-33)

## Better to be on God's good side

**Matt 5:10** "Blessed are those who are persecuted because of righteousness, for theirs is the kingdom of heaven."

**Luke 6:22** "Blessed are you when men hate you, when they exclude you and insult you and reject your name as evil, because of the Son of Man."

**John 15:20** "Remember the words I spoke to you: 'No servant is greater than his master.' If they persecuted me, they will persecute you also"

**Rom 8:35-36** Who shall separate us from the love of Christ? Shall trouble or hardship or persecution or famine or nakedness or danger or sword? As it is written: "For your sake we face death all day long; we are considered as sheep to be slaughtered."

"Well you're no fun anymore". Many a Christian has heard that statement from friends who remember them from yesteryear when they were the "life of the party". While we're to develop friendships with unbelievers and not be obnoxious, being called "Jesus freaks, Bible Thumpers" and more is hard to endure. We want folks to like us and accept us, but once we become a part of the family of God we can be sure that the world will not do either. Jesus told His disciples, **"If the world hates you, keep in mind that it hated me first."** (John 15:18) The world loves it's sin and therefore hates anything that reminds them of how vile they are. Satan is called the prince of the power of the air and as such he hates God and anything God loves. Therefore because God so loves us Satan hates us as much and wants to discourage us from living for the Lord. David said, **"Better is one day in your courts than a thousand elsewhere; I would rather be a doorkeeper in the house of my God than dwell in the tents of the wicked."** (Ps 84:10) Even if we do manage to be friends with the world it often finds a reason to reject us. The Prodigal son learned that; as soon as his money ran out he was alone. It is impossible to be true loyal friends with the world, but God will never let us down nor hurt us in any way.

## Oh the joy

**Col 1:3-5 We always thank God, the Father of our Lord Jesus Christ, when we pray for you, because we have heard of your faith in Christ Jesus and of the love you have for all the saints the faith and love that spring from the hope that is stored up for you in heaven and that you have already heard about in the word of truth, the gospel**

**Eph 1:15 For this reason, ever since I heard about your faith in the Lord Jesus and your love for all the saints,**

**3 John 3-4 It gave me great joy to have some brothers come and tell about your faithfulness to the truth and how you continue to walk in the truth. I have no greater joy than to hear that my children are walking in the truth.**

Both Paul and John found it good to remind their readers of the joy they had because those to whom they had preached were continuing in the truth of the Gospel. I think it could be compared to a parent who works and encourages their children to strive toward some objective. How proud they are the day that child accomplishes their goal and rightfully so. As a pastor I can attest that there is no greater joy for pastors than when the people we teach and work with grow closer to the Lord. The early church **"devoted themselves to the apostles' teaching and to the fellowship, to the breaking of bread and to prayer."** (Acts 2:42) They were wise enough to realize that what the apostles were teaching them was the way of life. As a result of such devotion, **"Everyone was filled with awe, and many wonders and miraculous signs were done by the apostles."** (Acts 2:43) Perhaps the reason we do not experience growth, closeness to the Lord and a million other benefits of our position in our Lord is that we are not devoted. If parents, the apostles and pastors are full of joy when they see in others a love and devotion to the Lord, imagine how God and the hosts of heaven rejoice when we act like we are really a part of His Kingdom.

## But, I'm not sure….

**Deut 31:6 Be strong and courageous. Do not be afraid or terrified because of them, for the LORD your God goes with you; he will never leave you nor forsake you."**

**Deut 31:23 The LORD gave this command to Joshua son of Nun: "Be strong and courageous, for you will bring the Israelites into the land I promised them on oath, and I myself will be with you."**

**Ps 27:14 Wait for the LORD; be strong and take heart and wait for the LORD.**

**Eph 6:10-11 Finally, be strong in the Lord and in his mighty power. Put on the full armor of God so that you can take your stand against the devil's schemes.**

Too many of us fear the unknown. We fear getting on an airplane, going to the market or any number of other things that have a hold on people; after all, you never know what might happen. Not overcoming these fears may deprive us of some temporal enjoyment, but being afraid to follow Jesus to the max will bring some very dire consequences. I've even heard of parents who try to persuade their children to choose a "safe" mission field in which to serve. (There is a song that says something to the effect, "please don't send me to Africa".) We do what God asks of us if it fits into our plans and schedules. Our employers can ask us to do most anything, our extracurricular activities can exact any requirements, but God better not take me out of my comfort zone or expect me to exert a lot of effort. I just have a full plate now and am unwilling to make adjustments to be or do what the One who died in my place asks of me. But remember, we need never fear or hold back for, **"God is able to make all grace abound to you, so that in all things at all times, having all that you need, you will abound in every good work."** (2 Cor 9:8) He will see us through if we will only follow Him.

## Unquestioning following

**Matt 4:19-20 "Come, follow me," Jesus said, "and I will make you fishers of men." At once they left their nets and followed Him.**

**Matt 9:9 As Jesus went on from there, he saw a man named Matthew sitting at the tax collector's booth. "Follow me," He told him, and Matthew got up and followed him.**

**Matt 16:24-25 4 Then Jesus said to his disciples, "If anyone would come after me, he must deny himself and take up his cross and follow me. For whoever wants to save his life will lose it, but whoever loses his life for me will find it."**

"Come follow Me". When the disciples heard these words they dropped what they were doing and responded to His call. None of them required a job description or explanation of where they were off to, they "at once followed Him". Some people today want to know just exactly what the Lord will require of them, then MAYBE they will think about it; but we must be like those of old and immediately follow. Jesus told the disciples, **"If anyone would come after me, he must deny himself and take up his cross and follow me."** (Matt 16:24) We should never wait nor hesitate, but rather go. It matters not where or what the Lord has asked of us, our response must be the same. The rich young ruler in Mathew 19 trusted his riches far more than he did Jesus and went away sad. He robbed himself of the joy of the Lord by loving this world. When Peter reminded Jesus that they had left all for Him He replied, **"I tell you the truth, no one who has left home or wife or brothers or parents or children for the sake of the kingdom of God will fail to receive many times as much in this age and, in the age to come, eternal life."** (Luke 18:29-30) To be rich in Him and in eternity we must be willing to leave everything here. So the only question is, will we? Oh how I pray that we all can answer, "Yes, Lord, I will follow.

*Just A Thought*

## What if it happened TODAY?

**Acts 1:11 "Men of Galilee," they said, "why do you stand here looking into the sky? This same Jesus, who has been taken from you into heaven, will come back in the same way you have seen him go into heaven."**

**1 Thess 4:16-18 For the Lord himself will come down from heaven, with a loud command, with the voice of the archangel and with the trumpet call of God, and the dead in Christ will rise first. After that, we who are still alive and are left will be caught up together with them in the clouds to meet the Lord in the air. And so we will be with the Lord forever. Therefore encourage each other with these words.**

Jesus came once as a babe in a manger but when He comes again He will arrive as the **"King of kings and the Lord of lords"** (1 Tim 3:15), and **"As surely as I live,' says the Lord, 'every knee will bow before me; every tongue will confess to God."** (Rom 14:11) Make no mistake about it; His second coming is evident by the signs of the times. Isaiah said, **"Woe to those who call evil good and good evil, who put darkness for light and light for darkness, who put bitter for sweet and sweet for bitter."** (Is 5:20) Our nation alone calls evil good and good evil. Sin is raising its ugly head and demanding to be acclaimed as normal and acceptable and Christians are being arrested and persecuted for loving God. His return is some two thousand years closer than it was in Bible times and could well be even today. In light of this two questions come to mind 1) "are we ready"? and 2) are we living so as to attract others to the security of being caught up with Jesus at that trumpet call? Even should He tarry another thousand years we need to be able to answer both questions with a resounding "YES".

## Hunger and Thirst

**Hag 1:2-4 This is what the LORD Almighty says: "These people say, 'The time has not yet come for the LORD's house to be built.'" Then the word of the LORD came through the prophet Haggai: "Is it a time for you yourselves to be living in your paneled houses, while this house remains a ruin?"**

Most of us live in pretty fine homes. We often paint and make repairs so that our residences look nice and protect us from the elements. The same applied to the Israelites. They had very fancy houses that were ceiled, referring to the fact that expensive wood paneling adorned their walls. However, at the same time the Temple still lay in ruins. God's people had become so focused on their own comfort that they forgot, or just plain neglected, the house of the Lord. One day King David realized this very thing and, **he said to Nathan the prophet, "Here I am, living in a palace of cedar, while the ark of God remains in a tent."** (2 Sam 7:2) This may well be a picture of the attitude some have toward God today. We have become ingrown and selfish. We make everything our god, from our homes, our possessions, our jobs and families, to even our particular belief system. David determined to rectify his situation by going to the work of preparing a place for the "Ark" and bringing it home. We need to work out our need of God by seeking Him and making Him our FIRST priority. Just one more thought; how about looking to Him for guidance in taking care of today's temples, our bodies (proper food, exercise, rest, nothing harmful etc.). **"Blessed are those who hunger and thirst for righteousness, for they will be filled."** (Matt 5:6) I would imagine that if you're like me, when your stomach says, "send food" you comply A.S.A.P; but do we as readily feed our spiritual needs? Do we **"hunger and thirst for righteousness"**?

# My Testimony In Brief

Rev. Ernest "Ernie" W. Jelliff was born in 1943 to Charles and Fannie Jelliff on a farm in Woodhull, New York. In 1949 tent meetings were held in Academy Corners, PA with the Reverend Elam J Daniels. The Jelliff family attended and when the call was given to accept Jesus Christ as Savior I told my dad that I needed to go to the altar. Dad replied, "Why? We are a Christian family." At age five and a half I said, "but that's not enough". My relationship with God grew and later in addition to secular employment I was privileged to serve the Lord in many ways, including teaching Sunday School and filling the pulpit. However, in 1989 I failed my Lord very miserably. Notwithstanding, I so praise Him that despite our sin, failure was not the end of service to Him. Following confession of our sin and repentance, experiencing God's forgiveness, writing numerous letters of confession and seeking forgiveness from our families and others, Ruthie and I were married in 1993 and rightfully continued to be disciplined by the local church, after which my dear Lord again started using me to teach and preach. In 2003 my wife and I felt called to plant a church, Daybreak Ministries, in our home. A number of people had urged us in this direction and together we all felt strongly led of God to begin a new work for His honor and glory, for the growing and equipping of His people and for a strong spiritual benevolent ministry to any and all who do not know Him. This came totally unexpected to us shortly after disability forced my retirement from the insurance industry but here we are over 6 years later. We have had a very exciting and at times scary ride but in obedience to our Lord one day at a time, we would not miss it for anything. God has done amazing things that we could never have imagined and our greatest joy is to see Him work in and through the lives of people as He continues to change and refine them and us. Very shortly after planting Daybreak I completed the requirements and became ordained with United Christian Faith Ministries (UCFM). About that same time the Lord urged me to begin writing a daily devotional that became "The Thought of the Day", which has been both my privilege and pleasure to continue sending out via email for several years now. "Praise the Lord, oh my soul; all my inmost being praise His holy name." Psalm 103:1 NIV

Just a Thought is a collection of daily devotionals which have been sent to the people of Daybreak Ministries, friends, family, and many others. These "thoughts" have not been written necessarily for the purpose of making one feel good or comfortable, but rather they are by design intended to spur the reader on to a deeper intimate walk with God and service to the King of kings.

Readers whose lives have been affected have asked for these devotionals in book form so they will be able to share them with others.

These thoughts have been sent as emails to all parts of the country and many have reported forwarding them on to others, who in turn have asked to be added to the daily list, enabling them to be received directly.

It is my earnest hope and prayer that you will be blessed, challenged and drawn closer to the Lord Jesus Christ as you read.

You can contact the author at:
Ernie Jelliff
165 Park Road,
Wellsboro, Pa 16901
ejelliff@ptd.net

Daybreak Ministries can be found on the web at www.daybreakministriespa.org